Rational Choice and British Politics

An Analysis of Rhetoric and Manipulation from Peel to Blair

Iain McLean

OXFORD
UNIVERSITY PRESS

OXFORD
UNIVERSITY PRESS

Great Clarendon Street, Oxford OX2 6DP

Oxford University Press is a department of the University of Oxford.
It furthers the University's objective of excellence in research, scholarship,
and education by publishing worldwide in

Oxford New York

Athens Auckland Bangkok Bogotá Buenos Aires
Cape Town Chennai Dar es Salaam Delhi Florence Hong Kong Istanbul
Karachi Kolkata Kuala Lumpur Madrid Melbourne Mexico City Mumbai
Nairobi Paris São Paulo Shanghai Singapore Taipei Tokyo Toronto Warsaw

and associated companies in Berlin Ibadan

Published in the United States
by Oxford University Press Inc., New York

First published 2001

British Library Cataloguing in Publication Data

Data available

Library of Congress Cataloging in Publication Data

Data available

ISBN 0-19-829530-8
ISBN 0-19-829529-4(Pbk.)

1 3 5 7 9 10 8 6 4 2

Typeset by Best-set Typesetter Ltd., Hong Kong
Printed in Great Britain
Biddles Ltd.,
Guildford & Kings Lynn

To Duncan

PREFACE AND ACKNOWLEDGEMENTS

This book is the product of many years of trespassing. Political scientists and historians inhabit neighbouring university departments. But they rarely enter one another's territory. They are usually in separate faculties; they do research in different ways; typically, they ignore one another's conclusions.

Some intellectual autobiography may help explain how this book came to be written. I studied history at university because it was what I had done at school. Being young and naïve, I did not even know when I left school that there was a neighbouring field labelled (in Oxford) PPE, for philosophy, politics, and economics. When I arrived at university, I decided that I was studying the wrong subject—I should have studied politics and economics instead. I know now that I could have changed subjects just by asking to; then, I did not know that I was allowed to ask. But the Oxford History school has its compensations. Its worship for primary sources can be one of them. So was the late lamented 'Peel Special Subject'. For many decades, undergraduates had the option of studying 'Financial and Economic Policy in the Peel Administration, 1841–6' from primary sources. Most Special Subjects required students to read sources in foreign languages. Just to ensure that Peel was not regarded as a soft option, the faculty threw in a Frenchman's description of Peel's England (Faucher 1845). But, French or no French (in later years, Faucher was set in translation), this was no soft option. The only point on which I would now fault the Peel Special Subject was its failure to focus attention on the Duke of Wellington and the House of Lords. Peel's administration grappled with subjects that mostly seem striking in their modernity—bank independence, utility regulation, factory safety, protection or free trade, social control, and famine. To understand where they succeeded and where they failed, students had to understand the subject-matter. It was a sharp lesson in social science as well as in history.

A historian might immediately condemn these remarks for anachronism. To regard a period or a politician as interesting because they dealt with problems that seem 'modern' is to privilege modernity. The past is another country; they do things differently there. Yes, that is true and must never be forgotten. But all historiography is selective. There is no harm in selecting events for study that are of enduring interest, so long as one remembers that contemporary actors approached them with different mentalities to ours. And while mentalities differ, rationality does not. Therefore, it is worth studying events in political history through the lens of rational choice, which has powerfully illuminated many actions in contemporary society. Rational-choice political scientists in the USA have made notable raids on American (and British—cf. e.g. Cox 1987) political history. Some of these raids are discussed in detail in this book. But, disappointingly, historians working in the field have paid little constructive attention to them, nor to some social scientists' empirical results, e.g. on the importance of religion in voting behaviour in Victorian and Edwardian Britain (Wald 1983). To a historian, the failing of the rational-choice raids is typically that they are too selective in their use of evidence. To a political scientist, the characteristic failing of political history is that it lays too much stress on the accidental and contingent. Historians are interested in the unique; social scientists in the repeatable, in modelling, and in observable implications from the case being studied to other cases (King, Keohane, and Verba 1994). Both are valid perspectives, and I have tried to see the world from both in this book.

My transition from historian to political scientist was gradual. My doctoral thesis, although submitted to a sub-faculty of Politics, was essentially historical, and it brought me face to face with another larger-than-life actor in this book, David Lloyd George. My detailed acquaintance with the other subjects of the book is more recent. William Ewart Gladstone I only started to see in any complexity when a co-author and I investigated a minor act of his—his regulation of the railways under Peel (see McLean and Foster 1992). But it is impossible to study any act of his, however minor, without becoming fascinated and intimidated by his huge and terrifying personality. In their different ways Disraeli, Salisbury, and Joe Chamberlain may all be defined by the respects in which they were not Gladstone. So Gladstone, although he does not have a chapter to himself, stalks through all the middle chapters of this book. As for Enoch Powell and Margaret Thatcher, I claim no privileged access. I have never met either except across the room at public meetings, but my fascination with them is widely shared.

What do the characters in this book have in common? Each of them faced a unique set of political circumstances. But each stood out from the general run of politicians for the way that he or she controlled events. Furthermore, each appreciated that politics could operate in more than one spatial dimension. This concept is explained in Chapter 1 and its use by each of the politicians in the book is the main subject of the chapters that follow. They are not the only outstanding politicians in Britain since 1832. But I believe that they are the full set of those who used politics 'heresthetically'. That is another term I explain in Chapter 1. It denotes a particular sort of manipulation—the art of making people believe that the world is as you say it is, in order to get your way. Britain's greatest twentieth-century Prime Minister, Winston Churchill, does not have a chapter to himself in this book because it is not about how to win a world war. (But he does have a cameo role as one of the British negotiators of the British–Irish Treaty of 1921). Aside from Churchill, however, my selection of leading politicians accords with the current historical consensus on which politicians have controlled events rather than let events control them.

A word on sources and methods. Historians may be critical of my limited use of manuscript sources. Political scientists may be surprised that I use them at all. An explanation to both is needed.

To the historians. Throughout this book, I stress politicians' private motivations, not their public explanations. Therefore, I have deliberately minimized my use of the UK public records. I have used the Irish public records for 1921–2, because the Irish leaders' private debate on whether or not to ratify the Treaty of 1921 is recorded there. As to my politicians' private papers, they fall into four classes. Those of Enoch Powell and Margaret Thatcher are not yet available to scholars. At the other extreme, some are so widely available in print, in reliable editions, that nothing would be gained from consulting the manuscript rather than the printed version. This applies to Peel and Gladstone. Disraeli and Salisbury are intermediate cases. Had I but world enough and time, I would have consulted their private papers for myself. But I have only one life, so I decided, regretfully, to depend on their biographers. Each is covered twice over—by a near-contemporary multi-volume 'Life and Letters' and by several modern Lives. Both have been well served. The six-volume *Life* of Disraeli by Monypenny and Buckle sparkles with his letters. Salisbury's daughter Lady Gwendolen Cecil never completed her filial biography, but it covers the parts of Salisbury's career that feature in this book. As for the moderns, Blake (1966) on Disraeli and Roberts (1999) on Salisbury each stands well clear of the pack. Finally, there is a class of my subjects where the private papers add the most value. These are Wellington, whose role in 1845–6 has been severely underestimated; Joseph Chamberlain, whose standard multi-volume Life is too partisan to be trusted; and Lloyd George, who unlike Gladstone has not yet found the biographer to match the subject. Among minor characters, the papers of Erskine Childers, his cousin Robert Barton, and A. J. Balfour's private secretary were most illuminating.

To the political scientists. Archives matter, and we do not use them enough, especially when we try to construct analytic narratives such as those in this book. It is too easy to ascribe plausible motives to the dead who cannot contradict us. What politicians say is evidence. What they say in private is better evidence than what they say in public. Authors of analytic narratives should test their narrative and their analysis against the available evidence.

In a sense, this book has been in the making since 1967, although I did not realize it then. But my first debt is to John Prest and the late Charles Stuart, who inducted me into the world of Peel and Wellington. Many people have commented on drafts and presentations, supplied me with data, or pointed me towards sources. Thanks to Andrew Adonis, Hugh Berrington, Michael Brock, the late Jim Bulpitt, David Butler, Gary Cox, Alasdair Crockett, John Darwin, Richard W. Davis, John Dunbabin, Ivan Ermakoff, Anna Gambles, Conor Gearty, Peter Gray, Ewen Green, Randall Hansen, Brian Harrison, Anthony Heath, Boyd Hilton, David Howell, Macartan Humphrey (my severest critic), Martin Johnes, Simon King, Moshé Machover, Gerry Mackie (my second-severest critic), Stephen P. Magee, the late Colin Matthew, Susannah Morris, Jack Nagel, Avner Offer, Brendan O'Leary, the late Mancur Olson, the late Bill Riker, Cheryl Schonhardt-Bailey, Ian Shapiro, Adam Sheingate, Richard Sinnott, David Stasavage, Donley Studlar, John Vickers, Kenneth Wald, Barry Weingast, Sir Michael Wheeler-Booth, and Stewart Wood.

At various stages Camilla Bustani, John Carney, Christopher Garner, Alistair McMillan, Burt Monroe, and Beata Rozumulowicz gave valuable research assistance. Support from the Nuffield Foundation, from the Economic & Social Research Council (under research grant R000234303), and from Nuffield College is gratefully acknowledged.

Draft chapters were tried out at several conferences and seminars. Thanks to the organizers of the conferences on the work of W. H. Riker, Norwich 1987 (Albert Weale) and on the political economy of trade policy, Washington University, St Louis, 1997 (Norman Schofield); the political economy seminar, University of California at Los Angeles, 1996 (George Tsebelis—special thanks for pointing out my failure to deal properly with the House of Lords); the Wellington Congress, Southampton 1998 (Chris Woolgar); the American History seminar, Cambridge University, January 1999 for its polite scepticism about W. H. Riker's origins of the Civil War (Tony Badger); several panels at both the Political Studies Association of the UK and the American Political Science Association since 1997, and most of all to those who attended my seminar series in Oxford, January–March 2000, when the whole book was aired in weekly discussions from which I profited a great deal. The nicest phrase I picked up from them was *The Santa Monica Revelation* for my sudden conversion to belief in the centrality of the House of Lords.

The staff of many libraries were unfailingly helpful. I acknowledge in particular all the libraries in which I consulted primary material (see References), and also the Library of Nuffield College. Extracts from the papers of Joseph and Austen Chamberlain are quoted by courtesy of the Director of Special Collections, University of Birmingham Library. I would like to thank the editors and publishers of *Wellington Studies III* and *Political Studies* to reuse material on Peel and Wellington which has previously appeared in these journals: I. McLean, 'Wellington and the Corn Laws 1845–6: a study in heresthetic', *Wellington Studies III* (Southampton: Hartley Institute 1999), 227–56, and I. McLean and C. Bustani, 'Irish potatoes and British politics: interests, ideology, heresthetic and the Repeal of the Corn Laws', *Political Studies* 47:3, 1999, 817–36, © Political Studies Association, 1999. I would also like to thank the Bodleian Library, University of Oxford for providing two black and white photographs for Figure 2.1 'Political Economy; or, Lord John Peel's Cloths' from volume XI *Punch*, July 1846 and Figure 3.1 'Moses in Egitto!!!' from *Punch*, volume 69, December 11th 1875, Reference (shelftmark), N. 2706 d.10.

My family have uncomplainingly put up with my long hours and absences. This book is dedicated with love and affection to Duncan, who was not born last time I had a chance to do this.

I. McL.
May 2000
Nuffield College, Oxford

CONTENTS

LIST OF TABLES

LIST OF FIGURES

1

Introduction

Majority Rule and Its Problems

This book is about politicians who have changed the number of political dimensions in British politics. And it is about politicians who play veto games. So, what is a political dimension? And how many of them are there usually? And what *is* a veto game?

A dimension is a way of organizing opinions. There is an infinity of possible policy platforms. Both politicians and voters need some way to evaluate them. A simple measuring rod is money. If I like health care to be publicly funded, then, other things being equal, the more money politicians promise to spend on public health care, the better.

But of course, other things are not equal. Politicians have to decide not only how much to spend, but how much to tax. And when they spend, they have to decide not only how much to spend on health, but how much on defence, education, roads, police, statues of famous men, and all the other things that governments spend taxpayers' money on.

The commonest way to make sense of this is to arrange possible policies along some line from the most extreme in one direction to the most extreme in the other. Politicians are well used to the terms 'left' and 'right' to label the ends of this line. Voters are less well used to the terms, but a wealth of evidence from surveys in many countries shows that they are comfortable with the line, or dimension, and that they are able to locate themselves, and the political parties, on such a line. (For contemporary evidence from Britain see the successive reports from the British Election Survey: Heath *et al*. 1985, 1991, 1994). A left-wing policy is one that gives priority to high spending, and a right-wing policy is one that gives priority to low taxation.

Politicians and voters alike make more subtle distinction. Within spending priorities there are 'left-wing' and 'right-wing' shades. People and politicians of the left give priority to health, social services, and overseas aid. People and politicians on the right give priority to defence and security. On both sides, people are aware that there is more to politics than taxing and spending, and they bundle their moral and ethical views into their evaluation of left and right, in ways that may seem to fit together less well than views on taxing and spending. For instance, opposition to restrictions on business is viewed as a 'right-wing' stance; but so is support for state enforcement of community morals. What about businesses that are believed to undermine community morals? Maximizing freedom to take, and trade in, drugs is viewed as a left-wing policy, but maximizing freedom to drive, and trade in, expensive cars is viewed as a right-wing policy.

This matters to political philosophers. It need not matter to political scientists, or to historians. What matters is whether bundles of policies, which may have no objective coherence, have subjective coherence to politicians, or to voters, or both. It is hard to judge how voters view bundles of policies. Only since the 1930s is there any survey evidence on how voters perceive policies and politicians; only since the 1960s have the surveys been sophisticated enough to give reliable information. For the rest of the period covered by this book, we have to guess. At least we know how politicians appealed to voters, which appeals seem to have succeeded, and which seem to have failed.

For politicians, the problem is a little more tractable. It can be tackled using both statistical and literary tools. The main statistical tool is roll-call analysis. This book uses it for the chapter on the 1840s, and in the background of the chapter on the 1880s, but not for the later chapters, because it has not been done on British data since then. Roll-call analysis examines the votes cast in a legislature—in our case, the House of Commons. How MPs vote on divisions is recorded, and this may open a route into understanding the ideologies of the dead. It can be shown that some votes are correlated, and others are not. For instance, how MPs in the Parliament of 1841–7 voted on the Corn Laws is correlated with how they voted on Ireland. It is not correlated with how they voted on factory reform. Those who wanted to keep the Corn Laws usually wanted to repress Irish unrest with force. Those who wanted to repeal the Corn Laws tended to be (slightly) more open to Irish dissent. But knowing where an MP stood on either of these sets of issues does not help us predict whether he favoured or opposed greater regulation of factories. The first set of issues stood on the main dimension of politics at the time. Factory reform did not.

Roll-call analysis is very big in American political science. It is almost invisible in Britain (and, as it happens, what there is has mostly been done by Americans). This may be partly because it is hard to do, and until recently required heavyweight computing power and familiarity with unfriendly programs—neither of these being resources that many British historians had at their fingertips. But it is due more to party discipline. Since the 1880s, most Commons division lists tell us nothing except which Members belonged to which party. Party discipline on the floor of the house has meant that any dissension is not expressed there. Ideologies are constrained by party, and roll-call analysis tells us nothing.

Where roll-calls are uninformative, we have to look at what politicians actually did and said. In this book, I rely both on what they said to the public, and on what they said to one another. Usually, the latter is more important. Of course, politicians, like anybody else, sometimes lie. So we need to ask ourselves all the time *To whom is he saying this? How likely is it to be true?* Most of the arguments of this book are built on what politicians privately said to one another, and to their friends rather than their enemies. I have assumed that politicians lie to their friends less often than to their enemies. Perhaps the most reliable evidence of all is what they say to their mistresses. But only two of the politicians at the heart of this book have had mistresses.

Is British politics since 1846, then, one-dimensional or multidimensional? The evidence is that normal politics is more or less unidimensional. Parties and politicians align themselves on the main salient issues of the day, so that those who are 'left' on one are 'left' on others, and those who are 'right' on one are 'right' on others. Although voters do not closely follow these ideologies, they follow them closely enough to be able to identify with one or another party, and to know how 'close' they are to each party. Note that I am not claiming that most people can identify how left-wing or right-wing they are. That is false, and unnecessary for my argument. *Left* and *right* have no objective meaning; they are defined purely in relation to the issues of the day. Thus, for example, support of income tax is a 'right' position in the 1840s, because it can be shown to align with support for the landed interest and indifference to Irish reform.

If politics is unidimensional, we can always draw a graph such as Fig. 1.1. In Fig. 1.1, the possible policies lie along the horizontal, x-axis, from the most 'left' to the most 'right'. The vertical, y-axis measures the number of people who like each policy the best. Thus the higher the line AB at any opinion point, the more people hold that opinion. In presentations of this theory, figures such as Fig. 1.1 are often drawn with a bell-shaped curve with a few people at each extreme and many at the middle. This may often be true, but it has caused a lot of confusion because it tends to mislead readers new to the theory as to what the 'median voter theorem' means. Therefore I have deliberately drawn Fig. 1.1 with an asymmetrical, non-bell-shaped, distribution of opinion.

Given the way in which Fig. 1.1 has been defined, we may take the area under any part of the curve AB to represent the number of people whose favourite position lies in the range between the points vertically below the ends of the curve. A very special position is defined by the vertical line MM'. This line cuts the area under the curve into two areas of exactly equal size. Any voter whose ideal position is M' is a, or the, *median voter*. The median voter has exactly as many other voters to her 'left' as to her 'right'.

Now let us suppose that there are two parties trying to win power by means of a national election. Suppose, further, that each of them regards ideology as only a means to an end. Both parties care not what policies they put forward, but wish only for the spoils of office. Then each of them will put forward an identical platform, which will coincide with what the median voter wants. Why? Because if the first to move, say party *J*, goes to any other

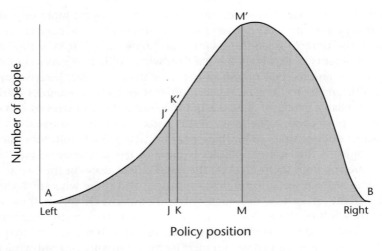

Fig. 1.1. The median voter theorem for one-dimensional issues.

issue position, then the other party *K*, need only nestle up to *J*, but just fractionally on the majority side of it. In that event, *K* will get the majority of the vote, and win the election. This is illustrated by the lines JJ′ and KK′ in Fig. 1.1. As all of this is common knowledge (or, if it is not, the parties soon find it out), the parties both move to, or try to occupy, the median voter's position.

It is time for a reality check. How far have conditions in Britain since 1846 corresponded to the simplicities of Fig. 1.1? First, it is obvious that there have been parties that do not seek nationwide power. By far the most important of these have been the Irish Party and its successors. Already when our story opens, most people in Ireland were hostile to the Union of 1800, which had incorporated the whole of Ireland into the United Kingdom. Some of the Irish MPs in 1846 described themselves as Repealers, interested only in Irish affairs. The Repealers weakened (in Parliament, though not out of it) in the 1850s and 1860s. But, starting in 1874, the Irish MPs became a cohesive nationalist bloc. By 1886, all the seats in Catholic Ireland were held by the Irish Party, which sought concessions for Ireland from a British Government of either party. It was not interested in governing a United Kingdom of which it did not approve.

By the time of Lloyd George, the united Irish Party had fragmented, but it was still true that Catholic Ireland elected politicians who were not interested in ruling the UK; the Treaty of 1921 marked their final withdrawal. However, parties that do not wish to form the government of the UK have remained. The Ulster Unionists have been such a party (or parties) ever since 1921. They have now been joined by the Northern Ireland nationalists, by the Scottish National Party (SNP), and *Plaid Cymru* ('Party of Wales'). Although Lloyd George seemed to solve the Irish Question by taking it out of British politics in 1921, it returned to haunt Britain again when violence restarted in 1968.

In a seminal work of comparative political science, Lipset and Rokkan (1967: ch. 1, quoted at p. 34) argue that European patterns of party competition are determined by the 'National Revolution' and 'the Industrial Revolution'. The Industrial Revolution is familiar. They argue that it generated class politics along the familiar left–right dimension. The National Revolution, they argue, set nation-building elites in the centre against those who resisted them in the periphery. Religion could in principle provide yet another dimension, although they argued that in many cases it aligned with the centre–periphery cleavage—the central elites belonged to one religion, and the resistant periphery to another. Furthermore, they argue, there is a lag between the development of cleavages (dimensions, in our terminology), and the development of party systems. Once a party system comes into existence along some dimension, there is a tendency for it to freeze up. The existing parties would rather adapt themselves to politics in the new dimension than allow new parties to come in and imperil their access to power. Therefore, old parties of centre and periphery may be more powerful, and new parties of class less powerful, than the issues of contemporary politics may lead one to expect.

Lipset and Rokkan's book appeared in 1967, at a time when all British political scientists accepted Peter Pulzer's (1975: 102—first published in 1967) axiom that 'Class is the basis of British party politics; all else is embellishment and detail'. Their idea that the centre–periphery dimension, although overlain by the left–right dimension, was still there started to gain acceptance with the relative decline of the Labour and Conservative parties and rise of peripheral parties in the 1970s. But it has never been as fully accepted as it should have been. Political scientists and historians are so used to looking at the British past through a retrospectoscope that they have tended to see things that were not there and missed things that were. They greatly exaggerated the importance of class in nineteenth- and early twentieth-century British politics at the expense of religion and centre–periphery politics.

The Lipset and Rokkan model fits British politics in most of our period. The centre wanted to extend British power all over the Empire. That meant, first, securing it in Scotland, Wales, Ireland, and even the north of England, which expressed varying degrees of discontent with London rule. Religious divisions strengthened the centre–periphery dimension and weakened the left–right dimension. The established churches—the Church of England and the Church of Scotland—were the churches of the centre. All the other churches were churches of the periphery. Most of Ireland was defiantly Catholic. Catholicism had been a badge of Irish identity ever since the seventeenth century. Wales was defiantly Nonconformist; Nonconformity was also stronger in northern than in southern England. Scotland had its own religious divisions, little understood by English politicians. The Church of Scotland split in 1843 on the lines of centre versus periphery within

Scotland, with the Free Church representing the spatial and socio-economic periphery and the established church the centre. The Free Church was strongest in the Highlands, and strongest of all where Highlanders had been evicted ('cleared') from their land. When Scots went overseas, as hundreds of thousands of them did to Ulster (many then going on to form a dominant religious group in the first century of the independent United States), they ceased to belong to an established church and became by definition Nonconformists. Struggles over church disestablishment and recognition—in Scotland in 1843, in Ireland from 1800 to 1869, and in Wales from 1910 to 1920—were as much centre–periphery politics as religious politics. In another seminal study by a non-Briton, Kenneth Wald (1983) showed that as late as 1910 religion was a better predictor than class of vote in Britain.

In normal times, the politics of centre and periphery could be bundled with the politics of left and right. As stated above, MPs in the 1840s had attitudes to Ireland (a centre–periphery issue) that lined up with their attitudes to the Corn Laws (a rural–urban issue generated by the Industrial Revolution). But the potential for disruptive changes of alignment was always there. At one level, the very presence of the Irish Party and its successors ensured that. The Irish Party did not seek power in the UK. But it held the balance in the House of Commons from 1885 to 1886, from 1892 to 1895, and from 1910 to 1918. Its successors as parties of the periphery (the Liberals, Scottish, Welsh, and Northern Irish Nationalists, and the Ulster Unionists) between them held the balance of power in 1974, from 1977 to 1979, and from 1996 to 1997. The presence of a potential second dimension enabled politicians such as Peel and Lloyd George to make the imaginative leaps discussed in the chapters that follow.

However, since 1900, or at the latest since 1914, there have been three parties in Parliament which *have* wanted to share in the government of the UK. The Labour Party won its first seats, as the Labour Representation Committee, in 1900. At first it was not clearly distinguished from the Liberals, and the two parties signed an electoral pact in 1903 which ensured that they did not run against one another in England. After the two General Elections of 1910, the Labour Party seemed to be in retreat, but the first wartime coalition of 1915 brought it into government. Since then, there has never been any doubt but that it sought to govern, even if in 1932 and again in 1980 that prospect seemed extremely remote.

The struggle between the Liberal and Labour Parties to form the opposition to the Conservatives lasted from 1918 to 1929; the Labour Party won, and the Liberals were driven back to the periphery, where they have continued to win most of their seats. In the early 1950s they almost died out altogether, appearing to confirm the truth of Duverger's Law:

[T]he simple-majority single-ballot system favours the two-party system. Of all the hypotheses that have been defined in this book, this approaches the most nearly perhaps to a true sociological law. (Duverger 1959: 217; stress in original)

The British electoral system would be more accurately described as a simple-*plurality* single-ballot system. In the Anglo-Saxon world it is also called 'First Past the Post'. This is another unsatisfactory name, because there is no fixed post for the first to pass. The electoral rule is that the candidate with the highest vote is elected, regardless of whether that candidate has won a majority of the vote. To distinguish 'the highest single vote, which may or may not be a majority of the votes cast' from 'the majority of votes', the former is called 'the plurality', and the British electoral system called the 'plurality system', throughout this book.

It is well known that the plurality system squeezes any candidate who is commonly believed to have little chance of winning locally. For such a candidate, being a perfect model of the opinions of the median voter is not sufficient; Duverger's Law puts a ruthless squeeze on her. Since the 1920s, this position has mostly been held by the Liberals, although in a few times and places it has been the Labour Party's turn to suffer, and in an even smaller number the Conservative Party's. These odd local situations account for the survival of the Liberals in the Commons from 1931 to 1964.

Nevertheless, unless the centre–periphery dimension is prised apart from the left–right dimension, they may collapse on one another. In that case, politics is unidimensional, and that is how British politics has appeared for most of the time since 1846. In unidimensional politics, it follows from the median voter theorem that parties will normally try to align themselves with the median voter. To do anything else is to risk catastrophic defeat. Some of the catastrophic defeats in British party politics during the period arise from parties being driven by their internal preoccupations to positions remote from the median voter, and/or from the electorate having sharply different views of the competence of the different parties. In 1931 Labour lost whatever reputation for competence at managing the economy it had had, as did the Conservatives in 1992. These factors account for the landslides of 1931 and 1983 (for the Conservatives) and 1997 (for Labour). These cases involved manoeuvres around (towards, away from) the median voter rather than her-esthetic moves into new dimensions.

But chaos is always possible. Here, 'chaos' has a precise definition. Whereas unidimensional politics is strongly stable around the position of the median voter, multidimensional politics is intrinsically unstable. Since 1785 it has been known (although often forgotten) that, whenever there are at least three voters and at least three options, option A may beat B by a majority, which beats C by a (different) majority, which likewise beats A. This is called a *majority-rule cycle*. If opinions can be arranged in one issue dimension so that nobody ranks the 'middle' option worst, then majority-rule cycles cannot exist. If not, then there is no median and majority-rule cycles are likely to be pervasive.

This situation is shown diagramatically in Fig. 1.2. Here the dimension 'left–right' is crosscut by the dimension 'slave–free'. Fig. 1.2 is intended to represent national politics in the USA from around 1800 to 1861. US national

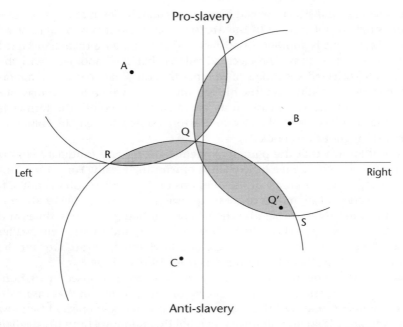

Fig. 1.2. Issue space in two dimensions: the non-existence of an equilibrium.

politics from 1800 to 1861 exhibited a broad 'left–right' division. These terms may be used only with the repeated health warning that they have no objective meaning. But there was a 'left' politics which appealed to the small farmer on the frontier, and a 'right' politics which appealed to the city non-farmer. The former was represented by the Republican-Democratic, later Democratic Party founded by Thomas Jefferson in 1800, and refounded by the frontiersman President Andrew Jackson in 1828. The latter was represented by a succession of relatively unsuccessful parties—Federalists and Whigs.

There is an important difference of notation between Fig. 1.1 and Fig. 1.2. The x-axis is the same. But in Fig. 1.2, the y-axis now measures, not the number of people on each position, but positions on a second issue dimension. As the two dimensions are, statistically, 'orthogonal'—which means no more than 'at right angles'—a politician may be in any of the four quadrants of Fig. 1.2. A politician is assumed to have a favourite point—such as the positions A, B, C in Fig. 1.2. Spreading out from each agent's favourite point are a set of *indifference contours*. One is shown around each of the points A, B, and C in Fig. 1.2. An indifference contour links all the points in two-dimensional space among which the agent is indifferent. Supposing that I am agent A, say, the further a set of policies is from my optimum point A, the less I like it. Policies can depart from my ideal point in any direction— more favourable to slavery, more hostile to it, more 'left-wing', more 'right-wing'. Assuming that I can rank any set of policies against any other, I can then draw an indifference contour to link any collection of policy positions that I like, or dislike, equally. An infinite number of indifference contours can be drawn: the further away they are from my ideal point, the less I like the policies they represent. The assumptions embodied in this paragraph are often summarized by the expression 'Euclidean space'. The space I have just defined has the properties first defined by the ancient Greek geometer Euclid (with notation from the seventeenth-century French philosopher and mathematician René Descartes).

Fig. 1.2 may be used to show why chaos is almost always possible in two dimensions. Consider the three politicians whose ideal positions are point A, B, and C in Fig. 1.2. If points A, B, and C were in a straight line, the situation could be reduced to that of Fig. 1.1. From that we would know that voter B, whose optimum was *B*, was the median voter, and that position *B* was unbeatable. It might seem intuitively obvious that there is a similar stability if the three points are not in line. There is not.

To illustrate this, look again at the three indifference contours drawn on to Fig. 1.2, and in particular at the three hatched areas *QP*, *QR*, and *QS*. The point Q where all three intersect, is the status quo: the current platform comprising a policy on slavery and a policy on welfare. From the definition just given, the area *QP* contains all the points which voters A and B prefer to the status quo Q. As A and B are a majority of the population, Q would lose to any point in this 'petal' (as these areas are called, for obvious reasons). Similarly, Q would lose to any point in the petal *QR*, by a 2–1 vote with A and C in the majority, or to any point in the petal *QS*, by a 2–1 vote with B and C in the majority. Suppose, without loss of generality, that Q is put to the vote against *Q′*. Compared to Q, *Q′* is inside the indifference curve of two out of the three voters. Therefore a majority of the electorate prefer it, therefore it is chosen. But, in an obvious sense, *Q′* is 'further away' from the electorate than the starting point.

But now the status quo point is *Q′*. A diagram similar to Fig. 1.2 could be drawn again, with three indifference curves coinciding at the new status quo *Q′*. I will not draw it, but leave it to the reader's imagination. Obviously, each of the petals is now larger. Therefore, the majority choice may wander yet further away from the original starting place. There is no bound to this process. Therefore, a sequence of majority decisions could take society arbitrarily far from its starting point.

This is not a formal proof of the now-notorious 'chaos theorems' that have been proved by Black and Newing (1951, in McLean, McMillan, and Monroe 1998); Plott (1967), Kramer (1973), McKelvey (1976, 1979), and Schofield (1983), among others. Nor is this book the place to prove or expound them— for that, see any intermediate or advanced social choice text such as Mueller 1989 or Saari 1995. The purpose of this little excursion into the geometry of social choice is to try to convince the reader that chaos is a real possibility whenever politics goes into two or more dimensions.

This may seem odd, since cycles are rarely observed. But politics is normally structured so as to hide them. Sometimes, however, it is in politicians' interest to bring them to the surface. In William Riker's (1982) canonical example, the Republican Party, created in 1856, deliberately revived the issue of slavery in US national politics in order to split the hegemonic Democratic Party into its northern and southern wings. In that, he claims, they completely succeeded, although at a heavy price. Once the issue of slavery cross-cut the 'left–right' alignment of the time, there was no stable outcome. In the Presidential election of 1860, there were four candidates. Under most plausible electoral systems, the northern Democrat Stephen A. Douglas would have won. But the system actually used—plurality vote filtered through the Electoral College—gave Abraham Lincoln a huge majority in the Electoral College, and successfully concealed, according to Riker, the underlying disequilibrium.

Riker built a great deal on this case—something for which he has been frequently criticized (see especially Green and Shapiro 1994, Mackie 2000). I am willing to concede a lot to the critics without conceding Riker's central point. In particular, I no longer accept Riker's claim that popular preferences were probably in a cycle among three of the four candidates (Lincoln, Douglas, and John Bell). As Mackie (2000) shows, this influential claim of Riker's depends on the assumption that most north-eastern Lincoln voters preferred Bell to Douglas (Riker 1982, Display 9–2, rows 1 and 2). Actually, most of them probably preferred Douglas to Bell, and with that switch Riker's cycle disappears. The chaos theorems are not quite as wide-ranging as they were believed to be when Riker (1982, 1986) wrote, and conditions for stability are a little more generous than he believed them to be. But his central insight remains valid. On critical occasions—however rare they may be— politics goes seriously multidimensional. When that happens, outcomes are extremely unpredictable. Given one set of rules, Lincoln won the 1860 election. Given most other sets of rules, Douglas would have won. The American Civil War might have had a very different course, or a different outcome, or perhaps not happened at all. The fate of slaves in the southern states might have been very different. We return to Riker's story in section 1.3, but first must introduce his distinction between heresthetic and rhetoric.

Rhetoric and Heresthetic

Rhetoric is the art of verbal persuasion. Heresthetic is the art and science of political manipulation. All politicians use rhetoric; some use heresthetic. In order to make this book manageable, I am concentrating on some specialized sorts of political rhetoric.

All politicians use rhetoric to praise their own side (and its policies) and to denounce the other (and its policies). This sort of rhetoric calls for no special comment, except when one politician exercises it much more skilfully than any other, thus giving his side an advantage. For instance, in the years leading up to the 1906 General Election campaign, discussed below, the Conservatives made a powerful rhetorical link between imperialism and xenophobia:

LET 'EM ALL COME

Is the Radical Cry

The Radicals, by their obstruction to the Aliens Bill, are evidently glad to see all foreigners who are criminals; who suffer from loathsome diseases; who are turned out in disgrace by their fellow countrymen; who are paupers; who fill our streets with profligacy and disorder.

The Radical Welcomes Them All

The Unionist Government wants to keep these creatures out of Great Britain. They don't want to see the honest Britisher turned out by these scourings of European slums. They brought in a Bill to check this evil flow of aliens.

But the Radicals said, No! we don't want to stop the foreign criminal and diseased outcast from coming into this country.

By obstruction, the radicals caused the postponement of the Government bill, which safeguarded British Workers.

Next Session, the Government will bring in the Bill again. Show your disgust of Radical tactics, and

SUPPORT THE UNIONIST GOVERNMENT

In the Policy of Fair Play

For your Countrymen

(National Union of Conservative and Unionist Associations, leaflet no. 325, 1904. Quoted in McKenzie and Silver 1968: 60)

But this was neutralized by the Liberal campaign in 1906, which managed to convince the electorate that Free Trade meant the Big Loaf and Protection meant the Little Loaf. (Liberal election agents even turned xenophobia to their advantage by putting a warm, freshly baked British Big Loaf next to a stale Continental rye-bread Little Loaf in committee room windows). Furthermore, the Liberals somehow conveyed the impression that the Conservatives would unleash a flood of Chinese labourers on Britain to take jobs from the British working man. Taking the period from 1895 to 1906 as a whole, therefore, neither side clearly gained the battle of xenophobic rhetoric.

There are, though, some cases in our period when one side gained a rhetorical advantage. The most clear-cut was during the battle between the Peers and the People—as one side called it—from 1909 to 1911. Nobody in our period could match Lloyd George at his peak:

The question will be asked 'Should 500 men, ordinary men chosen accidentally from among the unemployed, override the judgment—the deliberate judgment—of millions of people who are engaged in the industry which makes the wealth of the country?' That is one question. Another will be, who ordained that a few should have the land of Britain as a perquisite; who made 10,000 people owners of the soil, and the rest of us trespassers in the land of our birth . . . ? (Speech at Newcastle upon Tyne 10 October 1909, as quoted by *The Times* 11.10.09)

Lloyd George's purpose was a little bit heresthetical as well as rhetorical. He wished to infuriate the Tory peers so much that they would reject his budget. They did, playing into his hands.

At a deeper level, rhetoric consists of persuading everybody that the world is the way you say it is. It is usually quite easy to persuade your own side of this. Persuading the other side takes more skill. Sometimes you can cloak your argument in religion. There is no truth so final as religious truth. Unfortunately for rhetoricians, there has been no agreed religious truth in Britain during our period: as already discussed, religious alignments concurred with centre–periphery alignments. Religion could be a powerful weapon to rally your side, but not to persuade the other side to see the world as you saw it. Economics is more promising. Especially if Keynes's famous saying is true:

Practical men, who believe themselves to be quite exempt from any intellectual influences, are usually the slaves of some defunct economist. Madmen in authority, who hear voices in the air, are distilling their frenzy from some academic scribbler of a few years back. (Keynes 1936: 383)

The defunct economist in Keynes's sights was perhaps Adam Smith, but more likely David Ricardo or Alfred Marshall: the founder and refounder of the classical economics which Keynes sought to undermine. Classical economics was contested ground in the 1840s. Although Ricardo and his contemporaries argued passionately against the Corn Laws, it was not their voices that Peel (who was not mad) heard in the air. But by the 1860s, classical economics held an intellectual hegemony among British politicians that was not seriously dented until Keynes. That is not to say that all British politicians agreed with the classical prescriptions of free trade, cheap money, and low taxes. It is to say that those who disagreed were on the defensive. They started at a rhetorical disadvantage.

In this sense, the best rhetorician of our period is neither Peel nor Gladstone nor Disraeli nor Lloyd George, but Margaret Thatcher. During her Prime Ministership she evolved a novel economic policy that marked a radical break with the Keynesianism that had dominated British policy-making since 1945. She did not only say that the previous policies had failed. She said that *There is no alternative* to the policies she put in their place, and dumbfounded the critics within and without (Young 1990: 204–5). She said it so often that for a while her enemies nicknamed her Tina.

Riker's Narrative and Its Critics

The US Presidential Election of 1860, which was won by Abraham Lincoln for the new Republican Party, was beyond dispute the most important outcome in the history of presidential elections. Of the four candidates, Lincoln was the most firmly associated with maintaining the Union at all costs. He was opposed to the extension of slavery (although not, in 1860, to the institution of slavery itself). Militant abolitionists who did want to extirpate slavery from the South backed him. Lincoln's election led directly to the South's secession, led by South Carolina, and to the Civil War— by far the most destructive war in the history of the United States, in which many more Americans died than in either World War, Korea, or Vietnam. It also led to the Thirteenth, Fourteenth, and Fifteenth Amendments of the Constitution, which wrote the abolition of slavery and civil and voting rights into it.

Lincoln won with the lowest share of the popular vote[1] achieved by any winner in US presidential history—just under 40 per cent. That was enough to give him a comfortable victory in the Electoral College. The Electoral College, according to the US Constitution, is the body that actually elects the President. Each state has as many Electors as it has representatives in Congress. As every state has two Senators, this rule means that it has two Electors more than the number of its seats in the House of Representatives. Almost all states operated (and still do) a 'winner takes all rule' for their Electors: whichever candidate wins the most support in a state wins all of that state's Electors.

Lincoln and the Republicans had driven a wedge into the previously dominant Democrats, helping them to split into their northern and southern wings. Lincoln posed the following killer question to Douglas in 1858:

Can the people of the [should be 'a'] United States Territory in any lawful way, against the wishes of any citizen of the United States, exclude slavery from its limits prior to the formation of a state constitution? (At Freeport, Illinois, 27 August 1858. Holzer 1994: 96)

As Riker (1986: 2), says, 'To modern readers the question probably seems legalistic in sense and turgid in expression, and probably some are astonished by my description of it as a work of genius. However, it was not just the words themselves, but the setting, that honed this question stiletto-sharp.' Lincoln's question had the same effect as *Have you stopped beating your wife?* But it was harder to evade. Douglas was damned if he said *Yes* and damned if he said *No.* He said *Yes,* and then qualified his answer:

---

[1] Excluding the special case of 1824, another four-way fight, in which nobody won a majority of the Electoral College. Therefore the choice was made by the House of Representatives under the default procedure in the Constitution, for the second and last time in US history (the first was in 1800).

I answer emphatically, as Mr Lincoln has heard me answer a hundred times, on every stump in Illinois, that in my opinion the people of a Territory can by lawful means exclude slavery before it comes in as a State. . . . The people of a Territory have the lawful means to admit it or exclude it as they please, for the reason that slavery cannot exist a day or an hour anywhere unless supported by local police regulations. (Holzer 1994: 106)

As the white population spread across the continent beyond the original thirteen states of 1787, the newly settled areas were organized as Territories with a local legislature but not full statehood. Then, when they were judged to have a large enough population, Congress could vote to admit them as states. The original thirteen states were finely balanced between slave and free, and the Constitution reflects the messy compromises that were needed to get both classes of state to ratify it. The slave states had almost half of the population, and almost half of the seats in both houses of Congress. One of the messy compromises is that, at the demand of the southern states, slaves counted as three-fifths of a person each for the apportionment of congressional seats to the states, although of course they had neither votes nor any other rights. Despite this, it soon became clear that population was growing faster in the non-slave than in the slave parts of the country. So, in due course, the balance of seats in the House of Representatives, which are apportioned by population, would gradually swing to the disadvantage of the slave states. In the Senate, however, with two Senators per state regardless of population, the slave states could retain their block for longer (Weingast 1998).

Between 1791 and 1819, nine Territories were awarded statehood. Five of them were slaveholding (Alabama, Kentucky, Louisiana, Mississippi, and Tennessee). Four were not (Illinois, Indiana, Ohio, and Vermont). In 1819 a bill to admit Missouri was offered. A Representative from New York moved an amendment to prohibit slavery in Missouri. Both sides recognized the issue as momentous. The 77-year-old Thomas Jefferson wrote:

I had for a long time ceased to read newspapers or pay any attention to public affairs, confident they were in good hands, and content to be a passenger in our bark to the shore from which I am not distant. But this momentous question, like a fire bell in the night, awakened and filled me with terror. I considered it at once as the knell of the Union. It is hushed indeed for the moment. But this is a reprieve only, not a final sentence. (Thomas Jefferson Papers Series 1. General Correspondence. 1651–1827, Thomas Jefferson to John Holmes, April 22, 1820, read in facsimile on Library of Congress, Thomas Jefferson Papers website at http://memory.loc.gov/ammem/mtjhtml/mtjhome.html, 16.05.00. The printed version in Peterson 1975: 567–8, has minor punctuation errors.)

The knell was hushed by the Missouri Compromise, according to which Missouri was then admitted as a slave state, but balanced by Maine as a free state. Thereafter, states were admitted in pairs, one slave and one free (Arkansas with Michigan in 1836–7; Florida and Texas with Iowa and Wisconsin in

1845–8). As each state had two Senators, this meant that the balance of free and slave votes in the Senate remained undisturbed. The free states' share of US population, and hence of seats in the House of Representatives, had been growing rapidly through immigration. But a resolution to abolish slavery would have to pass both houses. It could not pass the Senate while the Missouri Compromise reigned.

From 1820 to 1850 the Missouri Compromise ensured the stability of the Union. In 1850 it broke down. California was admitted alone as a free state, and the South could foresee the end of its blocking vote in the Senate. The Wilmot Proviso (1846–8) had already threatened it. The Wilmot Proviso attempted to add a rider to resolutions voting money for war with Mexico, to stipulate that any territory gained as a result of that war should not permit slavery. Wilmot, like the promoter of the Missouri amendment in 1819, was a Representative from a northern district hundreds of miles from the nearest slave. He was moved by the concerns of his own district—to protect working-class whites from increased competition from blacks for jobs. However, to southerners, the whole point of war with Mexico was to gain territory in which slavery would be permitted, and therefore potentially more pro-slavery votes in the Senate. So the Wilmot Proviso was lethal for them. But the proviso itself could never have passed in the Senate. The admission of a free state without a balancing slave state was much more dangerous to southern interests. The war with Mexico led to a huge swathe of territory—modern New Mexico, Arizona, and California joining Texas, which had already declared its independence from Mexico—falling under United States control.

That unreliable guide hindsight sees the slide to war as inevitable from the breakdown of the Missouri Compromise. The Democrats, led by Douglas, tried to push the issue 'back into the localities so that it could not be agitated nationally' (Riker 1986: 4). They hoped to give the South a credible commitment to balancing California by admitting Kansas as a slave state. Their Kansas–Nebraska Act of 1854 ruled that those territories, which were rapidly gaining enough settlers to qualify as states, should decide for themselves whether to permit slavery. This led to a miniature civil war between slave and free forces in Kansas. Meanwhile, the southern-dominated Supreme Court destabilized the situation from the other side. In *Scott* v. *Sandford* (1857; 60 US 393), a slave, Dred Scott, had been brought to a state where slavery was illegal and then returned to Missouri, where it was legal. Scott sued, claiming that residence in a free state had freed him. The Court held that, according to the Constitution, blacks were not and could not be citizens of the United States, and federal law could not override the Constitution and make them so. This threatened to prevent any future federal attempts to outlaw slavery in Territories that were not yet states. Nevertheless, the Congressional Democrats came very close to securing a vote in both houses, in 1858, to admit Kansas as a slave state.

Democratic coalition. It also explains why Democrats from Jefferson onwards reacted with such fear and alarm at the attempts. It explains why so much of federal politics was concentrated on the apparently trivial issue of slavery in the Territories. Most of the Territories were very infertile ground for a slave economy, and nobody including slaveholders had any serious intention of introducing slaves to such places as Arizona or New Mexico. But if Territories were slaveholding, then future states would be slaveholding, and if future states were slaveholding, the balance rule for the Senate, introduced as the Missouri Compromise, could continue. And, given the rules for the passage of legislation through the bicameral Congress, the southern block on the Senate was absolutely central to preserving the peculiar institution in its heartland of the Old South.

In a word, the analytic narrative constantly recurs to the importance of institutions. Riker's version of it also lays great stress on heresthetic. Abraham Lincoln is celebrated as the greatest rhetorician in American political history. (Historians and literary critics remain fascinated by how he could craft the lapidary phrases of the Gettysburg Address while regarding it, and himself, as rhetorical failures). But Riker makes a plausible case for him as a heresthetician as well. He and others forced the dimension of slavery back into federal politics against the Democrats' increasingly desperate attempts to suppress it. And he blighted Douglas's future with his killer question at Freeport. It is now clear that Riker's attempt to portray each of the crises that led to the Civil War (especially the Wilmot Proviso and the 1860 election result) as an instance of cycling is unsuccessful. But his basic point remains sound.

Where there is equilibrium, it is (in the ungainly phrase) 'structure-induced equilibrium'. The underlying cycles that would lead outcomes to be unstable are suppressed because legislatures and constitutions are written in a certain way. The US Senate has a veto over all legislation not exclusively reserved to the House, and over all constitutional amendments. The two-Senators-per-state rule was therefore utterly crucial in the course of events leading to the Civil War. It distorted the slavery issue into an issue about the Territories. Other institutions that turn out to have been vital include the Democratic Party's two-thirds rule in its nominating convention; the practice (not a constitutional requirement) that most states give all their Electors to the party which wins a plurality of the electoral vote in the state; and the Twelfth Amendment's rules for dealing with the case where no presidential candidate gets a majority of the Electors' votes. All the games that politicians played in knowledge of these rules may be characterised as 'veto games'. We need to understand *veto players*, *extensive-form games*, *backward induction*, and *credible commitments*.

A veto player is simply one who has the right to make a move that cannot be overridden. The doctrine of parliamentary sovereignty, as taught to generations of students in or of Britain, states that Parliament can do anything except bind its successor. On the face of it, this turns the UK Parliament into a veto player in relation to the courts and the existing law (including laws

In 1858, when he posed the killer question,[2] Lincoln was fighting Douglas for a Senate seat in Illinois, a free state in which anti-slavery sentiment was growing. Those who know their *Huckleberry Finn* will recall that the plot turns on Huck and Jim missing Cairo, Illinois in a fog as they run away on a raft drifting down the Mississippi, so that they are carried deeper and deeper into the slave South. The constituency in which Douglas was running expected him to answer *Yes*; as the author of the Kansas–Nebraska Act he would be doubly embarrassed if he did not. But the 1858 campaign for the Senate mattered to Douglas not only for itself but also for his intended campaign for the Democratic nomination for the Presidency in 1860. To satisfy the nationwide constituency of Democrats with a voice in choosing their presidential nominee, Douglas would have to answer *No*. He could not credibly evade the killer question. He answered *Yes* and won the Senate seat. When he ran for the Democratic nomination for the Presidency in 1860, his campaign was so divisive that the party split down the middle. The Democrats had a rule that their presidential nominee must gain two-thirds of the vote at their nominating convention. This was designed to ensure (or at least had the effect of ensuring) that every Democratic presidential nominee had the support of both northern and southern Democrats. In the circumstances of 1860, it had no chance of securing unity. No Democrat, northern or southern, would be able to get two-thirds of the votes at the convention. The southern Democrats nominated John C. Breckinridge. The fourth candidate, John Bell, represented the southern wing of the old Whig party whose northern successors were the Republicans. According to the county election returns analysed by Lipset (1960: 348), Bell's strength in the South was in high-slave counties and Breckinridge's in low-slave counties. Lipset interprets this to mean that higher-status voters in the South continued to support the candidate whose former party had had most upper-class support.

Lincoln and Breckinridge were the extreme candidates. So it is safe to guess that almost everybody who voted for one of them ranked the other last. They were also strongly regional candidates–Lincoln of the Midwest (but with a strong following in New England and the Mid-Atlantic region as well), and Breckinridge of the South. Supporters of the two non-extreme candidates, Douglas and Bell, had regional, class, and slavery interests that pulled them in cross-cutting directions.

[2] The latest editor of the *Lincoln–Douglas Debates* disputes the long-held view that it was a killer question—a view which dates back at least to a 1901 novel cited by Riker (1986: 6–7). Holzer (1994: 89) points to Douglas's ready and fluent answer. It is true that Douglas's answer is ingenious. Good politicians must be good rhetoricians, and both Lincoln and Douglas, in their set-piece debates, were good rhetoricians. Douglas gets around the objection that *Dred Scott* forbade such action by saying that the legislature of a Territory could simply fail to police the fugitive slave laws if it wished to outlaw slavery in practice. But his unqualified first sentence gave Lincoln the weapon the Republicans needed to ensure that the Democrats would split at their 1860 nominating convention. Holzer does not mention the Democratic nominating convention's two-thirds rule (cf. Weingast 1998), which is probably crucial. Lincoln and the Republicans needed only to ensure that Douglas could not command two-thirds of the votes at the 1860 convention. Nobody could.

1845–8). As each state had two Senators, this meant that the balance of free and slave votes in the Senate remained undisturbed. The free states' share of US population, and hence of seats in the House of Representatives, had been growing rapidly through immigration. But a resolution to abolish slavery would have to pass both houses. It could not pass the Senate while the Missouri Compromise reigned.

From 1820 to 1850 the Missouri Compromise ensured the stability of the Union. In 1850 it broke down. California was admitted alone as a free state, and the South could foresee the end of its blocking vote in the Senate. The Wilmot Proviso (1846–8) had already threatened it. The Wilmot Proviso attempted to add a rider to resolutions voting money for war with Mexico, to stipulate that any territory gained as a result of that war should not permit slavery. Wilmot, like the promoter of the Missouri amendment in 1819, was a Representative from a northern district hundreds of miles from the nearest slave. He was moved by the concerns of his own district—to protect working-class whites from increased competition from blacks for jobs. However, to southerners, the whole point of war with Mexico was to gain territory in which slavery would be permitted, and therefore potentially more pro-slavery votes in the Senate. So the Wilmot Proviso was lethal for them. But the proviso itself could never have passed in the Senate. The admission of a free state without a balancing slave state was much more dangerous to southern interests. The war with Mexico led to a huge swathe of territory—modern New Mexico, Arizona, and California joining Texas, which had already declared its independence from Mexico—falling under United States control.

That unreliable guide hindsight sees the slide to war as inevitable from the breakdown of the Missouri Compromise. The Democrats, led by Douglas, tried to push the issue 'back into the localities so that it could not be agitated nationally' (Riker 1986: 4). They hoped to give the South a credible commitment to balancing California by admitting Kansas as a slave state. Their Kansas–Nebraska Act of 1854 ruled that those territories, which were rapidly gaining enough settlers to qualify as states, should decide for themselves whether to permit slavery. This led to a miniature civil war between slave and free forces in Kansas. Meanwhile, the southern-dominated Supreme Court destabilized the situation from the other side. In *Scott* v. *Sandford* (1857; 60 US 393), a slave, Dred Scott, had been brought to a state where slavery was illegal and then returned to Missouri, where it was legal. Scott sued, claiming that residence in a free state had freed him. The Court held that, according to the Constitution, blacks were not and could not be citizens of the United States, and federal law could not override the Constitution and make them so. This threatened to prevent any future federal attempts to outlaw slavery in Territories that were not yet states. Nevertheless, the Congressional Democrats came very close to securing a vote in both houses, in 1858, to admit Kansas as a slave state.

made by previous Parliaments). It can, and sometimes does, reverse the effects of court judgements by enacting laws that overturn them. Then, it is a veto player in a sense that, for instance, the United States Congress is not. But the UK Parliament is not a unitary actor. UK Acts of Parliament begin with the formula:

BE IT ENACTED by the Queen's most Excellent Majesty, by and with the advice and consent of the Lords Spiritual and Temporal, and Commons, in this present Parliament assembled, and by the authority of the same, as follows

Parliament, thus, has three parts: *the Queen's most Excellent Majesty* (the Crown), the *Lords Spiritual and Temporal,* and the *Commons.* Most studies of parliamentary manoeuvres, including this one, concentrate on the last. But we must consider the others as serious potential veto players.

Many readers will be familiar with so-called 'normal-form games'. In a normal-form game, the payoffs to each actor from each outcome are summarized as a single number in a matrix. However, game theorists have always known that the normal-form omits the sequence of play. To model the fact that players move in sequence, and that they either know or can guess one another's preferences, we need to represent the game of decision-making in a multi-chamber legislature by a *game tree,* also known as an *exten-sive-form game.* Fig. 1.3 is a simplified extensive-form game of British parliamentary procedure. There are three actors, Commons, Lords, and King, and they move in a sequence determined by the rules of parliamentary procedure. In the stylized example of Fig. 1.3, the Commons moves first. (A bill may be introduced in either house, but all important bills in our period were introduced first in the Commons). Having gone through its internal procedures (First Reading, Second Reading, Committee Stage, Report), it either produces a Commons bill c or votes it down. If a bill is defeated at this or any other stage, the status quo (sq) continues. If the Commons produces a bill, it goes to the Lords. The Lords consider the Commons bill through their internal procedures. At the end of those they either accept the Commons version c or substitute their version l. If they do the latter, the bill returns to the Commons, who either accept the Lords' amendments or reject them. If they accept some and reject others, they produce a modified bill c'. There is provision in the rules of Parliament for a conference of both houses to resolve disputes. Unlike other bicameral assemblies, however, the British Parliament had allowed these formal procedures to go out of use before 1846. In principle, then, a bill may shuttle between the two houses until it runs out of time.[3]

The final actor in the parliamentary game is the monarch, here labelled King. The monarch retains the power to reject bills, although this last hap-

---

[3] A further series of branches should be added to the tree in Fig. 1.3 to show these iterations, with the outcomes in which the bill runs out of time labelled *SQ*. This is important in the practical cases in later chapters, but omitted here for clarity.

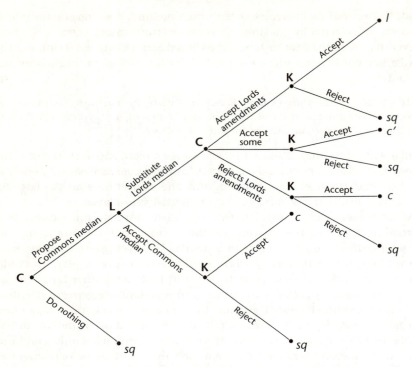

Fig. 1.3. An extensive-form game. The legislative process in a tricameral parliament.

    sq   *k*   *l*   *c′*   *c*

Fig. 1.4. Ideal points of the actors in Fig. 1.3.

pened in the early eighteenth century. However, this monarchical power
needs to be left in Fig. 1.3 so long as there is the remotest possibility that a
monarch might consider using it or—importantly—that one of the other
actors thinks he might. King George V toyed with the idea in 1910–14.

A device often used in studies of the US Congress, the European Union, and
other multi-player legislatures is to map each actor's favourite position in relation to the status quo. Fig. 1.4 is a stylized example for the data in Fig. 1.3.

Where the actors stand is an empirical matter. I have drawn Fig. 1.4 so that
everybody prefers some change to the status quo. In theory, the preferences
of the monarch can be inferred directly from what he says or does. The preferences of the two houses are a slightly trickier matter. At this point game
theorists appeal to the *median voter theorem* described above. According to the
median voter theorem, the preferences of the median member of each
chamber may stand for the preferences of that chamber. The reasoning is that
any position other than the median voter's favourite–that is, the 'median

optimum' for that chamber—will lose a binary vote to the median optimum. Therefore, the chamber's favourite position is its median optimum.

The player whose turn ends the game has different preferences to those of earlier players and has the options of accepting or vetoing the options presented to her. Let us assume for the time being that these preferences are common knowledge. Then, some options that earlier players might otherwise take become much less attractive to them because they know that the last player may veto them. Another way of saying the same thing is to refer to *the rule of anticipated reactions*.

If the political game really were as simple as that portrayed in Figs 1.3 and 1.4, the outcome would be clear-cut. The King is the veto player, and will veto any option that is further from his optimum K in Fig. 1.4 than from the status quo point sq. I have drawn Fig. 1.4 to represent a situation in which the Commons' median optimum is the furthest from the status quo and the King's is the closest. However, the King prefers the Lords' median optimum to the status quo. If the preferences were as shown, and the King were an unconditional veto player, then the outcome of the game in Fig. 1.3 is predetermined. We read it by going backwards along each branch of the tree from each outcome. It is common knowledge that the King prefers l to sq and prefers sq to c. Therefore, in the branches that end with the King making a choice between c and sq, he will choose sq: that is, veto the bill. In the branches that end with the King making a choice between l and sq, he will choose l—that is, accept the bill, as amended by the Lords. Now let us move back up the tree. If the Lords amend the bill, the Commons are the second-last actor. Do they reinstate their bill, which would enact c, or do they accept the Lords' amendments? They know that if they reinstate c, the King will veto the bill; if they accept l, he will accept it. They would rather have l than sq. Therefore, if the Lords amend the bill, the Commons will accept their amendments. Back up one stage to the Lords' decision. If they amend the bill, they can work out that it will be carried as amended. As that is their best possible outcome, that is what they will do. Back up finally to the first decision: do the Commons propose the bill at all, or do they abandon it? Well, they would rather have l than sq, so it is worth their while to propose a bill. Unless they want to make a point (which they probably do), they would save a lot of time by offering the Lords' median optimum l and not their own, c, nor any intermediate position c'. If the Lords have a veto, they would veto any compromise position such as c'. The Commons would then have fully anticipated the reactions of the other two players in the game.

This form of reasoning is called backward induction. It enables us to solve extensive-form games. Most real extensive-form games are much more complicated than Fig. 1.3. They are complicated, first, because the favourite positions of each player are not always common knowledge; second, because if underlying opinion is not single-dimensional, heresthetic politicians will try to regroup the issues so as to win on them. Third, and relatedly, it is arbitrary to say when a game ends. Persistent losers, as Riker says, always have an incentive to repackage the issues so that they come together in a way that turns the tables. How that works depends on the number of veto players.

The essential relationship between veto players and the dimensionality of the game is as follows. Veto players add stability, but at the expense of majority rule. A reorientation of national US politics around the new slavery agenda was held up, even though a majority of voters wanted it, because the Senate was a veto player. Up to 1911, many policies which could win a Commons majority, and a number which actually did, were vetoed in the Lords. Even in single-dimensional politics, that could mean the substitution of the median peer's optimum for the median MP's. In multidimensional politics, it meant that some points that could have been reached in a simple majority game were inaccessible. But it also meant that a politician who could restructure issues in order to win an unexpected Lords majority (Peel and Disraeli) or who could get rid of the veto itself (Lloyd George, with a little help from his friends), could achieve more than any other.

We need to look a bit more closely at the veto players in the British parliamentary game in our period.

The Crown

For most of our period, the monarch was a Tory. Queen Victoria started her reign under the wing of her first, Whig, Prime Minister, Lord Melbourne. In the 1830s, she disliked Peel, and prevented him from coming to power in 1839. However, under Prince Albert's influence, she changed her mind and approved of Peel's 1841–6 administration. From Disraeli's premiership onwards, she was firmly partisan, approving her Conservative administrations, and loathing her Liberal ones. In 1892, she wrote as follows to one of the leaders of the Unionist Party, which had just lost a General Election, about W. E. Gladstone, who had just won it:

The danger to the country . . . which is involved in having all these great interests entrusted to the shaking hand of an old, wild, and incomprehensible man of $82^{1}/_{2}$, is very great! It is a terrible trial, but, thank God, the country is sound, and it cannot last. (Victoria to Lord Lansdowne 12.08.92 in Newton 1929: 100. This letter was not included in the official edition of *The Letters of Queen Victoria*.)

Matthew (1995: 260–1) summarizes Queen Victoria's attitude to her Liberal governments in 1880–6 thus:

Victoria saw herself as an integral part of policy making, with the right to instruct, to abuse, and to hector. She corresponded about Liberal government policy and the content of the Queen's Speech with Conservative opposition leaders (but not *vice versa*); she continued to exclude certain Liberal MPs from Cabinet, and to object to lower-level appointment on grounds of policy; she expected revenge for Majuba; she opposed the Cabinet's withdrawal or reduction of British troops from Afghanistan and Egypt; she abused her ministers privately and, in the notorious case of the *'en clair* telegram' [discussed in Chapter 3] publicly over their handling of Sudanese policy; she objected to

Cabinet ministers' speeches; she offered to help Salisbury dissolve at the most propitious moment in 1885; she opposed Home Rule; and she did all these in her official capacity as Queen and Empress.

Edward VII was less partisan, although he did refuse to create enough peers to enact the 1909 Budget. George V, before becoming King, called Asquith 'not quite a gentleman' and Lloyd George 'that damned fellow' (both quoted by Bogdanor 1995: 67).

Was the monarch, then, a veto player in any of the games this book considers? Not in Peel's games: the queen supported him, but could not prevent him from resigning in June 1846. Not, effectively, in the games of Gladstone and Salisbury. Queen Victoria not only did as Matthew lists, but also tried to conspire with Gladstone's opponents in 1886 to form an anti-Home-Rule coalition (see e.g. her letters to George Goschen and his replies, in Buckle 1928, 2nd ser. iii. 712–13; 3rd ser. i. 22–7.) But they were quite capable of doing that on their own account. Gladstone's Home Rule Bills never got far enough for any question of a royal veto to be considered.

However, Edward VII and George V were more serious veto players, precisely because they were less extreme and somewhat wiser. Both were perturbed by some of the Asquith and Lloyd George administrations' policies: the 1909 Budget, reform of the House of Lords, and above all Home Rule. In 1914 George V seriously considered either refusing the Royal Assent to the Home Rule Act or dismissing the Liberal Government. He took advice from constitutional specialists, who happened to be Unionists. They confirmed him in his opinion that imposing Home Rule on Ulster was such a radical step that it warranted an equally radical reaction (Bogdanor 1995: 128–34). Fortunately, the First World War intervened.

Thus the game in Fig. 1.3 is not truly realistic. But it draws attention to something that is easy to forget if we do not think formally. George V could have refused assent to the Home Rule Bill or dismissed his government. We consider below the Australian crisis of 1975, where the Governor-General, that is, the representative of the Queen in Australia, did dismiss his government. But such actions by George V, like the real actions of Sir John Kerr, would not end the political game. Apart from anything else, they would call into question the legitimacy of the King himself. I consider this below in the section on the people as veto player.

The House of Lords

From the start of our period until 1909, all political actors assumed that the House of Lords was an unconditional veto player in every respect save one: that it could not reject a money bill. The almost silent passage of the Repeal of the Corn Laws in the Lords in 1846 is one of the most remarkable features of that remarkable episode, and one almost unnoticed by most of the modern commentators.

The House of Lords was an active veto player from 1846 to 1911. The Lords had an inbuilt Tory majority. By definition, it comprised the eldest sons (or other closest male relations) of previous peers, plus those newly created as peers. Almost all peers were extensive landowners at the time of their creation; those who were not almost all became landowners, or their heirs did. A ruthless non-Tory Prime Minister could try to change the partisan make-up by creating peers with rival vested interests—capitalists or labourers, for example. The only ruthless non-Tory Prime Minister to have done so in our period was Lloyd George (see Chapter 6). Neither Gladstone nor any Labour Prime Minister until Tony Blair did; whereas both Salisbury and Thatcher, the two most determined Conservative Prime Ministers of our period, freely created peers from their own side. According to a table drawn up for Gladstone in 1892, he had created eighty-four new peers since 1868; Disraeli and Salisbury, who between them had been Prime Ministers for the same length of time as he had, had created 101. Furthermore, Gladstone stayed with the traditional criteria of selection, so that most of his eighty-four peers were landed. Accordingly, many of them or their successors deserted the Liberals in 1886 of the thirty-three peers created by Gladstone between 1880 and 1885, 'at most eight were active Liberals after 1886' (Matthew 1995: 265). Thus the vested interest of the Lords was the landed interest. Throughout our period the Tory Party has been closer to the landed interest than have the other parties.

It was common knowledge between the parties in 1884 that the Third Reform Bill, which widened the franchise by bringing the county franchise in line with that in borough constituencies, would be rejected in the Lords. Salisbury therefore offered Gladstone a deal: if the Liberals would agree to a Redistribution Bill and a bipartisan commission would agree on the constituency boundaries under it, the Tory-dominated Lords would pass the Reform and Redistribution Bills together (see Chapter 3). Salisbury thus used the Lords' veto power to force redistribution on the Gladstone administration. The Lords rejected Irish Home Rule in 1893; they would have rejected it in 1886 if it had reached them, but it was defeated in the Commons before being sent to the Lords.

The events of 1909–11 both illustrated and checked the Lords' veto power. Like much of the rest of the British constitution, the doctrine that the Lords could not reject a money bill was not written down in any constitutional text. Therefore, on 30 November 1909, the House of Lords rejected Lloyd George's budget by 350 votes to 75. Roy Jenkins comments:

As is so often the case when the House of Lords is engaged in reaching a peculiarly silly decision, there were many comments on the high level of the debate and on the enhancement it gave to the deliberative quality of the chamber. (Jenkins 1968: 101)

The Lords had refused to vote supply. Therefore there was no money to pay the wages of public employees. So the Liberal government dissolved Parliament immediately. In the ensuing election, probably the most dramatic in twentieth-century Britain, the Liberals campaigned on the theme of 'the Peers against the People'. They succeeded in reversing the adverse trend of by-election results. Although their lead over the Conservatives was sharply cut from the huge lead they had had in 1906, so that the Irish Party held the balance, the parties hostile to the Lords (Liberals, Irish, and Labour) won a comfortable majority. The Liberals then introduced a bill to replace the absolute veto power of the Lords by a 'suspensory veto': that is, a provision that the Lords could reject a Commons bill twice, but if it was presented for a third time it would become law without Lords' approval.

This Parliament Bill then became the scene of another constitutional conflict which replayed that of the previous year. Forced by the breakdown of interparty talks (discussed in Chapter 6) to call another election, Asquith asked George V for a guarantee that, should the Liberals be returned again, he would be prepared to create enough Liberal peers to enact the Parliament Bill. This the King did very reluctantly: one of his private secretaries urged him not to; but the other clinched the issue by telling him (incorrectly) that if he refused to give the guarantees and Asquith resigned, the Tory leader Balfour would not form an administration—in which case the king would have been back with Asquith again.

Parliament was dissolved and a second election fought with exactly the same result, in aggregate, as the previous one. Though many seats changed hands, the changes cancelled one another out. The Parliament Bill was therefore enacted, finally passing the Lords on 10 August 1911 by 131 votes to 114. No creation of peers was needed.

The Parliament Acts of 1911 and 1949 (which reduced the suspensory veto from two sessions to one) changed the backward induction game. They divided it into two games, which may be called the post-election game and the pre-election game. In the post-election game, when a government has been newly returned, the Lords veto has no effect except delay. In the pre-election game, when a General Election is due before the bill in question had been back and forth the necessary number of times, the veto remains in effect absolute, as it was before 1911.

The structure-induced equilibrium in British politics is therefore complex. In the last two years before a General Election, the median peer remains a veto player. Early in the life of a Parliament, there is no veto player outside the Commons, with the uncertain exception of the people. Radical non-Tory governments can be radical early in their terms. The Lords did not obstruct the welfare and nationalization measures of the Attlee Labour government (1945–50), probably because they had learnt the lesson of 1911. But, as the model predicts, that government ran into increasing trouble from 1948 onwards, despite the 1949 Parliament Act. The Blair government elected in 1997 also got its radicalism in early. By 2000, even after the removal of the hereditary peers, it was sustaining frequent defeats in the Lords, some on civil libertarian issues, others on issues of traditional morality. The radicalism of Margaret Thatcher was unchecked by the Lords because she was a Tory radical.

The People: An Uncertain Veto Player

Up to now, we have been discussing the monarch and the Lords as unconditional veto players: that is, as players whose decision ends the game. The truth
is more complicated. In all the crises discussed in this book, the possibility
has always existed of an appeal to the people. If a General Election returns
the party that controlled the Commons at the time of the previous veto game,
the other players probably have to give way. Peel rejected the idea of a
dissolution and General Election in 1846 because he worried about the effect
on social order of an election held at such a heightened mood of public
opinion. For the two decades that Salisbury controlled the House of Lords,
he saw it as a bulwark against 'disintegration', by which he meant an attack
on (especially landed) property of which he accused the Liberals. Under his
leadership, however, the Lords defended property where it was safe to do so
and gave in where it was unsafe. It was safe to do so in places out of the public
eye, as for example in private bill committees, or in defence of legal monopo-
lies who extracted economic rent—solicitors, parliamentary agents, and so on
(Adonis 1993: chs. 4–5; on landed professions and rent extraction see Offer
1981). It was unsafe to reject anything politically popular. Salisbury's own colleagues thought he was playing a dangerous game of brinkmanship in this
way over the franchise reform bill of 1884, but he was saved by Gladstone's
unexpected capitulation to him (Chapter 3).

Après Cecil, le deluge. Salisbury's successors as Tory leaders in the Lords lacked
both his foresight and his control. The Liberals fought the election of January
1910 on the platform of 'the Peers against the People' and won more seats
than they probably would otherwise have done. Although Lloyd George
did not initially produce his budget as a deliberate provocation of the Lords,
their subsequent behaviour gave him an ideal platform for the anti-Lords
rhetoric that enlivened the autumn of 1909. The Liberal and allies' victory
forced the House of Lords to pass the 1909 Budget. In the summer of 1911,
the Conservative Lords divided between 'hedgers' and 'ditchers'. The 'ditchers' were prepared to die in the last ditch in defence of their own powers,
even if it meant forcing the king to create enough peers to pass the Parliament Bill. The 'hedgers' argued that that would change the character of
the Lords even more radically than would submission. As recorded above, the
'ditchers' gave way.

King George V did not actually do either of the things that would have
brought him into constitutional confrontation with Lloyd George and his
ministerial colleagues. In 1910 he agreed with great reluctance to create peers
if required after another election confirmed the Liberals in control of the
Commons (Jenkins 1968: 173–83; Bogdanor 1995: 117). And he did
not either refuse Royal Assent to the Home Rule Act or dismiss the Liberal
government in 1914. Had he done any of these things, a new and highly
unpredictable game would have begun. How it would have ended is unknow-
able. But it was common knowledge among the players that the stakes were

high. Kings and peers who exercised their veto power once might lose it a second time.

The nearest parallel to the actions that George V contemplated is the dismissal of the Labor (Whitlam) government in Australia by the Governor-General, Sir John Kerr, in 1975. The parallel is not exact, and too much must not be read into it. But it gives some hints about the game that might follow a royal or upper-chamber veto. The constitutional conflict began, as in Britain in 1909, when the upper house refused supply. The Australian Senate, unlike the British Lords, is an elected house. Sir John Kerr, after taking advice from the Chief Justice of Australia (a former minister from the opposition Liberal party), acted swiftly and secretly, improving the soundproofing of his office before his coup (Whitlam 1979: xi–xii). He summoned Gough Whitlam and the Opposition leader Malcolm Fraser to his office. Fraser, embarrassingly, arrived first and his driver was instructed to hide his car round the back so that Whitlam would not see that he was there (Whitlam 1979: 108). Kerr then dismissed Whitlam, and appointed Fraser Prime Minister. When the Speaker of the House of Representatives asked for an appointment to protest that Whitlam still had the confidence of the House, Kerr delayed seeing him until he had dissolved Parliament. He then told him 'that I had already dissolved both Houses of Parliament and that there would be an election for both on 13 December. There being nothing else of relevance to say the meeting ended' (Kerr 1979: 374). The Speaker protested to the Queen, saying that Kerr's actions 'will damage the standing of your representative in Australia and even yourself'. Her office told him that under the Australian Constitution the Queen had no power to intervene (see the letters quoted in Whitlam 1979: 175–7).

Fraser had foreknowledge of Kerr's veto play. In the short run it was successful for Fraser and his party: they won the ensuing General Election, in both houses, comfortably. In the long run, it has affected the two veto players quite differently. The legitimacy of the Senate has grown; that of the monarchy has shrunk. The final provocative chapter of Whitlam's (1979) provoked and provocative book is entitled 'Towards the Republic'. In fact, the Australians rejected a republic in their referendum of November 1999. But that is because the single alternative on the ballot was a head of state elected by both chambers of parliament, which the voters construed as a 'politicians' president'. A large majority of Australian public opinion was republican. Some royal advisers in Britain, but not all, have foreseen that controversial royal vetoes could similarly damage the legitimacy of the monarchy. This may have contributed to the failure of George V to exercise vetoes in 1910 and 1914.

In the days before opinion polls—that is, for all of our crises except the most recent–the People's move was unknown before it occurred. We cannot tell what the People would have done when a General Election was contemplated but rejected, for instance in 1846 or 1866. When a crisis led to a decisive General Election, as in 1886, 1906, and 1922, we have to ask whether the losing side anticipated the result. If it did, why did it allow the election to happen? If it did not, why not?

Leading from the Wrong Side

One common heresthetic move is 'leading from the wrong side'. This book will deal with two notable cases:

• Peel and Repeal of the Corn Laws
• Disraeli and the Second Reform Act

Peel led the agricultural party, which abolished agricultural protection. Disraeli led the rural party, which enfranchised the towns. Many upsets in democratic politics share this feature. General de Gaulle came to power in France with the support of those who wanted to keep Algeria French; he promptly gave Algeria its independence. It was the hawkish Israeli Prime Minister Menachem Begin, not his doveish predecessors, who was induced to come to Camp David and sign the first Arab–Israeli peace agreement. The Peronist Prime Minister of Argentia, Carlos Menem, demolished the protective institutions which had nurtured Peronism and which Peronism had nurtured.

Part of the explanation may be simply surprise. Disraeli never originally intended to widen the franchise by as much as he did. The previous Whig-Liberal government had failed to reform the franchise because of a split in its ranks—Disraeli moved swiftly and surprisingly. But this explanation does not fit more long-drawn-out stories such as Repeal of the Corn Laws. However, where politics is two-dimensional, leading from the wrong side is easier than when it is not. Peel and his allies put together a coalition that mustered enough support, first in the Cabinet, and then in each house of Parliament, on the second dimension to overcome its unpopularity on the main economic dimension of politics.

A politician who sits in the centre has less far to go than one who tries to lead from the wrong side. That does not necessarily mean that the centre is a good place to be. We shall argue in Chapter 6 that Lloyd George foresaw the marginalization of the Liberals. While politics is one-dimensional, a centre party may indeed espouse the median voter's favourite policies. But it may still be severely squeezed by the plurality electoral system. This was what Lloyd George feared. His fears were well grounded. At least, from his position in the centre, he was able to try out leaps in all directions without any one of them seeming quite as dramatic as Peel's or Disraeli's leaps into the dark.

What Is not in this Analytic Narrative and Why

Not all cataclysms are heresthetic. Since 1846, Britain has acquired and lost an empire and fought two world wars. Social and economic conditions have changed out of recognition. People are vastly richer and healthier than in 1846, but they have not grown richer or healthier as fast as those of some other countries. Even if we restrict ourselves narrowly to high politics, there have been cataclysms on which this book has nothing to say outside this brief section. Define a *landslide election* as a General Election in which the party which went on to form the government won 60 per cent or more of the seats. There were landslide elections in 1832, 1895, 1900, 1918, 1924, 1931, 1935, 1945, 1983, and 1997. (If the threshold for a landslide is set higher, at two-thirds of the seats, the cases are 1832, 1918, 1924, 1931 and 1935). Table 1.1 ranks General Elections since 1832 according to the proportion of seats won by the party which went on to form a government.

The first thing to notice about Table 1.1 is that it does not correspond to many people's perceptions. The General Election of 1906 was not a Liberal landslide (the Liberals won 59.7 per cent of the seats with 49.0 per cent of

Table 1.1. British General Elections 1832–1997, in descending order of winner's share of seats

Election	Seats to winner	Total seats	Winner's seat share	Election	Seats to winner	Total seats	Winner's seat share
1931	554	615	0.901	1955	344	630	0.546
1935	432	615	0.702	1859	357	654	0.546
1924	419	615	0.681	1880	352	652	0.540
1918	478	707	0.676	1874	350	652	0.537
1832	441	658	0.670	1979	339	635	0.534
1997	419	659	0.636	1970	330	630	0.524
1945	393	640	0.614	1837	344	658	0.523
1895	411	670	0.613	1992	336	651	0.516
1983	397	650	0.611	1951	321	625	0.514
1900	402	670	0.600	1950	315	625	0.504
1906	400	670	0.597	1964	317	630	0.503
1868	387	658	0.588	1974O	319	635	0.502
1886	393	670	0.587	1885	319	670	0.476
1835	385	658	0.585	1974F	301	635	0.474
1959	365	630	0.579	1929	288	615	0.468
1987	376	650	0.578	1847	293	658	0.445
1857	377	654	0.576	1910J	275	670	0.410
1966	363	630	0.576	1892	272	670	0.406
1865	370	658	0.562	1910D	272	670	0.406
1922	345	615	0.561	1923	159	615	0.259
1841	367	658	0.558				

Note to Tables 1.1 and 1.2: Omitting 1852, where the link between election result and government formation is too tenuous for data to be usable.

Source for Tables 1.1 and 1.2: 1832–95, Craig 1981: Table 1; 1900–92, Butler and Butler 1994: 213–19 (transposing final 2 columns for 1987 and 1992); 1997, Butler and Kavanagh 1997: Table A1–1.

the votes cast). Nor was that of 1979 a Conservative landslide (the Conservatives won 53.4 per cent of the seats with 43.9 per cent of the vote). On the other hand, the elections of 1924 and 1935, which are rarely analysed in detail, were both Conservative landslides.

In any case, the seats won by a party in a General Election are the product of two things: the votes cast for it, and the operation of the electoral system which maps votes cast into seats won. The British electoral system usually gives the winner an advantage: the winning party's share of votes maps on to a higher share of seats. Moreover, the winner's advantage itself varies from election to election. So perhaps the right way to characterize landslides is by votes cast. Although statistics for share of the national vote go back to 1832, they are highly misleading for elections before 1880 because of unopposed returns. Even from 1880 to 1918, they are distorted by unopposed returns in Ireland. But Table 1.2 can be interpreted with that caution in mind.

Define a *vote landslide* as a General Election in which the winning side won more than half of the vote. There have been vote landslides only in 1880, 1886, 1900, 1931, and 1935, and unopposed returns in Ireland cloud the interpretation of the first three. To connect vote landslides and seat landslides, we need a third concept, which I shall call a *power landslide*. A power landslide is the difference between the winning party's vote share and its seat share. It may be measured absolutely as (seat share – vote share), or relatively as ((seat share – vote share)/vote share). The relative measure is a better measure of the extra power delivered by the electoral system. In seven elections since 1880 the winner's seat share has exceeded its vote share by over one-third; in descending order these are 1997 (47.2 per cent bonus), 1922, 1983, 1918, 1924, and 1987.

Contemporary British historians still seem (despite some recent corrections) much more interested in the parties of the left than in the hegemonic Conservative Party, and therefore have failed to analyse such cases as 1924 or 1935. This is one reason for the disparity between the elections that are thought of as landslides and those that are actually landslides. Another is that people confuse landslide election outcomes with landslide consequences. This book is about consequences, not election results, and therefore the seat and power measures are more relevant than the vote measure. A landslide election may be important for giving the elected government leeway it would not have if it had been elected more narrowly, and thus more opportunity to change direction radically. At the time of writing, the 1997 Labour Government seems to come into this category. But the evidence is not all one way. Peel's large majority was a hindrance, not a help, to his radical change. Lloyd George's heresthetic was built on a small proportion of Commons seats.

Nevertheless, we must say *something* about the election landslides which did not lead to any change of direction. Disregarding 1832 (a landslide in every sense, but outside our time frame), there was only one nineteenth-century case, namely 1895. The 1895 election marked the clear rejection of the Liberal minority administration of 1892. But the Unionists who came to

Table 1.2. British General Elections 1832–1997, in descending order of winner's share of votes, showing bonus calculations

Election	Seats to winner	Total seats	Winner's vote share	Winner's absolute bonus	Winner's relative bonus
1931	554	615	0.670	0.231	0.344
1832	441	658	0.667	0.003	0.005
1859	357	654	0.657	−0.111	−0.169
1857	377	654	0.651	−0.075	−0.115
1868	387	658	0.615	−0.027	−0.044
1865	370	658	0.602	−0.040	−0.066
1835	385	658	0.574	0.011	0.019
1880	352	652	0.554	−0.014	−0.025
1847	293	658	0.539	−0.094	−0.174
1935	432	615	0.537	0.165	0.308
1837	344	658	0.517	0.006	0.011
1886	393	670	0.514	0.073	0.141
1900	402	670	0.511	0.089	0.174
1841	367	658	0.509	0.049	0.096
1955	344	630	0.497	0.049	0.099
1959	365	630	0.494	0.085	0.173
1895	411	670	0.491	0.122	0.249
1906	400	670	0.490	0.107	0.218
1924	419	615	0.483	0.198	0.411
1951	321	625	0.480	0.034	0.070
1966	363	630	0.479	0.097	0.203
1945	393	640	0.478	0.136	0.285
1918	478	707	0.476	0.200	0.420
1885	319	670	0.474	0.002	0.004
1970	330	630	0.464	0.060	0.129
1950	315	625	0.461	0.043	0.093
1892	272	670	0.451	−0.045	−0.100
1964	317	630	0.441	0.062	0.141
1874	350	652	0.439	0.098	0.223
1979	339	635	0.439	0.095	0.216
1910D	272	670	0.439	−0.033	−0.075
1997	419	659	0.432	0.204	0.472
1910J	275	670	0.432	−0.022	−0.050
1983	397	650	0.424	0.187	0.440
1987	376	650	0.423	0.155	0.368
1992	336	651	0.419	0.097	0.232
1974O	319	635	0.392	0.110	0.282
1922	345	615	0.382	0.179	0.469
1974F	301	635	0.371	0.103	0.278
1929	288	615	0.371	0.097	0.262
1923	159	615	0.305	−0.046	−0.152

power merely picked up their programme, and most of their personnel, from the 1886–92 government.

Following the fall of Lloyd George in 1922, there were three General Elections at annual intervals, in the autumns of 1922, 1923, and 1924. Lloyd George's failure left the Conservatives in a dominant position, as we shall see in detail in Chapter 6. But there were two opposition parties of roughly equal standing. British politics in the 1920s were in what Cox (1997) has labelled a 'non-Duvergerian equilibrium'. In many constituencies it was unclear which opposition party–Labour or Liberal–was best placed to beat the Conservatives. In addition, the Liberals were split between their Asquith and Lloyd George wings in 1922. These facts account for the Conservative power landslides of 1922 and 1924.

In 1931 the Labour government fell over a (partly self-imposed) financial crisis. Some of its leaders joined Prime Minister Ramsay MacDonald in forming a National Government with the other parties; most rejected him, and he was expelled from the party. Not surprisingly, the divided Labour Party scored one of its worst results in the ensuing General Election, in which the National Government parties' 2:1 vote lead was as usual exaggerated into an even greater lead in seats. Labour had by no means recovered in 1935, so once again there was a seat and power landslide for the National Government (that is, to all intents and purposes, for the Conservatives). These are unidimensional moves around the position of the median voter, which is why they get no further attention in this book.

For the same reason, this book has almost nothing to say about the man who, in a widely reported poll of historians at the start of 2000, was regarded as Britain's greatest twentieth-century Prime Minister. I agree with the poll's rankings (Lloyd George came second). But nothing that Winston Churchill did as Prime Minister from 1940 to 1945 was multidimensional, nor heresthetic. Rhetorical it certainly was, and Churchill gets more space in the dictionaries of quotations than do any of the subjects of this book. But Churchill's political rhetoric was for a different purpose to Lloyd George's or Thatcher's. It was rhetoric designed to unify the nation, not to win political advantage. Churchill's greatness is a different sort of greatness to that of Peel and Lloyd George.

2

Irish Potatoes and British Politics: Peel, Wellington, and the Repeal of the Corn Laws

The Puzzle

The Tory administration of Sir Robert Peel (1841–6) did two things that deeply offended many of its supporters. In both cases, some members of the legislature voted against their preferences. Both cases involved Ireland, and thus raised core–periphery as well as left–right issues. In both cases, a key actor whose role has hitherto been underrated was the leader of the House of Lords, the Duke of Wellington. The two cases were the Maynooth Grant (a grant of public funds to the Catholic seminary in Maynooth, Co. Kildare, west of Dublin) in 1845, and Repeal of the Corn Laws in 1846.

As noted in Chapter 1, religious and centre–periphery disputes reinforced one another. Most of Ireland was defiantly Catholic despite (perhaps because of) the efforts of Protestant politicians from Elizabeth I to Oliver Cromwell and William III to incorporate Ireland fully into the United Kingdom. Most of their unsuccessful attempts to impose Protestant supremacy had been bloodstained, Cromwell's most so. Ireland was a strategic weak point, from the point of view of nation-builders. Hostile Catholic powers could try invading Britain through Ireland, as Louis XIV had done in 1689–90. The French Directory tried again in 1796 and 1798, during the long Anglo-French war sparked off by the French Revolution. Arthur Wellesley, an Irish Protestant soldier born in 1769 and later, as the Duke of Wellington, Britain's most successful field commander against the French, remembered these events.

Wellington served as minister without portfolio and leader of the Lords during Peel's second administration. He intervened frequently on matters of military policy, rarely on others. But his infrequent interventions include the two crucial ones—Maynooth and the Repeal of the Corn Laws—in which he steered controversial government decisions, which he did not personally support, through the House of Lords. But for Wellington, the government would have lost the first in the Lords. If it had nevertheless survived, it would certainly have lost Repeal in the Lords.

Wellington wrote in November 1845, 'I believe that the disease in Ireland is the old incurable one, *Popery!*' (to Lord Alvanley, 28.11.1845, in Gray 1999: 203). And yet he had just ensured that the British state would pay towards the cost of training Irish Catholic priests. Maynooth had fallen into decay in 1845, and the Peel government's proposal to increase its grant from public funds infuriated hard-line Protestants. In the Lords, Wellington gave no ground to Protestant objections. His argument was purely based on public order. Ireland contained 8 million people (then about a third of the UK population), nearly 90 per cent of whom were Catholics: 'we cannot avoid their being Roman Catholics', he said with characteristic bluntness. Their priests had to be educated somewhere. If not in Ireland, they would be educated elsewhere in Europe, probably in another Catholic country. That would be worse. Priests were one of the main sources of political advice to the Irish people. It was important that they should be educated somewhere that the British government could watch over the doctrines they were taught (*Hansard*, Lords, 2 June 1845, cc 1160–74).

Many Tories had suspicions about their leaders. Peel and Wellington had already offended them by their approval of Catholic Emancipation in 1829, partly on grounds of public order in Ireland (Davis 1997). Maynooth made things worse. From the point of view of the historic centre—the Protestant landed aristocracy—it was but a prelude to a still more cataclysmic betrayal the following year.

In 1846, the government proposed, and both houses of parliament voted, to repeal the Corn Laws, which had provided protection for British agriculture by restricting the import of cereal grains. Farmers and landowners benefited from this protection; non-farm capitalists certainly suffered from it; non-farm labourers probably did. But the executive and both houses of parliament were dominated by the landed interest. Repeal therefore goes against all the standard accounts of political economy (see e.g. Schonhardt-Bailey 1996, 1997; Marrison 1998). Like the flight of the bumblebee, it could not happen. But it did. Peel was able to persuade not only the opposition but also a third of his own party in the Commons to support Repeal. And in the Lords, Wellington secured a comfortable majority for a policy that neither he nor most of his colleagues supported.

From Karl Marx to Sir Lewis Namier and all points in between, commentators assume that, at least most of the time, politicians are in office to promote their own material interests and/or the material interests of those who put them there. The most eloquent thing about Marx's commentary on Peel and Wellington is its absence. Marx wrote copiously about British politics from 1844 until his death. He regarded Repeal of the Corn Laws as a seminal event in the transition of power from the aristocracy to the bourgeoisie. All commentators since, whether Marxist or not, have followed his interpretation. Yet he can never quite explain how it happened. He treats most British politicians with withering scorn as he pins personal or class motivations on to all of their actions. But there are no personal comments on Peel or Wellington—dominant figures by anyone's reckoning.

Marx's explanation of Repeal embodies a classic fallacy and a classic mistake:

> The repeal of the Corn Laws in 1846 merely recognized an already accomplished fact, a change long since enacted in the elements of British civil society, *viz.*, the subordination of the landed interest under the moneyed interest, of property under commerce, of agriculture under manufacturing industry, of the country under the city. Could this fact be doubted since the country population stands, in England, to the towns' population in the proportion of one to three? (Marx 1852: 353)

The classic fallacy is to confuse class interests with individual interests. That a group of people share a class interest is not a reason why any individual member of the class should actively promote that interest. When (as sometimes in his writings) Marx makes Richard Cobden, the Lancashire cotton manufacturer and co-founder of the Anti-Corn-Law League, responsible for Repeal, he is supported by Cobden's own admission that Repeal favoured the interests of the manufacturing class. (Cobden 1870: i. 97). But he cannot explain why Cobden bankrupted and exhausted himself on the Anti-Corn-Law League rather than get on with printing calico and making money. At other times, when Marx admits that it was a Tory administration that repealed the Corn Laws, he is bereft of individual-level explanation altogether. He does not attempt to show that Repeal was good for Drayton Manor or Stratfield Saye, the country estates of Peel and Wellington.

The classic mistake is to forget that population was not electorate. The electorate of the House of Lords was, to an approximation, the same as its membership (Scots and Irish representative peers, and bishops, were (s)elected, but by very small electorates). The criteria for membership are very similar to the criteria for inheritance of real estate. The House of Lords was, by construction, a house of the landed interest. Because of variations in the franchise and (more important) in the size and location of constituencies, so was the House of Commons. Most constituencies were in small boroughs, and the industrial areas of the country were still severely underrepresented. The country electorate certainly did not stand, in England, to the towns' electorate in the proportion of one to three. Yet the unelected Lords and the Commons elected in 1841 passed Repeal.

Namierite historians have powerfully influenced the study of Parliament in the age of Peel and Wellington (Thorne 1986; Gash 1986). For Sir Lewis Namier, parliamentary politics was about position and personal benefit, not about ideology or class. But no Namierite has convincingly explained what was in it for Peel or Wellington, nor for those Tory MPs who voted with Peel in the Commons (in some cases voting to end their parliamentary careers), nor for the Tory peers who voted with Wellington, in many cases to the detriment of their estates.

Nor have modern political economists done any better. The dominant influence in historical political economy is the Chicago neoclassical school. For neoclassicists, as for Marx, politicians enact their material interests or those of their supporters. From this assumption springs what is called 'endogenous tariff theory' (ETT—see Magee 1997, and, for a test of it on the Corn Laws, Schonhardt-Bailey 1994). The level of tariffs is endogenous to— that is, can be read off directly from—the pattern of material interests. Exporting industry has an interest in low or zero tariffs. Industry that suffers, or would suffer, from import competition, has an interest in high tariffs. So far, so good: that fits the activities of manufacturing and agricultural lobbies in 1845–6. ETT then assumes that politicians are transparent carriers of their district interests into the legislature, regardless of party label. In the USA, that is plausible. In principle, we can then range the parliamentary constituencies from the most protectionist to the most free-trading. The constituency represented by the median MP will, by the median voter theorem, determine the level of protection in the economy. Because of the construction of both houses in 1846, the median member of both Commons and Lords sat for an agricultural 'constituency', the constituency of each peer being his estate. Therefore Parliament would maintain agricultural protection. This is a beautiful hypothesis destroyed by an inconvenient fact: Parliament did not.

If all explanations based on interest fail, what about ideology? One might argue that, despite his protestations to the contrary, Peel was a convert to the ideology of free trade. One cannot argue that for Wellington in the face of his plain words to the contrary:

I am one of those who think the continuance of the Corn Laws essential to the agriculture of the country in its existing state and particularly to that of Ireland, and a benefit to the whole community. ('The Duke's Memorandum' [to the Cabinet], 30.11.45, opening words. Peel 1856–7: ii. 198)

Boyd Hilton (1988) has recently revived interest in evangelical religion as the possible ideology of Repeal. He can make a good case for the Home Secretary, Sir James Graham, who thought that the Irish Famine was a visitation from Heaven, but not for Peel, nor Wellington, nor (on the statistical evidence) for the MPs who delivered Repeal in the Commons. (For fuller discussion of the Hilton hypothesis see McLean 1999c; McLean and Bustani 1999).

The crucial ideology was not religion, but public order and the Queen's government. Kemp (1962) was one of the first to point this out, but the implications of her argument have not been followed through. Wellington seems to have had an almost mystical belief in the Queen's government as a thing above party. His role as Commander-in-Chief was to protect the Queen's peace. In principle, therefore, it was his duty to do so whoever was in government. This led him into some odd contortions in 1845–6.

Repeal: A Narrative

The Corn Law of 1815 had excluded wheat from the UK until the domestic price was above 80 shillings per quarter. It was replaced by a sliding scale of tariffs in 1828. The retiring Whigs committed themselves to freer trade at the General Election of 1841, in the hope that Peel, the Tory leader, recognized by enemies as well as friends as by far the dominant figure in the Commons, would be trapped into a defence of the Corn Laws. Peel had probably already lost belief in them, but his party's vested interest lay most strongly in agriculture. He was not prepared to be pinned down, and won the election comfortably. Two decisions of 1842 increased his freedom to change course: a general reduction of tariffs, and the reintroduction of income tax. The ideological free-traders who staffed the Board of Trade (for whom see Brown 1958, *passim*) persuaded Peel and his able lieutenant W. E. Gladstone (vice-president of the Board of Trade, 1841–5) that the revenue from tariffs would rise if prohibitive rates were reduced and consolidated. The process of reducing tariffs exposed both politicians to rent-seeking coalitions of special interests, of which they were both utterly contemptuous. As Gladstone telegraphed to his diary,

B of Trade and House 12 3/4—6 3/4 and 9 1/4—1 1/2. [i.e. 12.45 pm to 6.45 pm and 9.15 pm to 1.30 am]. Dined at Abp of Yorks. Copper, Tin, Zinc, Salmon, Timber, Oil, Saltmeat, all are to be ruined, and all in arms. (W. E. Gladstone, Diary for 15.03.1842 in Foot and Matthew 1974: 187)

This contempt strongly coloured Peel's actions in 1845–6 (see e.g. his speech of 27 January 1846, conveniently reprinted in Schonhardt-Bailey 1996: 73–7).

In 1842, the public finances had been in deficit for four years running. Peel introduced a budget to put them into surplus (pointedly ignoring his Chancellor of the Exchequer, Henry Goulburn). He pointed out that tariffs were at a level that produced sharply diminishing marginal returns. Extending consumption taxes to new areas would either be divisive (as with railway travel) or would bring in only 'dribblets' from taxing 'pianofortes, umbrellas, or such articles'. Peel had an acute sense of the 'elasticity' (his own word—*Hansard*, Commons, 11 March 1842, cc 422–76, quoted at cols. 436 and 437) of revenue from income tax compared to the inelasticity of tariff revenue. He suggested that income from tariffs would rise when rates were cut—as was to prove correct. By reintroducing income tax, which had previously existed as an emergency measure during the Napoleonic Wars, Peel solved the chronic debt problem of the British state. Even where tariffs brought in considerable revenue (which the Corn Laws did not), he was now freer to reduce them.

In autumn 1845 came the first warnings of impending famine in Ireland. The Tory journalist J. W. Croker complained 'that Ireland has had anything to do with the grand convulsion [of the Tory party] . . . I cannot concede. Ireland has had no more to do with it than Kamschatka' (J. W. Croker to Sir

J. Graham, 21.2.46. in Jennings 1884: iii. 62). The charge is repeated in almost every history of Ireland or of the Corn Laws. But Peel, Wellington, and Sir James Graham, the three principal actors, linked Irish policy inextricably to corn policy.

On 13 October 1845, Peel wrote Graham, his Home Secretary:[1]

The accounts of the state of the potato-crop in Ireland are becoming very alarming. ... I have no confidence in such remedies as the prohibition of exports, or the stoppage of the distilleries. The removal of impediments to import is the only effectual remedy.

In a letter the same day, which crossed Peel's, Graham wrote:

Indian corn [i.e. maize] might be obtained from the United States readily, and on cheap terms, if the people would eat it; but unfortunately it is an acquired taste; and if we opened the ports to maize duty-free, most popular and irresistible arguments present themselves why flour and oatmeal, the staple of the food of man, should not be restricted in its supply by artificial means, while Heaven has withheld from an entire people its accustomed sustenance. Could we with propriety remit duties in November by Order in Council, when Parliament might so easily be called together? Can these duties, once remitted by Act of Parliament, be ever again reimposed? Ought they to be maintained with their present stringency, if the people of Ireland be reduced to the last extremity for want of food?

Many politicians did not yet take the blight seriously. Peel and Graham correctly foresaw that it would lead to a dearth of seed potatoes, and hence of food, the following season. Both immediately decided that the Irish crop failure dealt a mortal blow to the Corn Laws. Peel said so two days later to Lord Heytesbury, the Lord-Lieutenant of Ireland:

The accounts from Ireland of the potato crop, confirmed as they are by your high authority, are very alarming.

We must consider whether it is possible by legislation, or by the exercise of prerogative, to apply a remedy to the great evil with which we are threatened. The application of such remedy involves considerations of the utmost magnitude. The remedy is the removal of all impediments to the import of all kinds of human food—that is, the total and absolute repeal for ever of all duties on all articles of subsistence.

Peel's autobiography continues:

The Cabinet reassembled at my house on . . . Saturday, the 1st of November. On that occasion I read to the Cabinet the following Memorandum:—

[...] Inaction—the letting things take their own course—seems to me impossible.
...

[...] There will be no hope of contributions from England for the mitigation of this calamity. ... Before the meeting of Parliament we must be prepared with the measures to be proposed and the language to be held at its meeting.

---

[1] In all these extracts from Peel's memoirs Peel's commentary is in *italic*. Where not otherwise referenced, the source is Peel, *Memoirs*, (1856–7), ii, part III for the appropriate date.

We must indeed be so prepared, not merely before the actual meeting of Parliament, but before we finally resolve on the calling of Parliament for the despatch of business.

The calling of Parliament at an unusual period on any matter connected with a scarcity of food is a most important step.

It compels an immediate decision on these questions.

Shall we maintain unaltered—

Shall we modify—

Shall we suspend—the operation of the Corn Laws?

The first vote we propose—a vote of credit, for instance, for 100,000l, to be placed at the disposal of the Lord-Lieutenant for the supply of food—opens the whole question.

Can we vote public money for the sustenance for any considerable portion of the people on account of actual or apprehended scarcity, and maintain in full operation the existing restrictions on the free import of grain?

I am bound to say that we cannot. . . .

It is possible for us to take this course—to separate today under the strong impression that the meeting of Parliament on some day not later than the 27th of November is inevitable—to have a meeting of the Cabinet finally to decide our course at the latter end of next week . . .

Protection represented a fiscal transfer from consumers of grain to producers of grain. There was no hope of relying on private charity to feed the Irish because the English hated them. Therefore famine relief must come from public funds. But to spend public money on relief while protection kept prices artificially high was to waste public money. Peel, the most Gladstonian of early Victorian politicians, would not tolerate that. It would also concede the Anti-Corn-Law League's case, that the landlords were a privileged sectional interest, in the face of Peel's repeated statements that his administration was national, not sectional. But after a further meeting,

The Cabinet by a very considerable majority declined giving its assent to the proposals which I thus made to them. They were supported by only three members of the Cabinet—the Earl of Aberdeen, Sir James Graham, and Mr. Sidney Herbert

On 22 November, the Whig leader, Lord John Russell, declared that he was in favour of Repeal. On 26 November, Peel repeated that he could not accept the measures of Irish relief which the Cabinet had now instituted, 'and undertake at the same time to maintain the existing Corn Law'. He wrote directly to Wellington, for the first time saying what he was proposing and alerting Wellington to the renewed threat of the fall of the government:

My dear Duke,

In the inclosed memorandum are contained the Reasons which induce me to advise the Suspension of the existing Corn Laws for a limited period.

I will not ask you to express any opinion on the Subject in returning me this Paper. I only ask you to have the Kindness to read it—and to let me have the Box by the Post of tomorrow evening. I thought it right to mention confidentially to the Queen—that I feared there were serious differences in the Cabinet as to the Measures which the present Emergency requires. (Peel to Wellington, 29.11.45, Wellington Papers, University of Southampton (hereafter WP), 2/134/88).

At first sight this letter says nothing that Peel had not already said a month earlier. But Russell's letter had changed the situation. It made it clear that there was now a possible Commons majority for Repeal, comprising Russell's Whigs, the Irish members, and Peel with a small number of followers.

The Repeal of the Corn Laws became inevitable, not in May or June 1846, but on 30 November 1845, with Wellington's reply to this letter. After setting out his case for maintaining the Corn Laws, Wellington went on:

> [. . .] Here then comes the question which Sir Robert Peel has not discussed—I mean the Party view of it.
> The only ground upon which I think that view important is one upon which he must be a better judge than any one else; that is, whether he could carry on a Government for the Queen supposing the support of the landed interest were withdrawn from him. I am afraid he must reckon upon its being withdrawn from him, unless he should be able to show clearly the necessity for the measure in question.
> In respect to my own course, my only object in public life is to support Sir Robert Peel's administration of the Government for the Queen.
> A good Government for the country is more important than Corn Laws or any other consideration; and as long as Sir Robert Peel possesses the confidence of the Queen and of the public, and he has strength to perform the duties, his administration of the Government must be supported.
> My own judgment would lead me to maintain the Corn Laws.
> Sir Robert Peel may think that his position in Parliament and in the public view requires that the course should be taken which he recommends; and if that should be the case, I earnestly recommend that the Cabinet should support him, and I for one declare that I will do so.
> Wellington. (The Duke's Memorandum, 30.11.45. Peel, *Memoirs* ii. 200)

This marked the turning of the Duke. Once he was convinced that the question was not corn but the Queen's government, he never wavered from the self-imposed task of getting the Queen's government's measures through the House of Lords, as will be described below.

Russell inadvertently made Peel's position unassailable. Peel's threat to resign convinced Wellington, but not another key Cabinet member—Lord Stanley (the future 14th Earl of Derby)—of the need to subordinate corn to government unity. Peel, having rejected the idea of a General Election on public order grounds, therefore brusquely resigned. Note that in early November he persevered although only three Cabinet members supported him. Now, he resigned although all but two supported him. The Queen asked Russell to form a government. At that point, there was probably a Commons majority for Repeal. Russell could have carried it with the votes of the radicals, the Irish Repealers, the Whigs, and Peel and one or two of his close followers. He would be unable to carry it in the House of Lords. While Russell was trying to form a government, he asked Peel for support in carrying through Repeal, and the Queen appealed to Wellington to continue as Commander-in-Chief of the Army under Russell. Both refused. Wellington professed total loyalty to the Queen but said he 'could have no relations' with Lord John Russell (Queen Victoria to Wellington, 12.12.45 and two replies, same day. WP 2/134/118, 119, 123). Russell told the Queen on 20 December that he was unable to form a government. Peel had elicited promises from Wellington, Stanley, and the Duke of Buccleuch (the other holdout from Peel's proposals of 6 December) not only that each of them was unwilling to form a protectionist government, but that each of them thought that nobody else should. Peel swept back into office with undisguised delight, in unchallengeable possession of the field.

While Russell was trying to form a government, Protectionist peers were writing to Wellington to ask him to lead the protectionist party, now that it had become common knowledge that Peel had doubts. Lord Redesdale, a Tory whip, wrote that as Russell, 'one of the most mischievous and reckless politicians' in the country, might 'lean to the *republican* party for support . . . [i]t is above all things necessary that our party in the House of Lords should be kept together'. He described the Tories as a powerful army 'whose staff and materiel have been surrendered to the enemy by their commander. . . . I am in the position of one in charge of a very large and important division of that army', which needed a leader. 'The integrity of the Church' was also at risk. Redesdale urged Wellington to put himself at the head of this army.

Despite Redesdale's military choice of metaphor, Wellington would have none of it. He replied with a carefully phrased paean to Peel: The 'lamentable condition' of public affairs was due

to the Reform Act, which tended to deprive nearly every Member of the House of Commons of his real Independance, and with very few exceptions, of whom Sir R. Peel is one, has placed nearly every Member in a state of dependance for his political existence. (Redesdale to Wellington, 14.12.45; Wellington to Redesdale, 16.12.45. WP 2/134/130–131)

Wellington's tactics were to turn Tory rhetoric against Tories. According to Tory rhetoric, the independence of legislators was lost in 1832 when they became beholden to their constituency interests. It was ingenious rhetoric for Wellington to use. Had he been intelligent enough, Redesdale might have retorted that it was the very dependence of MPs on re-election, threatened as many of them were by the Anti-Corn-Law League in their constituencies, that was one of the causes of the crisis. He merely huffed off with an angry snort.

Thus Wellington was signalling even during the Russell interregnum that he would stay with Peel, despite disagreeing with him on the Corn Laws. But Peel blocked off all exits for both Russell and the protectionist Tories. Peel's heresthetic, linking Corn Law with the Famine, had put together a coalition for Repeal that would not otherwise have existed. Passage of Repeal in the Lords depended on Wellington. That is why Peel's heresthetic also had to include references to public order and the Queen's government, Wellington's favourite themes. In a perfectly judged letter to Wellington when he heard that Russell had failed, Peel wrote:

Lord John Russell declines, after having accepted to form a Government. I am going to the Queen—I shall tell her at once, and without hesitation, that I will not abandon her—whatever may happen I shall return from Windsor as Her Minister.

It is necessary that we should have a Cabinet as soon as possible.

Will you have the goodness to attend a Cabinet in my room *in Downing Street*—at nine o'clock this Evening? (Peel to Wellington 20.12.45. WP 2/135/9. Original underlining and punctuation.)

Peel returned from Windsor as Her Minister and Wellington his most loyal lieutenant.

In Wellington's view, the issue had ceased to be the Corn Laws, and had become the continuance of the Queen's government. How was he turned? The best evidence comes in an exchange between him and Stanley in February 1846, by which time they were the leaders of the opposite benches in the Lords. But they shared a concern for public order, and agreed that it required the speedy rebuilding of the Tory Party in safe hands. They did not think that the Commons leaders of the Protectionists had safe hands. Benjamin Disraeli, who was making witty, slashing, and venomous attacks on Peel's change of stance, was an adventurer of dubious origins and finances. Lord George Bentinck had shown no interest in anything except racing until Disraeli recruited him as the violent figurehead of the Protectionists. Therefore the two Tory leaders agreed that Wellington was right to stay in government and that Stanley would vote but not speak against the Corn Bill, and would not lead opposition to it in the Lords.

Stanley wrote:

We cannot disguise from ourselves that the unfortunate measure now under consideration has, for the time at hand, completely dislocated and shattered the great Conservative party in both Houses. . . . But when, with that disregard of yourself which you have shown throughout your life, you advise that I should now endeavour to rally the Conservative party, I am forced to remind you that in the present state of affairs and feeling, they could only be so rallied in opposition to the measures of your own Government. I may be compelled, by my strong sense of the impolicy of the present measures, to give my vote against them; but I have resisted, and I shall continue to resist, entreaties that I would take an active part, and put myself at the head of a movement to throw them out.

Wellington replied:

That which I look for therefore is, the holding together in other hands the great, and at this moment powerful, Conservative party; and this for the sake of the Queen, of the religious and other ancient institutions of the country, of its resources, influence, and power. . . . It is quite obvious that I am not the person who can pretend to undertake, with any chance of success, to perform this task. . . . You will see, therefore, that the stage is entirely clear and open for you, and notwithstanding that I am, thank God, in as good health as I was twenty years ago, I am as much out of your way, as you contemplated the possibility that I might be when you desired to be removed to the House of Lords.

In a 'memorandum upon the leadership of the Conservative Party in the House', apparently addressed to Stanley, he added, 'I am *most anxious* for Lord Stanley's success. He will always find me ready to promote his views for [the] consolidation of the Conservative party'. Wellington conceded that 'my position is certainly anomalous', but added that he had taken the same line while leader of the Tories in the Lords during the Whig administrations of the 1830s. (Stanley to Wellington, 18.2.1846; Wellington to Stanley, 19.2.1846; [Wellington], Memorandum upon the leadership of the Conservative Party in the House of Lords [February 1846]. WP 2/138/15–44. The letters are in Gleig 1864: 413–22.)

Peel's package was presented to Parliament in January 1846. It contained proposals for rate (property tax) relief for landowners, to compensate for the loss of protection. Disraeli and Bentinck fiercely attacked Peel in the Commons. But the result there was never in doubt. The crucial vote, on May 15 1846, went in favour of Repeal by 327 to 229. The entire opposition— Whig, Radical, and Irish—supported Peel, as did about a third of the Tories. The other two-thirds under Disraeli voted against Repeal.

The House of Lords held a veto, which could not then be overridden by the Commons. When Wellington came to defend Repeal, his strategy was the same as over Maynooth. He said not a word in favour of free trade. The reasons he gave were constitutional:

- The Bill was recommended by a speech from the Throne
- It was passed by a majority of the House of Commons
- Were the House of Lords to reject it, it would be the only branch of the legislature to do so. He reminded his audience that without the House of Commons and the Crown the House of Lords could do nothing
- The House of Lords had vast influence on public opinion
- If it did not pass Repeal then, it would merely be postponing it to the next Parliament, where it would come up again (*Hansard*, Lords, 28 May 1846, cc 1401–05).

Assisted by Stanley's decision not to obstruct it, Repeal passed in the Lords by 211 to 166 on 28 May 1846. That was as crucial as the Commons vote.

Disraeli then made a Faustian pact with the Whigs and the Irish Repealers to vote down the government's Irish Coercion Bill, which was going through Parliament at the same time. Peel rejected appeals from Wellington and Cobden among others to call a general election. He offered his and his Cabinet's resignation, and the Peel administration came to an abrupt end. The imposing Peel gave way to the diminutive Russell (Fig. 2.1). In his parting remarks, Peel caused yet further, and quite gratuitous, offence to his party. He said that neither he nor Russell, but Cobden, deserved most credit for Repeal: 'one who, acting, I believe, from pure and disinterested motives, has, with untiring energy, made appeals to our reason, and has enforced those appeals

Fig. 2.1. Political Economy; Or, Lord John in Peel's Clothes. *Punch*, July 1846. Original caption: 'The Queen: Well! It is not the best fit in the world, but we'll see how he goes on!

with an eloquence the more to be admired because it was unaffected and unadorned.' This was remarkable on two counts. First, relations between the two had until shortly beforehand been extremely bad. Second, it was unhelpful to Wellington, who had frequently told wavering Tory peers that if they did not support Peel they would get Cobden. It is hard not to conclude that Peel, who had achieved what he most cared about, had recklessly lost interest in his former supporters. The diarist and gossip Charles Greville noted, 'Peel fell with great *éclat*, and amidst a sort of halo of popularity, but his speech . . . gave inexpressible offence. . . . Almost every part of it offended somebody; but his unnecessary panegyrick of Cobden . . . above all deeply offended the Duke of Wellington' (Greville 1938, v. 329–30). Conservative historians have never forgiven Peel for that speech.

Interests and Ideology in the House of Commons
Data

This is the only case study in the book where roll-call analysis can be used systematically, to study what sorts of Tory MPs supported and opposed Peel. I use the merged datasets of Aydelotte (1970) and Schonhardt-Bailey (1994), with some extra variables. Over twenty years from 1955 to 1975, the late W. O. Aydelotte assembled a unique database of rollcalls in the 1841–7 House of Commons. For each of the 815 men who sat in that House, Aydelotte recorded his vote or non-vote on the 186 principal divisions. He also collected up to 200 pieces of contextual information on each MP from contemporary sources. Most of these record the member's networks (club membership, relationship to the aristocracy, school attended) and material interests (business interests, military service, wealth at death . . .). Schonhardt-Bailey collected further data intended to facilitate a direct test of endogenous tariff theory. Accordingly, her data record the economic interest of each constituency and the degree of portfolio diversification since 1815. Of her variables, the one reported below, now called CSBDPREF,[2] records the expected trade orientation of each constituency. The more it depended on industry vulnerable to imports (specifically agriculture), the more its MP could be expected to have a constituency interest in voting for protection. Conversely, the more it depended on exporting industry (such as textiles, machinery, or cutlery), or on international transport (docks), the more its MP could be expected to have a constituency interest in voting for free trade.

Both the Aydelotte and the Schonhardt-Bailey variables concentrate on interests rather than ideology. Material interests are easier to measure, but we have been able to import a few measures of ideology to the database. From Hilton (1988) and his sources, we marked all those known to be religious evangelicals (and the few known vocal opponents of evangelicalism). From the records of the *History of Parliament*, which end in 1832, we coded for the attitudes of the longer-serving MPs in our set to the religious and constitutional crises of 1829–32 over the position of the Catholic and Anglican churches. And from the 1851 census we add details of religious attendance

---

[2] This is a revision of her earlier variable DISTPREF, the results from which have been reported in both her and my earlier work. Some dubious cases have been reclassified with new data, and the new variable gives better results.

in England, Scotland and Wales (1851 being the only time in British history that these data have been recorded). There was no census of religious attendance in Ireland, but the 1851 census yields data of excess mortality for the Irish census districts, 1841–51, which we have coded as a new variable DEATH for Irish members. (It is not significant in the analyses below, perhaps because the horror of the Famine had not yet struck in full force by June 1846.)

Parliamentary procedures are majoritarian. Therefore, at least in the long run and assuming that legislators are moderately well informed, the opinion of the median legislator will prevail in each house, and political manipulation cannot shift voting from this robust equilibrium position. This is well documented in studies of the US Congress (especially Poole and Rosenthal 1997), and it underlies endogenous tariff theory, reviewed above. However, when opinion is multidimensional, the median voter theorem does not hold. A heresthetician knows that no outcome in multidimensional space is stable under majority rule. So he structures the world so that he can win for his favourite option. Repeal of the Corn Laws was one such case. By linking Repeal with Ireland, and by taking advantage of Russell's indecision, Peel structured the world so that almost the whole of the opposition in the Commons voted for Repeal. (Only ten non-Tory MPs voted against Repeal in the third reading vote, on 18 May 1846, on which this analysis is based. All of them represented deeply agricultural seats).

The Aydelotte dataset encompasses votes not only on Repeal but also, *inter alia*, on railway, bank, and factory regulation; political reform; educational reform; working-class distress; individual railway proposals; and the abolition of flogging in the army. It can therefore be used to test, not only the roles of interest and ideology in determining MPs' votes, but also whether the number of issue dimensions was high enough to promote chaos and heresthetic. Elsewhere (McLean and Foster 1992; McLean 1995; McLean and Bustani 1999; McLean 1999c) we have explored the dimensionally of rollcall voting in the 1841 House. That work confirms Aydelotte's original finding that politics in that Parliament were multidimensional. Aydelotte originally found no fewer than twenty-four dimensions to the voting, using Guttman scaling. This is both too many and too few. It is too many in that most of the scales are inadequately labelled, uninterpreted, and seriously overlapping. (Nevertheless, Aydelotte's work is extraordinarily adventurous for its time, given the techniques and hardware then available.) It is too few in that it does not pick up the dimension of regulation. An MP's position on Aydelotte's Big Scale, which links the Corn Laws, Ireland, and relief of working-class distress into a single ideological dimension, fails to predict his position on regulation. For instance, if he was 'right-wing' on the Big Scale, he was equally likely to be 'right-wing' or 'left-wing' on regulation. This is not too surprising, as it was then as now not clear whether being in favour of stringent government regulation is a right-wing or a left-wing position.

However, regulation is not a big enough exception to the generalization that opinion among MPs was one-dimensional. Although it is true that Peel threatened to resign if factory legislation he opposed were carried, and it is also true that the Ten Hours Act 1847 was carried by a 'left-right' coalition to punish the repealers of the Corn Laws, Peel's threat was not really credible. Governments did not stand or fall on issues of regulation. Therefore the answer to the question, *Does the Aydelotte dataset show that opinion in the Commons during the Corn Law crisis was inherently two-dimensional?* is *No*. Nevertheless, Peel managed to carry the house, as the following subsections show.

Results of Bivariate Analysis

All the analyses reported below take the dependent variable as vote on the third reading of the bill to repeal the Corn Laws, on 15 May 1846. (The vote on the second reading, on 27 March 1846, was almost identical—the analysis is not affected by choosing one vote rather than the other.) The first step is to take likely predictors one at a time. MPs who voted for Repeal sat for more urban seats than those who voted against. Viewing the data the other way round, the probability of voting for Repeal rose for each class of constituency except the last (there was no difference in vote between MPs representing moderately free-trade and strongly free-trade constituency interests). Table 2.1 summarizes the main results.

Table 2.1 gives reasonable support to endogenous tariff theory (ETT). The probability of voting for Repeal varies in the expected direction for constituency characteristics, and also for whether the MP was an active businessman. It also shows that ideology mattered: for instance, either MPs' attitudes to the constitutional questions of fifteen years earlier coloured their attitudes to Repeal, or both were coloured by some common background factor. The influence of evangelicalism fits an inverted U-shaped pattern predicted by Hilton, although this effect is less strong and there is some risk of circularity in the data. Hilton's hypothesis is that 'moderate' evangelicals welcomed Repeal whereas 'extreme' ones merely saw in the famine evidence for God's punishment for Britain's wickedness (rather blasphemously implying that God has a poor aim—punishing the English by killing the Irish). But in such data there is a risk of defining evangelicalism from public statements made during the Corn Law crisis, thus reversing the direction of causation.

However, although the trends are as predicted by ETT, the outcome is not. True, the more rural the constituency, the likelier was its MP to vote against Repeal. But in all categories except the most rural, a majority of Members voted for Repeal. Disregarding coding errors and missing data,[3] the median constituency is in category 2 (next-to-most protectionist). But Table 2.1 shows that a majority of Members who sat for category 2 constituencies voted for Repeal. Second, the analysis so far assumes that party is irrelevant. This is in the tradition of ETT and of American roll-call analysis. In these traditions,

---

[3] The variable CSBDPREF is defined only for English seats. Introducing it to the analysis therefore leads all non-English cases to be discarded. However, the non-English constituencies were not more urban than the English ones.

Table 2.1. The probability of voting for Repeal. Bivariate analysis: all votes

Variable	Value	Prob. of voting for Repeal	N. of cases	df	F	Sig. F
Predicted trade orientation				4	26.844	0.000
	1 (most protectionist)	0.19	99			
	2	0.56	176			
	3	0.72	79			
	4	0.89	36			
	5 (most free trade)	0.86	22			
Evangelicalism				3	2.625	0.050
	Anti	1.00	3			
	No info	0.58	573			
	evangelical	0.79	14			
	Extreme evang.	0.30	10			
Business				1	9.180	0.003
	Not active bus'man	0.55	498			
	Active bus'man	0.72	102			
Catholic emancipation				2	9.704	0.000
	Was against	0.24	33			
	No info	0.59	525			
	Was pro	0.71	42			
Church and state				4	9.843	0.000
	1 (Strongly anti reform)	0.42	24			
	2	0.33	3			
	3 (no info)	0.54	498			
	4	0.80	20			
	5 (Strongly pro reform)	0.93	55			

Source: enhanced Aydelotte dataset.

party is treated as an intervening variable, which confuses more than it clarifies. As it is an assumption of ETT that the MP for a district votes his district's interest in the same way regardless of his party label, it ignores party as a control variable. Even in the weak party system of the 1840s, that approach is wrong for UK data. True, there is a reasonable association (tau-β 0.345) between rurality and Toryism, but it is far from perfect. The strong

Table 2.2. The probability of voting for Repeal. Bivariate analysis: Tory votes only

Variable	Value	Prob. of voting for Repeal	N. of cases	df	F	Sig. F
Predicted trade orientation				4	8.189	0.000
	1 (most protectionist)	0.10	86			
	2	0.38	116			
	3	0.46	41			
	4	0.64	11			
	5 (most free trade)	0.40	5			
Evangelicalism				2	2.719	0.067
	No info	0.31	337			
	evangelical	0.67	9			
	Extreme evang.	0.22	9			

Source: enhanced Aydelotte dataset.

NB. Only 10 non-Tories voted against Repeal. They were all from deeply agricultural seats (mean value of the trade orientation variable = 1.67; mean trade orientation for non-Tory pro-Repeal voters = 2.89). Taking the vote as the dependent variable, trade orientation was the only significant predictor for the non-Tories (F = 8.189 for 4 df; sig. of F = 0.000).
For Tories, attitudes to Catholicism or church and state, and whether the MP was an active businessman, were not significant predictors of vote on Repeal.

Tory government was a strong constraint on those whose party label was Tory, even though it could only induce a third of them to vote with the government.

Therefore, we repeat the analysis of Table 2.1 for Tories only. Peel's heresthetic, and Russell's failure to form a government, had delivered all the Whig, Liberal, Reform, and Repealer votes, bar ten, to the government. If they would have voted for Repeal under Russell, it would be perverse not to vote for it under Peel. The swing voters would be those Tories who, torn between their government and their interests, chose the former. Table 2.2 shows the results of repeating the analysis of Table 2.1 on just the Tory MPs.

In Table 2.2, three of the five predictors drop away. These variables are themselves strongly associated with party, so their significance in the all-MPs analysis tells us nothing about the comparison between the swing voters (the Peelites) and the protectionist Tories. We are left with trade orientation and evangelicalism, both of them still subject to the qualifications just mentioned. Note in particular that the median MP in this category still sits for a seat with the next-to-most protectionist trade orientation. As expected, a majority of them, like a majority of all Tory MPs, voted against Repeal, but 38 per cent of them voted in favour—roughly the same proportion as among Tory MPs at large, and enough to secure Peel his Commons majority.

Logistic Regression Analysis

If bivariate analysis tells us little about the Peelites, can multivariate analysis do any better? All the variables that were tried for the bivariate associations reported above were tried again, including those found not to be significant in the bivariate model (since bivariate analysis can conceal true associations as well as reveal misleading ones). As the dependent variable (vote on the third reading of the Corn Law Bill) is binary, we use logistic regression. The full results and diagnostics are in McLean and Bustani 1999. The best-fitting model is good at predicting negative votes (that is, votes against Repeal), but bad at predicting positive votes, in favour of Repeal. It successfully predicts only 40 per cent of these.

Of the four predictors that work in this model, one is ideological, one relates to personal interests and the other two are environmental. Most of the work is done by the constituency variable TYPECON2, which distinguishes county members from the rest. Note that in this model, small borough members do not behave distinctively from anybody else. Being in a constituency with a high proportion of Anglican churchgoers on census Sunday 1851 predisposes the member against Repeal. The personal-interest variable that works is GENTRY. Earlier work had shown that the relationship between Repeal vote and membership of the landed interest was non-linear. The very largest landowners in the Commons actually voted in a majority in favour of repeal. They were likelier to have diversified asset holdings than the next class down, classified as GENTRY, the only set of landowners to vote by a majority against Repeal. This finding is consistent with earlier economic history (e.g. Moore 1965. See the anthology in Schonhardt-Bailey 1997, vol. 4). Support for Catholic emancipation in 1828–30 predisposes a Member in favour of Repeal. This backs our (and Kemp 1962's) argument that Maynooth and Repeal were constitutional disputes as much as political or economic ones, and that sufficient Tories saw them in that light for both to be carried. The variables relating to district trade orientation and evangelicalism have dropped out. In this model, there are very few incorrectly predicted votes against Repeal. There are a lot of incorrectly predicted votes for Repeal. The best available multivariate model cannot account for fifty-five out of the ninety-three Peelites for whom data are available. Tory MPs, faced with the choice of Repeal followed by defeat or defeat followed, in all probability, by Repeal, chose unpredictably between these unpalatable alternatives. But some of them chose the option which certainly brought them no material satisfaction, that of voting with Peel. The usual materialist explanation—namely, that office-holders support the government in order to keep their jobs, and others vote for the government in order to get jobs—cannot apply. It was common knowledge that Peel would soon be defeated, if not on the Corn Laws, then on something else.

Thus we are led to a conclusion with which only Namierites, Marxists, new trade theorists, and public choice theorists could disagree: ideology and interests both matter.

The Heresthetic of Peel and Wellington

Peel, Wellington, and Graham constructed only a temporary winning coalition, which did not outlive the Repeal vote. After 1846 there was a Commons (though not a Lords) majority for a free-trading capitalist coalition but Peel did not lead it. If he had not fatally fallen from his horse in 1850 he, rather than his follower Aberdeen, would have become Prime Minister in 1852, and a Peel Administration would surely have handled the Crimean War more competently than did Aberdeen. After the fall of the Aberdeen ministry, the Peelites lost what coherence they had had as a group. Gladstone and others went into the Liberal Party. What we call 'Gladstonian' policy—liberal, capitalist, opposed to military adventures abroad—should perhaps rather be called 'Peelite'.

Conventional Downsian political science (cf. Downs 1957) both misspecifies Peel's utility function and fails to understand how a politician's utility function may change over time. Having achieved Repeal, he was delighted to cease being Prime Minister and no longer have to 'listen to such trash in the House of Commons' (Peel to Gladstone, 13.07.46, in Foot and Matthew 1974: 559). In August 1846 he wrote to Aberdeen:

I do not know how other men are constituted, but I can say with truth that I find the day too short for my present occupations, which chiefly consist in lounging in my library, directing improvements, riding with the boys and my daughter, and pitying Lord John and his colleagues. (Peel to Aberdeen, 14.08.46, quoted by Gash 1986: 616)

But he had resumed office in December 1845 with extreme alacrity. In early November he had insisted on staying though only three of the Cabinet supported him; in late November he insisted on resigning though all but two supported him. He probably did not guess that Russell would fail in the precise way he did, but he created the conditions for it by refusing to write Russell a blank cheque of support, and getting promises from Wellington and Stanley that they would neither form a protectionist government nor support anyone else who tried. Perhaps Russell used a squabble between two of his colleagues as an excuse to duck the responsibility for repeal; but he could not carry the Lords unless Peel and Wellington let him. Peel would give him no such promise, thus manoeuvring himself into the position that only he could form an administration. The protectionist Tories in both houses then faced a dilemma: to accept Repeal from Peel, or to defeat him and accept the risk of a radical victory in the ensuing election, and then have Repeal and many other disagreeable things forced on them anyhow.

Was Ireland really no more relevant to Repeal than Kamchatka? Croker, who made the allegation, was editor of the protectionist *Quarterly Review* and almost the only person who could write to Wellington in colloquial, bantering, tones. Wellington agreed with him. In his analysis of the Famine (see McLean 1999c), he anticipated by over a century Sen's (1981) theme that famine is usually a failure of entitlement, not a failure of food. The crop failure was worst in the east of Ireland; the famine was worst in the west. The east was in a cash economy, which gave the poor some entitlements to alternative food. The west was not. But Wellington did not foresee the depth of the famine, nor did his prescient analysis of entitlement failure lead to any policy conclusion. Peel's and Graham's insight, in simultaneously seeing in October 1845 that the crisis was desperate, was deeper. Graham was moved by his gloomy evangelicalism. Peel was not an evangelical. His adoption of Ireland as the peg on which to hang the conversion to free trade he had already intellectually made was heresthetical. However, he was sincere in his wish to minimize the famine:

Are you to look to and depend upon chance in such an extremity? Or, Good God, are you to sit in cabinet, and consider and calculate how much diarrhoea, and bloody flux, and dysentery, a people can bear before it becomes necessary for you to provide them with food? (*Hansard*, Commons, 27 March 1846, col. 217; see also his peroration of 16.2.46, col. 1043).

Wellington was alarmed at the effect of the Famine on Peel and Graham. As he reportedly said to Henry Pierrepoint, who passed the *bon mot* on to Greville, 'Rotten potatoes have done it all; they put Peel in his d—d fright' (Greville 1938, v. 282). A Tory MP recounted a meeting with Wellington in September 1846, when Wellington reportedly said that

He had done everything in his power to open Peel's eyes—that he never saw a man in such a state of alarm—he was hardly himself—the potato disease seemed to occupy his whole mind. Sir James Graham seemed to have frightened him. The Duke related to me all that as passed in the Cabinet. He had done everything in his power to prevent Peel from taking the course he determined to pursue. (Knatchbull MSS U951/F21. Kent Record Office, Maidstone. I am very grateful to Anna Gambles for finding this reference. See also Wellington's letters to J. W. Croker of 11.12.45, 14.12.45, 26.12.45, 28.12.45, 29.12.45, 6.1.46, and 6.4.46. Jennings 1884: iii. 38–65)

However, once everything in the Duke's power proved insufficient, his ideology of service to the Queen took hold, even *before* Peel's resignation and Russell's abortive attempt to form a government in December 1845. From November 1845 to June 1846, Wellington was unbreakably tied to Peel in spite of their fundamental disagreement. How they got into this curious knot is a case study in heresthetic.

Repeal, Endogeneity, Ideology, Interest, and Heresthetic

We have shown that none of the standard explanations of Repeal works well, except the very old-fashioned idea that two determined men did what they did because they thought it was right, and a third consented because he thought it conduced to public order. Yes, Peel was absolutely pivotal. But so was Wellington, whose role has been overlooked. Peel's change of mind was dramatic but not abrupt—he lost faith in the Corn Laws over a long period starting before 1841. What was abrupt was his decision that the famine killed the Corn Laws. Croker, and the modern writers who follow him, are right up to a point. Yes, Peel seized the Famine heresthetically as an issue on which to change the dimensionality of politics, and hence force Repeal through, which he could not otherwise have done. But no, Ireland was much more relevant to Repeal than was Kamchatka. Peel, and even Wellington, saw connections which Croker and modern trade theorists did not; and Peel did care about the Famine as a substantive issue.

Another of Croker's complaints has more substance: against Peel's delay in telling Wellington and the other protectionist ministers what he was up to. After a conversation with Wellington at Stratfield Saye in December 1846, Croker wrote:

he (the D.) was not at all in the secret of [Peel's] change of opinion, and knew very little of what was going on or intended. He was much surprised to hear that I had long suspected that Peel had modified his opinion on *his own* Corn Law. My suspicion—I might indeed say my proofs—were long anterior to the alarm about the potato crop, but the Duke had no suspicion of any other motive at the time (16.12.46; Jennings 1884: iii. 89).

Croker is not always a reliable witness. But this charge is justified, as became clear as soon as Peel's memoir was published in 1857. To Graham and Heytesbury Peel had confided in October that the Corn Laws must go entirely; to the rest of the Cabinet, he proposed only their modification or suspension. From November till January, Wellington insisted to the Protectionist peers that he had no knowledge of what exactly Peel would propose. It was probably convenient for both that he did not know too much detail, but it is surprising that Peel told so little to the man on whom all depended in the Lords.

The Aydelotte data enables us to check whether it was the inherent multidimensionality of Commons opinion that enabled Peel to work his heresthetic. We have found that it was not. The votes for and against Repeal aligned MPs along the main dimension of politics. But they nevertheless voted for an outcome that the median MP disliked, and the median peer disliked still more. Peel had structured the world so that, for these swing voters, that was the lesser evil.

Interests and ideology both played a great part. But, for elites as well as for legislators, ideology was probably the greater. And ideology has to be modelled in a more sophisticated way than in mainstream political economy, or in mainstream historiography. Mainstream political economy tends to see it as 'shirking' (Kalt and Zupan 1984), that is as adopting positions that differ from one's constituents. But this terminology ignores the Burkean idea of representation, which mattered a good deal to Peelites and others who 'gave no pledges'. (See Wellington's letter to Redesdale for a heresthetic use of Burkean representation theory.) Neither, curiously, recognizes the true achievements of Peel and Wellington.

In his parting shot, Redesdale responded to Wellington's 'Queen's government' line:

> But who brought her into difficulty? What has placed her in a position which rendered it almost necessary for her to call in the republican party to assist her to govern the country?—a position in which only one other sovereign of the realm has ever been placed—and he had his head cut off very soon after. Charles I's difficulties arose from his having attempted to govern without a Parliament. It is strange, but if practically looked into it is true, that Peel's arise from the same source. (Redesdale to Wellington, 1.1.46. WP 2/135/90)

He had a reasonable point. Wellington's ideology did not allow him to draw a line beyond which a policy was so unTory that he would refuse to support it. And Wellington's tactic of warning the protectionists that if they did not accept Peel they might get Cobden was cruelly undermined by Peel's 'panegyrick' of Cobden. On the other hand, Wellington, obsessed as he was by the threat to public order in Ireland, decided that concessions were appropriate. He and Peel infuriated the Ultras, as they had done in 1829–32 over Emancipation and in 1845 over Maynooth. The one time in our period when Ultras controlled the House of Lords without challenge was from 1909 to 1911. The record of these years suggests that Peel and Wellington had a longer-term view than did Lord Redesdale and the Tory Ultras.

APPENDIX 2.1

Variables Used in the Rollcall Analysis

1. *Measures of MP's ideology*

Variable Name	Source	Description
BIGBIGSC	2	Scale position on Big Scale
CATHOLIC	5	MP's attitude to Roman Catholics
CHUSTATE	5	MP's attitude to church–state relations
DENOM	5	MP's denomination if not C of E
EVANGEL	5	MP's attitude to evangelicalism
MILITARY	2	Any military service
PARTYBK5	1	Five-way party breakdown
PEELITE	2	Tory who voted with Peel in May 1846 in favour of repealing the Corn Laws
PLEDGE	5	whether MP gave pledges

2. *Measures of constituency ideology*

Variable Name	Source	Description
COFE	4	(C of E attenders/population, 1851)*100
PROTDISS	4	(Protestant dissenters/population, 1851)*100
RC	4	(Roman Catholics/population, 1851)*100
RELIGIOS	4	(total attenders/population, 1851)*100

3. *Measures of MP's interests*

Variable Name	Source	Description
AGE1841	1	MP's age in 1841
BANK1	1	MP had interests in banking
BUSINT	1	MP had any business interests
CONTEST	1	Election to 1841 parliament contested
GENTRY	2	Member of gentry
PATRON	2	N. of livings of which patron
SOCCLSUM	1	Social class—summary
WEALTH	1	Wealth at death

4. *Measures of constituency interests*

Variable Name	Source	Description
CSBDPREF	6	District trade preference
DCDIST	3	Nature of district
DIVS15CO	3	Diversification score 1850
EOVRSSUM	1	Electors per seat in the constituency
NENGLAND	2	Constit. in England/Wales north of line from Wash to Avon
POVRESUM	2	Population/electorate in the constituency
SCOTLAND	2	Constit. in Scotland
SIRELAND	2	Constit. in Ireland excl. Ulster
TYPECON2	1	Type of constituency: county, small borough, large borough, or university
ULSTER	2	Constit. in Ulster

Note: England south of Wash/Avon line was taken as the reference category in running regional regressions (not reported in this chapter).

Source codes:
1. Aydelotte.
2. Aydelotte, recoded or regrouped.
3. Schonhardt-Bailey 1994.
4. 1851 Census of Religious Attendance, coded by us from the county tables.
5. Our data (see text).
6. Schonhardt-Bailey, revised data 1998.

3

Dishing the Whigs: Disraeli, Salisbury, and the Relaunching of the Tory Party 1846–86

The Start of Recovery

Stanley and Wellington had agreed while leading the opposite sides of the House of Lords in 1846 that the preservation of the Conservative Party was essential to public order, and also to the interests of land and the Established Church. Yet, however much they both wished to minimize the effect of Peel's great smash, it seemed to have overwhelmed the Conservatives. Most of the ablest Conservatives became Peelites; over the next two decades those of them who stayed in politics drifted into the Liberal ranks. The rump of the Conservatives seemed like a narrow interest group, and furthermore one whose interest would get narrower and narrower with economic and political change. The party of the land was in an uncomfortable position at a time when the balance of population and wealth was shifting to the industrial north of England. True, power in the legislature stayed with the south and with the land, because the north was un- or under-represented, and because the land still held its veto in the House of Lords. But intelligent Conservatives could see that this situation could not be protected forever. As to the Church, the 1851 census was a rude shock. For the only time in British census history, a census of religious attendance ran alongside the population census. There were more non-Anglican than Anglican attendances in England and Wales on census Sunday (Table 3.1).

Anglican prelates spin-doctored the results, claiming that Dissenters had inflated their counts because they were dishonest and couldn't count. Their propaganda has misled some scholars into mistrusting the 1851 results. But, having studied the large number of round numbers (such as 100) indicative of estimated congregation sizes, Crockett and Crockett (forthcoming) concluded that the Church of England (and some older dissenting denominations) inflated such rounded estimates quite substantially, while the insurgent

Table 3.1. Church and chapel attendance on Census Sunday, 1851, England and Wales

	Number	Percent of total
England		
Anglican	4,745,510	50.3
Roman Catholic	351,252	3.7
Jewish	5,431	0.06
All other [i.e., total Dissenting]	4,327,613	45.9
Wales		
Anglican	189,706	19.3
Roman Catholic	8,373	0.9
Jewish	78	0.008
All other [i.e., total Dissenting]	784,117	79.8
England & Wales		
Anglican	4,935,216	47.40
Roman Catholic	359,625	3.45
Jewish	5,509	0.05
All other [i.e., total Dissenting]	5,111,730	49.09

Source: computerized database of registration district returns, by kind courtesy of Alasdair Crockett.

Methodists did not. The net effect of such practices was to flatter the Church of England's popularity relative to Nonconformity. Without Anglican inflation, the Established Church might have recorded a minority of attendances even in England itself. That the results were such dynamite is probably the main reason why the 1851 religious census was never repeated. Over Maynooth, Wellington had come close to conceding that the position of the established Anglican Church of Ireland was not tenable in the long run ('we cannot prevent them from being Roman Catholics'). The Established Church accounted for only a fifth of attendances in Wales. In Scotland, the Established Church split in 1843, with the dissenting Free Church taking off the majority of ministers and congregations. The Conservatives could not simply remain the party of stubborn resistance to all of these trends. They would have to broaden their social base. The task must start immediately after the defeat of Peel.

The leaders of the Conservative Party after the Peel debacle were an ill-matched pair. Stanley,[1] despite his early nickname (conferred by Disraeli and his friends) as 'the Rupert of parliamentary discussion', had faded. Of all leading Victorian politicians he is probably now the least known, having neither a contemporary three-decker biography with letters, nor a compre-

---

[1] Lord Stanley became the 14th Earl of Derby in 1851. In this book, he is named by the title he held at the time under discussion. The 15th, 16th, and 17th Earls of Derby were also politicians, and also held the title Lord Stanley before succeeding to the earldom.

hensive modern study (but see Robert Stewart 1971). He said and did very little that made a mark after he became leader of the Conservatives, even though he somehow managed to be Prime Minister three times. Even his hagiographer in the old *Dictionary of National Biography* admits, 'He was not a statesman of profoundly settled convictions or of widely constructive views. He was a man rather of intense vitality than of great intellect.' As his son wrote to Disraeli in 1853, 'the Captain does not care for office but wishes to keep things as they are and impede "progress"' (Stanley to Disraeli 20.1.1853, quoted by Blake (1966): 354). Disraeli complained in 1853 that 'My despatches from Knowsley [the stately home of the Earls of Derby] have only taken the shape of haunches of venison' (to Lord Londonderry Sept. 1853, in Blake 1966: 357. See various other amusing expressions of Disraeli's frustration with Derby, loc. cit. 357–60). However, he published a translation of *The Iliad* which went through six editions in his lifetime.

On the other hand, there has never been much doubt about the character of Benjamin Disraeli. Among British politicians, his ability to invent his past, to get into financial and sexual misadventures, and then miraculously escape from them, is rivalled only by Lord Archer of Weston-super-Mare (see Crick 1995). Unlike Lord Archer, he was never caught. Maurice Cowling (1967: 327) calls him 'a destructive showman . . . combin[ing] . . . the uncaptivable combination of contrived ordinariness, controlled geniality, brazen insincerity, and bitter verbal unscrupulousness'. He also wrote novels.

Most of Disraeli's early misadventures, though highly entertaining, are irrelevant to our analysis. From the mishaps described with loving care by his biographers, of whom the best remains Blake (1966), we mention only those which either imperilled his relationship with Stanley or throw light on his political philosophy and/or his capacity for heresthetic.

In 1830 and 1831 Disraeli went on a grand tour encompassing Spain, Turkey, and Egypt. This introduced Disraeli to the romance of the East and undoubtedly coloured his later attitudes to foreign policy. For instance, he approved of the relaxed attitude to Jews that he found in Istanbul. His travelling companions included James Clay, described by Blake (1966: 62) as 'a handsome youth with the complexion of a ripe peach'. He later became a radical Liberal MP and an authority on whist. More important, during the 1867 reform campaign, he acted as a channel between the radicals and Disraeli, bypassing Gladstone (F. B. Smith 1966: 63, 101). Clay and Disraeli engaged in adventures with sex and drugs, one of Clay's letters describing them being 'unprintable even in this liberal era' (Blake 1966: 62). On the ship home from Egypt Disraeli met and befriended Henry Stanley, Lord Stanley's younger brother. When they reached London, Stanley disappeared. In the words of Disraeli's solicitor writing many years later, 'he was eventually run to earth at Effie Bond's, the Keeper of the Hell in St James's Street where he had taken up his quarters and to which it was alleged Disraeli had introduced him' (Sir Philip Rose, quoted by Blake 1966: 71). Disraeli was probably innocent of this particular charge, but his character did not inspire the elder Stanleys to trust him.

Disraeli's early politics were equally colourful. In his first parliamentary contests, he did not mind whether he stood as a Tory, a Radical, or both; the one thing he was clearly not was a Whig. In 1833, he sent his sister a newspaper gossip column which said:

Someone asked Disraeli in offering himself for Marylebone, on what he intended *to stand*. 'On my head' was the reply. (To Sarah Disraeli, 8.4.1833, in Blake 1966: 92)

In 1834 he ran, unsuccessfully, as a Radical for Wycombe against the two sitting Whig members. He received £500 in funds from the Tories, who thought he had more chance of unseating the incumbents than a Tory would have done. After losing, he wrote to Wellington:

I am now a cipher, but if the devotion of my energies to your cause, *in* and *out*, can ever avail you, your grace may count upon me, who seeks no greater satisfaction than that of serving a great man

to which Wellington replied cautiously in the third person that he 'very much regrets the result of the election at Wycombe' (Disraeli to Wellington, 7.1.1835 and reply, in Blake 1966: 123). When Peel was forming his administration in 1841, Disraeli sent him a letter which ended:

I confess [that] to be unrecognised at this moment by you appears to me to be overwhelming, and I appeal to your own heart—to that justice and that magnanimity which I feel are your characteristics—to save me from an intolerable humiliation (To Peel, 5.9.1841. In Parker 1891: ii. 486).

No job resulted, nor did one for Disraeli's brother for which he asked Graham in 1843. When Graham told Peel about the request, Peel replied:

I am very glad that Mr Disraeli has asked for an office for his brother. It is a good thing when such a man puts his shabbiness on record. He asked me for office himself, and I was not surprised that being refused he became independent and a patriot. But to ask favours after his conduct last Session is too bad. However, it is a bridle in his mouth (Graham to Peel 21.12.1843 and reply, 22.12.1843; in Parker 1891: iii. 424–5)

It was not. But it cannot have done him any good in his relations with Stanley. As a Cabinet colleague of Peel, Graham, and Wellington until December 1845, Stanley certainly knew about Disraeli's twists, turns, and importunities. His most astonishing escape actually came after Stanley had changed sides, in the Corn Law debates. Disraeli, who had earlier said, 'a Conservative Government is an Organised Hypocrisy',[2] attacked Peel for his change of mind and contrasted it with his own steadfastness. Peel asked why then was Disraeli 'ready as I think he was, to unite his fortunes with mine in office'? Disraeli replied:

I never asked a favour of the Government, not even one of those mechanical things which persons are obliged to ask. . . . I never directly or indirectly solicited office. (Hansard, 3s v. 86: 689, 709, 15.5.46)

---

[2] Hansard, 3s 78: 1028, 17.3.45. The quotation is usually taken out of context. Disraeli did not mean that any Conservative government was an organized hypocrisy. He meant that Peel's Administration was.

An eyewitness (Lord Lincoln) stated that Peel had Disraeli's letter of 1841, in which he directly solicited office, in his dispatch box on setting out to the debate (Blake 1966: 238–9). Peel's failure to destroy Disraeli on the spot is mystifying. The bridle was in Disraeli's mouth; the reins were in Peel's hands; he did not pull on them.

It is not surprising that, immediately after the crash of 1846–7, Stanley (Derby) should have had so little faith in Disraeli that he tried twice to appoint nonentities as Commons leaders of the Conservatives after Bentinck's unexpected death in 1848. He asked Disraeli to 'give a generous support to a leader of abilities inferior to your own' (Stanley to Disraeli 21.12.48, in Blake 1966: 265–6). Not until the end of 1851 did Disraeli formally become the Conservative leader in the Commons. By this time, he had already written to James Clay, 'Protection is not only dead, but damned' (1850; Monypenny and Buckle 1929: i. 1057. Clay had suggested that protection, like Lazarus, was not dead but asleep). Derby clung to protection for longer. But when he formed his first minority government in 1852, he appointed Disraeli Chancellor of the Exchequer. Disraeli's budget made no attempt to reintroduce protection, although it introduced tax concessions for the victims of Repeal. It was defeated, after being savaged by Gladstone in the Commons, and the government resigned, Disraeli saying as he went, 'England does not love coalitions'.[3] But the coalition that defeated him did not include the protectionists.

Derby and Disraeli formed three minority administrations, in 1852, 1858, and 1866. After the crash of 1846, no party held a majority in the Commons except in 1857 (when it soon crumbled) and 1868. All attempts to compile a table of party shares for these years are defeated by the independence of MPs. A few sources attempt, with great labour, to calculate the number of Peelites and of independent Irish MPs. Nobody has ever attempted to divide Liberals into their factions. Those who supported Palmerston might sometimes vote with the Tories. Those who supported Russell would not. Table 3.2 is the best we can do. It purports to show a Liberal majority in 1857, 1859, and 1865. But the 1859 election was called in the aftermath of Palmerston's defeat, and the 1865 Parliament did not meet till after his death. Therefore there was no Liberal unity.

The Heresthetic of Reform 1866–7

The making of the Second Reform Act in 1866–67 is one of the most exhaustively analysed events in British political history. Four notable monographs (F. B. Smith 1966; Cowling 1967; P. Smith 1967; Feuchtwanger 1968) came

---

[3] Hansard, 3s 123: 1666, 16.12.52. This is also usually taken out of context. Disraeli meant, 'I do not love the coalition that I know is about to defeat me', but he managed to express himself in more generalized terms.

Table 3.2. UK General Election results, 1847–68

Year	Tory Seats (%)	Peelite Seats (%)	Liberal Seats (%)	Irish nationalist Seats (%)
1847	276 (42.07)	48 (7.32)	294 (44.82)	38 (5.79)
1852	280 (42.81)	50 (7.65)	278 (42.51)	46 (7.03)
1857	264 (40.37)		378 (57.80)	12 (1.83)
1859	297 (45.41)		342 (52.29)	15 (2.29)
1865	288 (43.77)		350 (53.19)	20 (3.04)
1868	271 (41.19)		387 (58.81)	

Sources: Craig 1977 for overall totals of Conservatives and Liberals. Craig does not attempt to guess Peelite or Irish home rule numbers. Peelites from Conacher 1972. Irish numbers from Walker 1978. 'Nationalist' = Repealer or Confederate (1847); Lib. Independent (1852); those who attended a meeting of the National Association in Dublin, 05.12.65 (1865).

out on the centenary, the first two of them exclusively about the making of the Act and the second two about its consequences. This section has no startling discoveries to add to these standard sources. But it does consider the main attempts at reform in the light of the models introduced in Chapter 1.

The Peelites collapsed as a governing force after the failure of the Peelite Aberdeen to run the Crimean War efficiently. He was succeeded in January 1855 by Lord Palmerston, who remained Prime Minister for ten years, apart from a brief Derby–Disraeli interlude in 1858–9. Palmerston was nominally a Whig, but was most notable for his aggressive foreign policy. There would be no parliamentary reform from a Palmerston administration. Disraeli took up the issue of reform as a possible means of restoring the fortunes of the Tories. Disraeli suggested to Derby in 1857:

whether a juster apportionment of M.P.s may not be the question on which a powerful and enduring party may be established. . . . [T]he present arrangement, which leaves the balance of power in small boroughs, which are ruled by cliques of Dissenters, seems fatal to the maintenance of the present aristocratic and ecclesiastical institutions. . . . [T]he question of the suffrage may be dealt with extensively, but in an eminently conservative manner. If fifty members were added to the counties, by reducing the small borough to one member, and every ten-pound householder in the county population were annexed to a borough constituency, you would . . . greatly increase the Conservative power at the same time . . . Our party is now a corpse, but in the present perplexed state of affairs, *a Conservative public pledge[d] to Parliamentary Reform*, a bold and decided course might . . . put us on our legs.[4] (Monypenny and Buckle 1929: i. 1479)

Derby rejected the idea opting for 'a safer course' of tacitly supporting Palmerston against Lord John Russell, now regarded as the leader of the Radicals.

---

[4] Stress in original. The source has 'pledged' but Disraeli probably meant to say 'pledge'.

However, Disraeli and Stanley drafted a bill in the autumn of 1858, adopting the principle of assimilating the county franchise with the borough franchise by introducing a £10 rating qualification for the counties, redistributing fifty-two seats to the counties away from the boroughs, and disenfranchising between sixty and ninety small boroughs. Disraeli further sought information on the effect which a lowering of the ratings qualification would have for Conservative electoral strength, writing to many Conservative agents for their opinions.

The result of the inquiry was the Disraeli and Rose memorandum (F. B. Smith 1966: 41), which declared that the Conservatives' objective should be 'a fair impartial contrasting scheme to [John] Bright's' that would enable them to appeal to the country if necessary. It should also promise finality, but 'that this can only be attained by removing anomalies in the elective franchise and so defining it to embrace the influences of property, station and intelligence without regard solely to population'.

The Conservative bill of 1859 was defeated on a motion by Lord John Russell:

that this House is of the opinion, that it is neither just nor politic to interfere in the manner proposed in this Bill, with the Freehold Franchise as hitherto exercised in the Counties of England and Wales; that no re-adjustment of the Franchise will satisfy this House or the Country, which does not provide for a greater extension of the suffrage in Cities and Boroughs that is contemplated in the present measure. (Hansard 3s 153, 405, 21.03.1859)

This motion was designed to attract both ends of the spectrum: the radicals and the Palmerstonians. Palmerston had described Disraeli, in French, as 'a democrat under the skin of a conservative' (in Monypenny and Buckle 1929: i. 1605). The motion was 'too mild to cause the government to dissolve if they were defeated, but strong enough to make them resign'. Derby and Disraeli resigned and Palmerston resumed office, to reign untroubled by reform until the next election was legally required, in August 1865.

The Commons majority elected in 1865 in support of the anti-reformer Palmerston, who died three months after the General Election, rejected a Reform Bill introduced in 1866 by the succeeding Russell–Gladstone ministry. The ministry resigned, to be succeeded by a minority Tory administration under Derby, with Disraeli as Commons leader and Chancellor of the Exchequer. The same House as had rejected Gladstone's bill passed Disraeli's much more radical one in 1867; it then passed almost unhindered through the House of Lords. This summary implies that a heresthetician was at work. The median member of both houses was against reform. The median member of the 1865 Commons was a Palmerstonite, opposed to reform. Any reform would entail some reduction in the authority of the Lords, whose median member therefore also opposed reform. Gladstone failed to introduce reform while leading a majority government, whereas Disraeli succeeded while leading a minority government. Both the failure and the success must therefore be analysed.

All reformers in the 1860s, including both Gladstone and Disraeli, shared
a mental map of the British population. In the social orders below those who
already held the franchise lay some who were respectable and some who were
not. The respectable held enough property to give them a stake in society.
Owning property had two consequences. First, it was associated with higher
standards of morality—the property-owner was less likely to be bribed than
the propertyless. (There was no objective evidence for this, nor is there a good
a priori reason why it should be so, but all reformers at the time believed it.)
Second, if the propertyless were enfranchised, they would enact confiscatory
legislation. They would expropriate the assets of the propertied and give them
to themselves. This was a fear as old as Aristotle (*Politics* Book IV, esp. 1292a;
Sinclair 1962: 154–60). All contemporary commentators, from J. S. Mill on
the left to Robert Lowe and Lord Cranborne (later Salisbury) on the right,
shared it (for examples of their writings see Chapter 4). Therefore, all attempts
at electoral reform from 1832 to the initial 1867 proposals attempted to find
some legally defensible line to draw between the propertied and the propertyless. The obvious criterion was freehold ownership of a house or other
real estate. But this was too narrow. Most even of the middle class were
tenants, not freeholders. Liability for poor rates (local property tax) at some
minimum annual level, and payment of a certain minimum annual rent, were
the two marks of property that reformers sought. Both were extremely shaky
bases for a legal distinction between voters and non-voters. Property is a stock;
rent and rate payments are both flows. The reformers wanted to enfranchise
just those who had enough of the stock—of property. But the only information available was unreliable, and it concerned flows. Even in an administra-
tively perfect world, it would be very hard to deduce the size of a stock from
the annual flows related to it. The market with all its local peculiarities determined rent levels. Annual rate payments varied according to local practice,
especially with regard to compounding. A compounder was a tenant who paid
a single bill, covering both rent and rates, to his landlord. The landlord then
paid on the rates to the Poor Law authorities, usually at a concessionary rate.
The landlord's, not the compounder's, name would appear on the rating list.
Therefore, if the rating list remained the eligibility criterion, most compounders were ineligible for the vote. Politicians' guesses as to how many
people would be enfranchised by any given rent or rate threshold were subject
to wild variations. Therefore, an amendment to substitute 'ratal' for 'rental'
or *vice versa*, or to raise or lower a rate or rent threshold, could leave even
well-informed politicians floundering, quite unable to guess how it would
affect the franchise. No wonder Disraeli called franchise reform a 'Serbonian
bog'.[5] This made for ideal heresthetic conditions.

In 1866, Gladstone found himself battling on two fronts: Bright and the
reformers to his left, the Palmerstonians to his right. The Gladstone bill,

---

[5] Hansard, 3s, 186: 15, 18.03.67 *Serbonian bog*: Milton's name for Lake Serbonis in Lower Egypt,
a marshy tract (now dry) covered with shifting sand. Hence used allusively (*OED*, CD-Rom edn).

produced after much confusion and argument in the Cabinet, introduced a rent threshold of £7, and addressed the problem of compounders by directing rating books to declare their names. In the counties, new voters must demonstrate £50 in savings or occupancy of a household valued at £14 per annum rental. Gladstone said,

the number of persons properly belonging to the working class and having £14 rental . . . will be so small . . . as not to be worth taking into calculation. Or at least . . . that portion of the newly enfranchised . . . as may belong to the labouring class, will be tenants of small holdings of land in immediate connection with the landed class. (Hansard, 3s, 182: 30, 13.03.66)

Disraeli let the Palmerstonian Whigs make hostile amendments and then fell in behind them. Bright nicknamed the anti-reform Whigs 'the Cave of Adullam' (Hansard, 3s, 182: 219, 12.03.66), and the nickname has stuck (See Old Testament, 1 Samuel 22: 1, 2). The first wrecking amendment came from the Adullamite Earl Grosvenor, who said that it 'has not been framed or worded by a Tory hand' (Hansard, 3s, 182: 1156. 12.04.66). The Grosvenor amendment was clever. It called for franchise extension to be delayed until 'the entire scheme', including a redistribution bill, had been proposed. Redistribution would inevitably make enemies of all who stood to lose their seats, and might lose the government its majority. The Grosvenor amendment was lost by only five votes. Thirty-five Whigs voted for it, balanced only by one Tory who hoped to become a baronet and voted for the government in the hope of being noticed (F. B. Smith 1966: 90, 255–6; *Hansard* 3s 183, 152, 27.04.66). The government contemplated resigning, but decided to soldier on. It introduced a botched redistribution bill, which was furiously attacked by the 'dying swans' (as one of them labelled himself[6]) who stood to lose their seats. Any redistribution bill created as many new issue dimensions as the number of seats it abolished, and therefore greatly increased the prospects of multidimensional chaos. Each MP had a distinct issue dimension—his own survival. A series of amendments to the main bill was lost by narrow majorities, each time with about twenty-five Adullamites voting for it.[7] Meanwhile, Lord Derby drew up a list of Whig peers who were likely to vote against the bill in the Lords and kill it there (F. B. Smith 1966: 108). Finally, the Adullamites triumphed in the Commons with another 'ratal for rental' amendment, which they won by 315 votes to 304 (*Hansard* 3s 184, 639. 18.06.66). As Gladstone recorded, this was done with 'violent flourishing [of] hats and other manifestations which I think novel and inappropriate'. (Gladstone, diary for 18.06.66, in Matthew 1978). The Russell administration resigned, despite urgent requests from the Queen that they should stay on.

---

[6] F. D. Goldsmid (Palmerstonite, Honiton). *Hansard* 3s 183, 1554, 31.05.66.
[7] Stanley's amendment lost by 287 to 260; Walpole's amendment lost by 297 to 283; Ward Hunt's amendment to substitute 'ratal' for 'rental', lost by 280 to 273. *Hansard* 3s 183: 2072; 183: 2126; 184: 405; F. B. Smith 1966: 102–10.

The Adullamites seem to have thought that as they had shown that their group contained the median Commons voter, they should lead the next administration. Derby, Disraeli, and the Queen would have none of that. The Queen sent for Derby, who formed a minority Tory government. The Adullamites who had put them in refused office, after not being offered the premiership (Monypenny and Buckle 1929: ii. 176). Although without a majority, Derby and Disraeli were under no immediate pressure, as Parliament adjourned in July to shoot grouse until November.

On 29 July 1866 Disraeli wrote to Derby,

Suppose, instead of discharging the order of the day on the Reform Bill, you took up the measure where it stops: £6 *rating* for boroughs; £20 rating for counties, to be brought up on report; the northern boroughs to be enfranchised; no disfranchisement of any kind. You could carry this in the present House, and rapidly. It would prevent all agitation in the recess; it would cut the ground entirely from under Gladstone; and it would smash the Bath Cabal [i.e. anti-reform Tories led by the Marquis of Bath], for there would be no dangerous questions ahead. (Monypenny and Buckle 1929: ii. 186–7)

'To be brought up on report' may imply that the rating clauses were not to be introduced until the bill had reached report stage, half way through its Commons progress. If so, this letter accurately foreshadows Disraeli's improvisations of 1867. But Derby was more cautious. He proposed not a bill but a series of resolutions. His thinking, too, was tactical. If Parliament voted down the resolutions, those who voted against them would face huge pressure from reformers at the ensuing General Election. If it voted for them, this would give Derby and Disraeli the maximum authority to draft a bill, at leisure, which might unite the Conservatives. Derby wished the matter to go to a Royal Commission, which would have given the minority government a year's breathing space:

If we get the House pledged to our *principles*, we shall be in a much better position for hereafter discussing details; and it will be difficult for the Radicals, either to escape from Amendments, or so to frame them as not to clash with moderate Liberals, and widen the existing breach. (Derby to Disraeli, 09.10 66, Disraeli Papers '14 Derby', quoted in F. B. Smith 1966: 135)

This approach would, he argued, 'place us on velvet'. Disraeli agreed, noting that,

if the House . . . gets involved in the discussion, the Liberal party will probably be broken up. If as is more likely, Mr. Gladstone meets the Ministerial motion by a general resolution in favor of immediate legislation, it is not impossible he may be defeated, which will establish the Government. But if he succeed it will probably be by a narrow majority, and the dissolution will then take place on an issue between Bright's policy and our programme. (Disraeli to Derby, 18.11.66, in Monypenny and Buckle 1929: ii. 194)

Derby's resolutions, introduced to the Cabinet on 8 November 1866 against the background of massive Reform demonstrations in Birmingham, Leeds,

Manchester, and Glasgow, embodied the principle of enfranchisement for rated householders tempered by a 'fancy franchise' of plural votes for the landed classes. The idea was that extended borough suffrage on the basis of 'personal rating', with its radical implications, would be tempered by an equal and opposite dose of plural votes, to banish the spectre of a confiscatory working-class majority. However, again the problem of incomplete information created much friction within the Cabinet as everyone seemed to have different estimates of the effects.

The resolutions were presented to the Commons on 14 February 1867, with the promise of a £6 rating for boroughs. The next day Disraeli checkmated Gladstone, who had come to the House prepared with a motion to vote down the resolutions, by withdrawing the resolutions (F. B. Smith 1966: 158). In place of the resolutions Disraeli introduced the Reform Bill, offering a £6 rating, providing 'personal payment of rates', plural votes for the landed classes, and a three-year residency requirement.

Disraeli's introductory speech was designed to counter Gladstone's desire for a £5 rating, as well as placating those who feared that the bill was a step toward democracy.

[O]ur object is not only to maintain, but to strengthen, the character and functions of this House [by] . . . establish[ing] them on a broad popular basis. . . . I attribute the sentiment of alarm associated with [the bill] to a misapprehension of its meaning, and to that perplexity of ideas which too often confounds popular privileges with democratic rights. (Hansard, 3s 186: 6, 18.03.67)

He lauded personal payment of rates as (implausibly) a fundamental part of the British constitution.

Gladstone immediately pointed out the flaws in the bill, including its incongruence with the 1832 Act. Rather than counter these attacks directly, Disraeli conceded nothing to Gladstone while in the same breath conceding to other Liberals and Reformers. This had the effect of isolating Gladstone within his own party, bringing those who wanted a settlement of the issue into Disraeli's camp. Clay advised a meeting of Liberal and Radical MPs that their interest lay in keeping the Tories in office, because they would get a better deal from them than from Gladstone (F. B. Smith 1966: 166).

The problems embodied in the bill were becoming increasingly evident through debate. Not only was it incongruent with the 1832 Act, it was also complicated by incomplete record keeping in the parishes and boroughs, the exclusion of compounders, and the seeming unworkability of the fancy franchises of education and plural voting. However, as Gladstone offered up a number of amendments to the bill, Disraeli resorted to the unusual step of writing to *The Times*, intimating that the government would resign if any were passed.

Disraeli's first dilemma was over Ayrton's (Lib.) amendment seeking to reduce the residency requirement from two years to one. Disraeli agreed to this amendment as it would bring on side the Radicals and independent Liberals, but he knew it would split his Cabinet. He stood back from debate on the principle that if the amendment passed he would placate the Liberals and Radicals with the acceptance of the amendment, and placate his own side with the knowledge that the amendment did not emanate from Gladstone. The amendment was passed with no debate. Only specialists would be able to guess, and then not necessarily accurately, how many extra voters this would add.

Disraeli could not master the Cabinet as effortlessly as the Commons. Three ministers including Cranborne (later Salisbury) resigned in protest at the increasing radicalism of the bill. Cranborne had done his homework, and worked out that Disraeli's proposals would enfranchise far more lower-class people than Disraeli had assumed (Roberts 1999: 90–1). Despite losing three ministers, Disraeli carried the Tory backbenchers, who endorsed the bill at a meeting in the Carlton Club. Even though by then it embodied house-hold suffrage in the boroughs, the Tory MPs were placated by the supposed counterweights of plural voting, or by the thrill of the chase, or both. One by one, the counterweights fell off, as it became clear that there were no acceptable lists of taxpayers, or personal ratepayers, or savings account holders, on which to base the plural franchises. Disraeli pressed on regardless, leaving his followers with only the thrill of the chase. Nowhere was this more notable than on the Hodgkinson amendment. Grosvenor Hodgkinson (Lib., Newark) moved that 'no other person other than the occupier shall . . . be rated to parochial rates in respect of premises occupied by him within the limits of a Parliamentary borough, all Acts to the contrary now in force notwithstanding' (*Hansard* 3s 187: 708, 17.05.67).

Both legally and politically, the Hodgkinson amendment was breathtaking. Legally, it purported to solve the problem of compounding simply by repeal-ing all the legislation that permitted it (thus throwing local government finance into chaos). Politically, it enabled Disraeli to claim blandly that he could now at last implement the principle of personal payment of rates. In a thin house, which Gladstone had left for dinner expecting an official Liberal amendment to be moved which would have achieved the Hodgkinson aim by more legally defensible methods, Disraeli simply accepted the Hodgkinson amendment. This episode was quickly followed by Disraeli's withdrawal of the fancy franchises, and passage through third reading, all without division. In the words of F. B. Smith (1966: 207), 'within the space of an hour, the results of fifteen years' work to devise a set of qualifications supplementary to the old tests of occupation and citizenship were scrapped, and with their disappearance went the last chance of introducing any coun-terweights within a mass electorate.' The best clue as to why Conservative MPs accepted Disraeli's extraordinary manoeuvres lies in the toast proposed to him at the Carlton Club on 12 April: 'Here's [to] the man who rode the race, who took the time, who kept the time, and who did the trick!' (Monypenny and Buckle 1929: ii. 267)

The bill now went to the House of Lords, where Derby repeated Wellington's feat of 1845 and 1846: he persuaded a majority of voting peers to vote against their material interests and pass the bill. There was no co-operation between the Tory (Cranborne) and Whig (Adullamite) rebels. About twenty to thirty backwoods Tories who never normally came to the House turned up for the rare pleasure of supporting a Tory government (F. B. Smith 1966: 209). The Lords inserted two substantial constitutional amendments and one political one. The first ended the automatic dissolution of Parliament when the sovereign died. The second ended the requirement for Commons ministers to resign their seats and fight by-elections on appointment. The third was the much-misunderstood (even by F. B. Smith 1966: 212, and Cowling 1967: 226–7) Cairns amendment that instituted the 'limited vote'. The limited vote amendment created three-member seats in the big cities, but gave each elector only two votes. The idea was to give the Conservatives a toehold in the overwhelmingly Liberal cities. Most historians believe that it failed to work, because Joseph Chamberlain's Liberals organized their Birmingham caucus so effectively that the Liberals won all three seats there in the general elections of 1868 to 1880. He divided the city into thirds and in each third told his followers to vote for a different pair of Liberals. But that is merely the rational strategy for an informed and disciplined party. If the Cairns amendment is considered from a game-theoretic perspective, as Lewis Carroll was the first to do (Dodgson 1884; McLean, McMillan, and Monroe 1996), it may be seen as a surprisingly effective device for proportional representation. The Liberals won all three seats in Birmingham despite and not because of the Cairns amendment, but because they controlled over two-thirds of the vote there. The only politician to understand this, however dimly, was Lord Salisbury in 1884, and he rescued the Tories not by proportional representation but by careful attention to district boundaries (see below).

Disraeli accepted the Lords amendments, and proceeded to a redistribution bill. He avoided the dying swan trap that the Adullamites had set for Gladstone in 1866. Only thirty seats were abolished—seven of them from boroughs that had been disenfranchised for corruption, and therefore had no defenders in the House. The other twenty-three were in small boroughs, reduced from two seats to one each. The boundary commissioners he appointed to oversee the redistribution were Tories, and they secretly reported to the Tory agents before reporting to Parliament (Blake 1966: 473; F. B. Smith 1966: 219). Disraeli's ways of doing public business differed from Gladstone's.

The only other politician in this book to pull off a coup remotely comparable to Disraeli's in 1867 was Lloyd George with the Irish negotiations in 1921. On these occasions a majority of each House voted against their interests and their ideology. The same happened in 1845 and 1846, but Peel's and Wellington's methods differed greatly from Disraeli's and Lloyd George's. The destructive triumph of 1866 was shared with the Adullamites, and is not too

surprising, given that a majority of each House was against reform. Disraeli
let the Adullamites destroy Gladstone and then scooped the resulting win-
nings. The constructive triumph of 1867, apart from some nimble footwork
by Derby at the beginning, was Disraeli's alone. He did it by smoke and
mirrors, or, as he called it, 'all the black devices . . . I applied' (to working
men's meeting, Edinburgh, 31.10.67, quoted by Cowling 1967: 311). Even the
experts—even Disraeli himself—could not calculate the electoral effects of
amendments as they were considered and moved. Did a £5 rating threshold
enfranchise more or fewer people than a £5 rental threshold? Clay and some
of the Radicals probably realized how far Disraeli was going, and correctly saw
that their interest lay in keeping the Tories in, so that they would get more
from Disraeli than they would have done from their own leader. The Tories,
in both houses, seem to have responded simply to the thrill of the chase and
to Disraeli's unprecedented mastery of the Commons, without paying attention to the substance of the legislation. It is usually unsatisfactory to attribute
differential information levels to different members of the legislature (see e.g.
Mackie 2000 for attacks on Riker 1982 on these grounds). But here the empirical evidence is strong. Clay was a master of statistics. So was Cranborne. Disraeli was not. He blithely accepted the Hodgkinson amendment with no care
for its huge consequences, just to wrongfoot the absent Gladstone. And his
followers loved him for it. In the short term, it was brilliant heresthetic. But
was it part of a grander plan?

Disraeli's Political Philosophy

Disraeli's politics may have been something more than pure opportunism. He
expressed a consistent view of British political history which contained a
more or less coherent ideology. At least, it was quite clear what he was against;
less clear what he was for. The fullest statements are in his early *Vindication
of the English Constitution* (Disraeli 1835/1969); his 'Young England' novels
Coningsby (Disraeli 1844/1983) and *Sybil* (Disraeli 1845/1985); and his life of
Bentinck (Disraeli 1852).

   From the very first, he struck one consistent note:

A Tory and a Radical I understand; a Whig—a democratic aristocrat—I cannot com-
prehend. If the Tories . . . are sincere in their avowal that the state cannot be governed
with the present machinery, it is their duty to coalesce with the radicals, and permit
both political nicknames to merge in the common, the intelligible, and the dignified
title of a National Party. (*What is He? by the Author of Vivian Grey*, 1833, quoted by Blake
1966: 92–3)

He frequently characterized the Whig aristocrats as people who built their
dynasties on the plunder of the Church in the sixteenth and seventeenth centuries. Not they, but the Tories, were the true friends of democracy and
religious freedom, because in the seventeenth century

[D]ivine right and passive obedience resounded from our Protestant pulpits, echoed with enthusiasm by a free and spirited people who acknowledged in these phrases only a determination to maintain the mild authority of their King and their Church. (Disraeli 1835/1969: 177–8)

Coningsby and *Sybil* continue the theme. Both novels have entire chapters of history and ideology in with the drama and romance. The Whig coup, as Disraeli now saw it, deprived the Crown of power and substituted a 'Venetian constitution' in which the king was as powerless as the doge of Venice and the Whig oligarchy ruled in the name of the 'people'. (Disraeli's view of the Venetian constitution was as distinctive as that of the British constitution.)

Disraeli has his heroes say of the Tories in 1837:

'And yet', he [Buckhurst] added, laughing, 'if any fellow were to ask me what the Conservative Cause is, I am sure I should not know what to say'.

'Why, it is the cause of our glorious institutions' said Coningsby. 'A Crown robbed of its prerogatives; a Church controlled by a commission; and an Aristocracy that does not lead'.

'Under whose genial influence the order of the Peasantry, "a country's pride", has vanished from the face of the land', said Henry Sydney, 'and is succeeded by a race of serfs, who are called labourers, and who burn ricks'.

'Under which.' continued Coningsby, 'the Crown has become a cipher; the Church a sect; the Nobility drones; and the People drudges.' (Disraeli 1844/1983: 283)

So too in *Sybil*, where the rich and the poor have become two nations, mutually uncomprehending. It hints at an alliance between land and labour against capital which occasionally took shape in the 1840s. For instance, the devout evangelical (and landowner) Lord Ashley sponsored the Ten Hours' Bill, restricting the hours of factory labour. A romantic, Disraelian view of such regulation is that the rich were reaching out to the poor. A materialist view is that the interests of each factor of production differed, and that therefore each alliance of any two against the third was possible. We are to infer from *Coningsby* and *Sybil* that when labourers were peasants, they and their superiors understood each other perfectly and lived in perfect harmony. Or are we? You can never be sure with Disraeli, who has a talent for mocking his own positions, as for example in the character of the embarrassed Catholic landowner Lyle in *Coningsby*: 'But not a heart there that did not bless the bell that sounded from the tower of St Geneviève!' (Disraeli 1844/1983: 170)

Disraeli formed a parliamentary group of young aristocrats, Young England, to act out the ideals of *Coningsby* in the Parliament of 1841–7. Young England, like the Fourth Party of the 1880s, was a small group of unorthodox Tories with high opinions of themselves and considerable capacity to cause trouble to their own leaders. Of the other members of Young England, Lord John Manners (later the Duke of Rutland) wrote a *Plea for National Holy-Days* and a poem containing the couplet

> Let wealth and commerce, laws and learning die,
> But leave us still our old Nobility

George Smythe, the model for Coningsby, accepted a job under Peel in January 1846. By then, Young England was already dead as a practical ideology (if it had ever been one), as the Young Englanders had split up over the Maynooth grant in 1845.

The most telling theme in the young Disraeli's ideology is his attack on Tory pragmatism. Into Lyle's mouth he puts this scarcely veiled attack on Peel and Wellington:

The Duke talks to me of Conservative principles; but he does not inform me what they are. I observe indeed a party in the State whose rule is to consent to no change, until it is clamorously called for, and then instantly to yield; but these are Concessionary, not Conservative principles. This party treats institutions as we do our pheasants, they preserve only to destroy them. (ibid. 172)

But while this was fine as ideology, it was difficult as practical politics. For twenty years, Disraeli was yoked to Derby, whose politics (as his correspondence with Wellington in 1846 so eloquently shows) were precisely those mocked by Lyle. And whatever Disraeli was, he was not a reactionary. He knew that majorities could not be built without flexibility. In 1867, despite much flannel about preserving our ancient institutions, he engineered a reform much more sweeping than that of 1832.

Did Disraeli Really Rebase the Party?

In a celebrated phrase, *The Times* wrote soon after Disraeli's death that

In the inarticulate mass of the English populace, [he] discerned the Conservative workingman as the sculptor perceives the angel prisoned in a block of marble. (18 April 1883)

McKenzie and Silver (1968) used the striking image as the title of their study of working-class Conservatism. Disraeli often claimed that Conservatism implied national unity. The Conservatives were the national party, he said in his first successful election campaign:

By the Conservative cause I mean the splendour of the Crown, the lustre of the Peerage, the privileges of the Commons, the rights of the poor. I mean that harmonious union, that magnificent concord of all interests, of all classes, on which our national greatness depends (Speech at Maidstone, (?) 1837, in Edwards 1973: 173; cf. also Monypenny & Buckle 1929: i. 376–7)

Most historians (notably Blake 1966; F. B. Smith 1966) have been thoroughly sceptical of these claims. How far was Disraeli personally responsible for the great escape of the Tory Party from the ghetto into which he (or, as he would say, Peel) took it in 1846?

One fact is quite clear. Disraeli extracted the Conservatives from the dead-end of protection. It was a dead-end in the 1850s because it was inextricably linked with the interests of the land. The interests of the land were bound to become a smaller and smaller proportion of the interests represented in Parliament, with or without electoral reform. Economic geography and demographics would see to that. Disraeli was infinitely suppler than his co-leaders Bentinck and Stanley (Derby).

What did he get it into? The main (linked) claims are that Disraeli invented Tory democracy and militant (jingo[8]) imperialism.

Tory democracy certainly takes some ideas from Disraeli. The ruling idea is that the Tories are the true promoters of national unity and class harmony. Their opponents (Liberal, Labour, Irish, Scottish or Welsh nationalist) are petty, factional, and anti-national. This idea has been very long-lasting. McKenzie and Silver (1968) show how it has been a constant theme of Conservative electoral propaganda from the earliest days of the National Union of Conservative and Unionist Associations (founded with Disraeli's blessing in 1867—see McKenzie 1963: 150–4) until the time they were writing. It has resurfaced since then, especially during the Falklands and Gulf wars and in Conservative attacks on the Labour proposals to devolve power in Scotland and Wales in the 1970s and 1990s.

But did Disraeli contribute anything beyond words? The 1867 Reform Act was tactical, not strategic, heresthetic. Disraeli brilliantly conjured up a parliamentary majority for a bill that was more radical than one the same Parliament had defeated. But he did not have any organizing principle.

What about party organization? Disraeli paid some attention to it, but not as much as has been claimed. The best-drawn caricatures in *Coningsby* are Tadpole and Taper, the party managers. Taper always wanted 'a cry' (in modern jargon, a catch-phrase—in *Coningsby* they settle for 'a sound Conservative government . . . Tory men and Whig measures'—Disraeli 1844/1983: 129). Tadpole preferred registration of new electors. They may have been modelled on Peel's agent Francis Bonham. They do not suggest that the Disraeli of the 1840s was a friend of party agents. The greatest Conservative achievement was not the National Union but the strangely neglected Primrose League. As Pugh (1985: 2) points out, the tiny Independent Labour Party (6,000 members nationwide in 1900) has received hugely more attention from historians and political scientists than the Primrose League (6,000 members in its Bolton, Lancs. branch alone in 1900). Lord Randolph Churchill, who was to the Fourth Party of the 1880s as Disraeli had been to Young England, built up the Primrose League in 1883. His aim was to advance his own career rather than provide a mass Conservative organization. However, Tadpole and Taper soon displaced him. Disraeli

---

[8] 'Jingoism' comes from this music-hall song: *We don't want to fight, but, by Jingo if we do / We've got the ships, we've got the men, we've got the money too / We've fought the Bear before, and while Britons shall be true / The Russians shall not have Constantinople.* It was first performed in 1878, during Disraeli's Eastern campaign.

was the posthumous inspiration of the Primrose League (see below and Pugh 1985: chs. 1 and 2).

Paternalistic legislation to improve working-class conditions did take place during Disraeli's lifetime, and Conservative propaganda made much of it. McKenzie and Silver (1968: 44) report that 'the most frequently republished booklet in the Conservative archives has been *How Conservatives Have Helped the British People*', (10th edition 1963). This edition begins with a quotation from Disraeli, 'Power has only one duty—to secure the social welfare of the people', and cites the trade union legislation of 1875 and 1876, and the Public Health Act 1875. However, there is no evidence that Disraeli took much personal interest. The social reform legislation of his 1874–80 government was the work of an energetic and (then) competent Home Secretary, Richard Cross. Disraeli did not initiate it and rarely commented on it.

What about Disraeli the originator of popular imperialism? Here too, revisionists have been at work. In early life, although Disraeli was interested in the Middle East, he showed no particular interest in the British Empire, once notoriously calling the colonies 'a millstone round our necks'. As late as 1866 Disraeli, as Chancellor of the Exchequer, complained to Derby, 'what is the use of these colonial deadweights which *we do not govern* . . . Leave the Canadians to defend themselves; . . . give up the settlements on the west coast of Africa; and we shall make a saving' (Disraeli to Derby, 17.10.66, in Blake 1966: 455). Under Palmerston there was no space for ultra-imperialism—the Tories could not outdo his aggressive popular imperialism, exemplified by the Don Pacifico affair in 1850 (for which see Ridley 1970: 374–87). Disraeli's imperialism could not flower until after Palmerston's death in 1865. It had, at least in retrospect, three main components—Suez, India, and the Eastern Question. They were all linked.

In 1875, Disraeli purchased a block of shares in the Suez Canal Company, to keep them out of French hands (Fig. 3.1). The Suez Canal offered the shortest route to India. But Disraeli's purchase can be overrated, as it colourfully was by Disraeli himself. Control of the Canal Company did not imply control of the canal, which was governed by an international agreement guaranteeing access to shipping of any nationality. Another colourful incident was the Royal Titles Bill in 1876, which declared Queen Victoria to be Empress of India. However, although Disraeli arranged it with his usual panache, the idea was the Queen's, not his (Blake 1966: 562–3). Disraeli became deeply embroiled in what contemporaries called the 'Eastern Question' during his premiership from 1874 to 1880. At the heart of the Eastern Question was the competition between the European powers for control of the Balkans. The eastern Balkans were part of the Turkish (Ottoman) Empire, which was fast losing its grip over its European territory. The governments of Russia and Austria coveted parts of it, and the government of Prussia joined them in the *Dreikaiserbund* (League of Three Emperors). Disraeli and Salisbury, whom Disraeli made Foreign Secretary in 1878, wished to restore the balance of power that they felt would be upset if the other European powers grabbed too much

PUNCH, OR THE LONDON CHARIVARI.—December 11, 1875.

"MOSÉ IN EGITTO!!!"

Fig. 3.1. Mose in Egitto!!! John Tenniel's comment on Disraeli's acquisition of Suez Canal shares. First published in *Punch*, 11 December 1875.

Turkish territory. Their policy culminated in the Congress of Berlin in 1878, from which Disraeli said that he brought back peace with honour. As the Austrians and the Russians coveted Turkish territory, Disraeli wanted to sustain the Turkish regime. This provoked the fury of Gladstone, because of Turkish abuses of human rights in the Balkans. He demanded that Turks should 'one and all, bag and baggage, . . . clear out from the province they have desolated and profaned'. In 1876 Gladstone returned from retirement to launch a campaign of furious oratory against Disraeli's Eastern policy. When the Liberals won the 1880 General Election, Gladstone thus found himself again in power.

The Balkans were never part of the British Empire. But in Disraeli's mind, the Eastern Question had a connection with India, because British politicians and writers saw Russia as a threat to British rule in India. He suggested in 1877 to Queen Victoria that 'the Empress of India should order her armies to clear central Asia of the Muscovites, and drive them into the Caspian' (Disraeli to Victoria, 22.07.77, in Monypenny and Buckle 1929: ii. 1027). Disraeli was a perfect target for his own colleague Salisbury's put-down:

A great deal of misapprehension arises from the use of maps on a small scale. As with such maps you are able to put a thumb on India and a finger on Russia, some persons at once think that the political situation is alarming and that India must be looked to. (Hansard 3s 234: 1565, 11.06.77)

A number of small colonial wars also broke out under Disraeli—in Abyssinia in 1867, in Afghanistan (twice) and Zululand between 1876 and 1879. And several territories were annexed to the British Empire, including the Gold Coast (now Ghana—1874), Fiji (1874), the Malay States (1875), Transvaal (1877 and soon regretted), and Cyprus (1878). On the face of it, Gladstone's description of Disraeli's policy as 'territorial aggrandisement, backed up by military display' (quoted by Eldridge 1996: 37) was justified. Yet many of these were accidental. The Afghan and Zulu wars were both started by British proconsuls without authority. Disraeli backed them in public but attacked them furiously in private. The Abyssinian war looks in retrospect like a politician's perfect war—a victory against black men to distract attention from trouble at home. But retrospect is just what that is. Militarily, it was extraordinarily rash to strike off for hundreds of miles through hostile roadless terrain in pursuit of no more than the rescue of a consul, three soldiers, and a number of missionaries. Most of the accessions to the Empire were made by the Colonial Secretary, with Disraeli merely sending vaguely encouraging letters. The exception is Cyprus, occupied as part of a secret deal with Turkey backed up with the despatch of Indian troops through the Suez Canal to Malta. Although this was dramatic, Disraeli's claims that 'Constantinople is the key of India' (Monypenny and Buckle 1929: ii. 956) and that 'In taking Cyprus, the movement is not Mediterranean, it is Indian' (Eldridge 1996: 47) seem to arise from the use of maps on a small scale.

Finally, the fame of Disraeli's Crystal Palace speech in 1872, in which he defined the aims of the Conservatives, is mostly posthumous. Disraeli reiterated old themes about the nation and the monarchy. He did not say much about the Empire. In his earlier career, he had occasionally brought up the idea of the Empire as a trading bloc, and he repeated it at the Crystal Palace ('self-government . . . ought to have been accompanied by an Imperial tariff'—Kebbel 1882: ii. 523–35). But making a policy out of imperial preference was left to his successors.

Disraeli's imperialism, like his social reform, was thus largely a posthumous construction. Nevertheless, Disraeli himself played a vital role. His personality, his writings, his aura of romance—these provided a cloak for his great heresthetic manoeuvre, continued by his successors. When Disraeli became joint leader of the Conservative Party, it was a sect, promoting the declining fortunes of the land and the Established Church of England. When he died, it claimed to be not just *a* national party, but *the* national party—a claim it has continued to make from that day to this.

The Strange Career of Lord Salisbury

Robert Gascoyne Cecil, 3rd Marquess of Salisbury, seems an unlikely co-founder of the modern Conservative Party. Aloof and disdainful (in 1874 Disraeli called him 'a great master of gibes and flouts and jeers'), he opposed the Second Reform Bill and detested Disraeli until the latter sent him to the Constantinople conference on the Eastern Question in 1876, making him Foreign Secretary in 1878. He succeeded Disraeli smoothly as Conservative leader in the Lords in 1881. With the fall of Gladstone's Liberal administration in June 1885, Queen Victoria sent for Salisbury rather than the Commons leader Northcote. This exercise of royal veto has been attributed (e.g. by Roberts 1999: 318) to the Queen's wish to appoint 'the man best placed to save her from her ultimate political nightmare—five more years of William Ewart Gladstone'.

It was not the first unexpected twist in Salisbury's career. Lord Robert was the third (second surviving) son of the 2nd Marquess of Salisbury, with whom his relations soured in his schooldays and got worse when his father cut him off without funds because he disapproved of Lord Robert's choice of a wife. He was born two months premature. There are persistent but unproved stories that his real father was the Hatfield family doctor. His mother died when he was 9. He was sent to a succession of appalling schools, or at least schools at which he was treated appallingly. This culminated at Eton, a school romantically celebrated the novels of Disraeli, who did not go to it:

Really now Eton has become insupportable. Just multiply ten times the bullying I got under C——and you will have some faint idea of what I get at present. I am obliged to hide myself all the evening in some corner to prevent being bullied, and if I dare venture from my room I get it directly. . . . I am obnoxious to them all because I can do verses [i.e. compose Latin poetry as a school exercise], but will not do them for the others, not choosing to sacrifice my liberty at the bidding of one lower than myself. They call me stingy because I won't do the verses and take it out in bullying. (Cecil to his father, 13 and 15 May 1844, in Cecil 1921: 13)

He went on to Christ Church, Oxford, where he had a mental breakdown, left early with a fourth-class degree, and toured the world in order to try to restore his mental stability. Throughout life he was a gloomy misanthropic depressive. He entered the Commons, unopposed, as MP for the family seat of Stamford in 1853 immediately on his return from the world tour. He never had to contest an election. In 1865 his invalid elder brother predeceased their father. This event turned Lord Robert Cecil into Lord Cranborne and the heir to the marquisate.[9] He succeeded as 3rd Marquess in 1868 and went to the House of Lords.

An intriguing hypothesis about British Prime Ministers is that 'If it is lonely at the top, it is because it is the lonely who seek to climb there' (Berrington 1974: 369). Berrington built on Iremonger's (1970) *The Fiery Chariot*. Iremonger believes that political leaders are like the fiery charioteer Phaeton in Greek legend. The son of the sun god by a sea-nymph, Phaeton demands proof that his father really loves him. On being told that he can have whatever he wants, he chooses to drive the sun across the sky. He crashes to his death. Iremonger claims that a huge proportion of British Prime Ministers were bereaved in childhood. Though her statistics are wrong, there is still a strong effect after correction (Berrington 1974: tables 1–4). Prime Ministers are much more likely to have been bereaved than either the general population or a comparable social group such as peers or Cabinet ministers, but the closer one gets to the premiership (among Cabinet ministers or near-misses), the commoner childhood bereavement becomes.

Even after Berrington's reworking, the hypothesis stands on shaky statistical ground, and it suffers from the usual tendency to claim too much and to manipulate the evidence in its favour. But there is an irreducible core of truth in it. Politics does attract more than its fair share of lonely, disturbed individuals, even though it seems to require just the opposite character trait of thick-skinned gregariousness. Of the Prime Ministers in this book, Salisbury is the only one who fits the Iremonger personality type. Others in the book who failed to become Prime Minister—including both Enoch Powell and Sir Keith Joseph—also shared it. But in modern conditions, it is hard to imagine how an Iremonger type ever becomes Prime Minister. With Salisbury, it is easy. He never faced a contested election to any post, even that of Prime Minister, for which the Queen, not his party, chose him.

Both Salisbury's personality and his political views are evident from the extensive journalism of his early maturity, which he wrote for money after his father had cut him off for marrying below his station. In his journalism (Salisbury 1905; Pinto-Duschinsky 1967; P. Smith 1972), Cecil set out the philosophy of 'the rising hope of [the] stern and unbending Tories'—the label that T. B. Macaulay had unpresciently pinned on Gladstone in 1839. In an essay that several scholars (e.g. Pinto-Duschinsky 1967: 28; Taylor 1975: xi; Roberts 1999: 838–44), have seen as autobiographical, Cecil eulogized Lord Castlereagh, the depressive Foreign Secretary after the Napoleonic Wars. Reviled by radicals including Shelley and Byron, Castlereagh committed suicide in 1822. For Cecil, Castlereagh's refusal to court popularity insulated him from having to 'swallow a string of prejudices dictated to him by an unreasoning and passionate herd of ignorant men'. As Wellington had told Lord Redesdale in 1845–6, the 1832 Reform Act had 'deprived almost every

---

[9] Therefore, as with the Stanleys (Derbys), this book calls Salisbury by the appropriate name— Cecil to 1865, Cranborne from 1865 to 1868, and Salisbury thereafter.

Member of the house of Commons of his real Independence' by making him subject to contested elections. A future Castlereagh would lack the freedom of manoeuvre he had to '[find] Europe at war and . . . [leave] it at peace' ([Cecil] 1862: 221, 206).

Therefore Salisbury bitterly opposed extending the franchise. The wider the franchise, the more dependent would politicians become—and the more agonizing would electioneering be for people of his personality. Of the 'shy person', he wrote in 1863, 'Most people who do not happen to be afflicted in that way look upon it as a deliberate offence against themselves, planned for their especial annoyance' ([Cecil] 1863: 272). He followed Disraeli's twists and turns in 1867 with mounting horror, believing that Disraeli was trying to 'hustle and cheat' him (Cecil 1921: 268). He showed that Disraeli's original proposals would enfranchise more and different people than Disraeli claimed. They would be 'the ruin of the Conservative party'. Disraeli's action was 'a political betrayal which has no parallel in our Parliamentary annals' (Cecil 1921: 233–4; Hansard 3s 188: 1539, 15.07.67).

How then could Salisbury not only work with a man for whom he had such contempt but continue his work of electoral reform? Disraeli was extraordinarily thick-skinned. He assumed that the insults others hurled at him were as evanescent as those he hurled at them, and therefore had no qualms about offering office to the great master of gibes and flouts and jeers. Salisbury said of Disraeli in 1880: 'As a politician he was exceedingly short-sighted though very clear-sighted' (Roberts 1999: 253). Salisbury was equally clear-sighted but tried to take a longer view.

Salisbury and the Crisis of Conservatism

In the early 1880s the longer view was an exceedingly gloomy one. His article 'Disintegration' (Salisbury 1883) sets the tone.

Things that have been secure for centuries are secure no longer. Not only is every existing principle and institution challenged, but it has been made evident by practical experience that most of them can be altered with great ease. . . . Churchmen, landowners, publicans, manufacturers, house-owners, railway shareholders, fundholders, are painfully aware that they have all been threatened. . . . The collapse of principles formerly looked on as immovable has been so complete, the changes of front executed by parties and individuals have been so astounding, that no one can foresee into what unexpected region of political doctrine the Legislature will make its next excursion. (In Smith 1972: 344–5)

For one who never had to face an election, Salisbury was remarkably interested in electoral statistics. His article 'The value of redistribution: a note on electoral statistics' (Salisbury 1884) is the most impressive piece of psephology ever written by a practising UK politician. He points out that in the 1880 General Election, the Liberal lead in votes had produced an exaggerated lead in seats. Unless the 1884 extension of the franchise were to be accompanied by a redistribution of seats the result could be the destruction of the Conservatives in Parliament, even if the franchise extension reduced their share of the vote only slightly or not at all. Salisbury (1884) imagined a seventeen-seat legislature with single-member districts split between imaginary parties which he named 'Catholics' and 'Liberals' in the proportion eight to nine. The 'Liberals' would win all seventeen seats in two cases: where the population was exactly evenly mixed, and where it was completely segregated (say into a 'Liberal' city surrounded by 'Catholic' countryside), but constituencies were drawn in such a way (in this case, radially from the city centre) that each constituency contained the same ratio of 'Catholics' to 'Liberals' as the population.

Ireland was even more threatening. Since 1874 and especially since 1880, seats in Catholic Ireland had been falling to militant supporters of Home Rule, who used every procedural means open to them to disrupt Parliament. The franchise reform of 1884 proposed to extend the franchise in Ireland, as in the rest of the country, to rural householders. Would this not mean a great boost to Charles Stuart Parnell, the Home Rule leader, with consequent threats to public order and the unity of the UK?

Salisbury (1884) shies away from what seems to the modern reader the obvious conclusion he should have drawn, namely that the salvation of the Conservatives, and the Irish Unionists, would lie with proportional representation (PR). In an odd meeting of minds from different intellectual spheres, Salisbury discussed PR in 1884 with Lewis Carroll, in his real guise of C. L. Dodgson, mathematics tutor at Christ Church, Oxford. Carroll was a political Conservative as well as a temperamental conservative. He met Salisbury and his family in 1870, uncharacteristically using his fame as the author of *Alice* to obtain an introduction to Salisbury's wife and daughters (Cohen 1979: 211). Despite the gulf of class, Carroll spent the New Year at Hatfield several times in the 1870s and 1880s. In July 1884, Carroll sent his scheme to Salisbury saying 'How I wish the enclosed could have appeared as *your* scheme. . . . That *some* such scheme is needed, and much more needed than *any* scheme for mere redistribution of electoral districts, I feel sure.' Salisbury replied immediately, acknowledging the need for electoral reform but stressing the difficulty of getting a hearing for 'anything . . . absolutely new . . . however Conservative'. Carroll replied the next day. After congratulating Salisbury for a speech in the House of Lords in which he had insisted that the Conservatives would not accept franchise reform unless it was linked with redistribution, Carroll went on '*please* don't call my scheme for Proportionate Representation a "Conservative" one. . . . *all* I aim at is to secure that, *whatever* be the proportions of opinion among the Electors, the *same* shall exist among the Members' (McLean, McMillan, and Monroe 1996: xxiii–iv; Cohen 1979: 544–5). Salisbury did as he had threatened. He used the Conservatives' veto in the Lords to return the Franchise Bill to the Commons, insisting that it must be 'accompanied by provisions for so apportioning the right to return members of parliament as to insure a true and fair representation of the people' (quoted by Hart 1992: 107). There are some hints that, before then, he may have wished to preserve the limited vote clause in the 1867 Act (A. Jones 1972: esp. 184–5, 193–4; Hart 1992: 111). Salisbury understood, better than Disraeli (or some modern commentators), that it helped the Conservatives in the cities, although he is unlikely to have understood Lewis Carroll's mathematical proof of the point. His Lords' veto in November 1884 took him down a different road.

Salisbury's use of the veto was the most successful during our period. Other Conservatives thought it could lead to a 'Peers against the People' election, for which the radical Liberal Joseph Chamberlain was enthusiastically preparing. But Gladstone gave in completely to Salisbury's demand not to proceed with the franchise extension unless it was coupled with a redistribution. In 1866, as both politicians must have remembered, the Adullamites used the same device (the Grosvenor amendment) to wreck Gladstone's Reform Bill. This time, Salisbury could not stop the franchise extension. As he himself (as Lord Cranborne) and Lowe had warned in 1866–7, the 1867 Act enfranchised all male householders in borough constituencies but not in county constituencies. But no principle, however Conservative, could justify this anomaly continuing, and so the 1884 Franchise Bill removed it by introducing household suffrage, on the 1867 basis, in county seats. The Commons passed it without difficulty—the Liberals had a secure majority on this subject, if not on others. The impasse caused by the Lords' rejection of it in June lasted until Gladstone unexpectedly capitulated in November. Most observers seem to have thought that Salisbury would blink first, or be deserted by his frightened supporters.

Gladstone and Salisbury met to discuss the outlines of redistribution. The meeting was amicable, even though the Queen's private secretary had predicted that if they were 'locked up together[,] nothing would be found but a beard and a pair of collars next morning' (quoted in Roberts 1999: 305). Each leader nominated a group of supporters to negotiate an agreed settlement. All witnesses agree that only two of the negotiators were on top of the arguments—Salisbury for the Conservatives, and Sir Charles Dilke for the Liberals.

Dilke and Chamberlain were the two leaders of the radical wing of Liberalism. They were both social reformers and both imperialists, and had made a pact in 1880 that neither would serve in government without the other. By 1884 both of them were in government—the Queen's efforts to block Dilke, who had queried the amount of public money she got to support her relatives, had ultimately failed (Jenkins 1958: chs. 4 and 5 *passim*). Dilke's description of the first draft he agreed with Salisbury is admirably clear:

[T]he Tories proposed and we accepted single-member districts universally in counties, boundaries to be drawn by a commission who were to separate urban from rural as far as possible, without grouping and without creating constituencies of utterly eccentric shape. . . . The Tories proposed single-member districts almost everywhere in boroughs, and only positively named one exception—the City of London—but were evidently prepared to make some exceptions.

Within the Liberal ranks, Dilke wrote 'that Chamberlain and I and Mr Gladstone were the only three people who understood the subject, so that the others were unable to fight except in the form known as swearing at large' (C. Dilke, 'Memorandum', Dilke Papers, British Library Add. Mss. 43938. Quoted in Jenkins 1958: 192). The Whigs knew that Dilke had undercut them, but only dimly understood how. They insisted that the final agreement—which became known as the 'Arlington Street compact' after the address of Salisbury's London house—should allow more two-member borough seats to survive. This they did in the medium-sized cities, some of them until 1950.

The Arlington Street compact was the work of the extremists on each side— Dilke and Salisbury. How was it so easy for them to agree? Because they both envisaged the development of two-party, two-class politics. If constituencies were divided, in the phrase given to the boundary commissioners, 'according to the occupation of the people', this would create socially homogeneous units. Abolishing double-member seats would end the uneasy Liberal compromise whereby the Liberals put up one Radical and one Whig together. Dilke was happy with this, as the Radical domination of the new Liberal machinery for nominating candidates would ensure that the Radicals won the nominations in the successor seats. His partial defeat by the Whigs on this point did not, as it turned out, staunch the flow of Whigs out of the Liberal party. The events of 1886, which we discuss below, drove them out anyhow. The remaining two-member seats were, however, to provide a lever for the new Labour Party after 1903. Instead of Whig–Radical pairs, the Labour and Liberal parties nominated Liberal–Labour pairs, and most of the Labour MPs of 1906 were returned in two-member seats as a result of this arrangement. As the Labour Party ultimately replaced the Liberals, even the survival of some two-member borough seats did not benefit the centre in the end.

While it is easy to see why the terms of the Arlington Street compact benefited the radical wing of Liberalism, it is harder to see why they benefited the diehard wing of Conservatism. The answer lies in two of Salisbury's insights. The first was his psephological insight (Salisbury 1884). Unless seat boundaries were drawn so as to make each seat socially homogeneous, the expected Conservative defeat would be a Conservative wipeout in urban Britain. Either the continuance of multi-member borough seats or the creation of socially mixed single-member seats could have this result, as Salisbury had proved. Given that he failed to support PR, the next-best option from a Conservative point of view was to propose socially homogeneous seats. This would not secure a Conservative majority, but it would prevent a wipeout.

To secure a majority, Salisbury and his allies would have to do something more. We shall argue in Chapter 4 that he needed to move British politics off the one-dimensional line from left to right—terms which were then coming into use for the first time in the modern sense. He had to introduce a new dimension such that the material interests of lower middle-class or working-class electors did not always prevail. He pinned his hopes, such as they were, on the 'villa vote'. 'I believe there is a great deal of Villa Toryism which requires organization', he wrote to his co-leader Northcote in 1882 (quoted in Cornford 1963: 52). 'Villa Toryism' was not a complimentary phrase. The word *villa* had been debased, like the thing, from an Italian gentleman's farmstead to a suburban middle-class street. As one of its defining quotations, the *Oxford English Dictionary* cites a letter from the writer Charlotte Yonge in 1865, 'My sister lives at Little Worthy, the next parish . . . It has a railroad in it, and the cockneys have come down on it and "villafied" it.'

However villafied, the suburbs were the only possible route away from Disintegration. To conquer them, Salisbury needed to take over institutions that he had not created—the Conservative Party machine and the Primrose League. The mercurial and immature Lord Randolph Churchill, with whom Salisbury had to work until the end of 1886, created both. Salisbury then took advantage ruthlessly of one of Lord Randolph's many resignation threats by accepting it, and then leaking their correspondence to the press, while denying that he had done so (Roberts 1999: 415–19). Churchill had seen both institutions as the vehicles to carry him to the leadership of the Conservatives as the darling of the rank and file. This was always an unrealistic ambition. The National Union of Conservative and Unionist Associations gave the leadership access to workers in the constituencies, but not *vice versa* (McKenzie 1963: 22–4, 146–75). However, the Primrose League was far more important. Lord Randolph endowed it with a riot of mock-medieval and mock-Disraelian romanticism, which that great ham would have loved. It got its name from the Queen's sending 'his favourite flowers from Osborne' to Disraeli's funeral (Blake 1966: 752). On the second anniversary of Disraeli's death, in April 1883, some rather obscure Conservatives got the idea of forming a league in his honour, and shrewdly encouraged florists to stock up on primroses (Pugh 1985: 20). Disraeli's last masterstroke had been to die just at the end of the primrose season. Florists were naturally delighted at an opportunity to shift old stock. Churchill soon took over the League as another vehicle for his ambition; Salisbury agreed to be a patron. He regarded the Primrose League as 'if I may say so without irreverence . . . , the preaching friars of the message' (quoted in Steele 1999: 7–8). The League regarded itself as:

This creation of a Tory democracy . . . raised from the spirit of . . . chivalry. Hence the Primrose League was formed on the basis of the old orders of knighthood (1887, quoted by Pugh 1985: 20).

A physical link with Disraeli's Young England even survived in Lord John Manners, he of 'But leave us still our old Nobility', who duly became a patron of the League. But what was to keep the Tory democracy supporting the Tories? Here lay Salisbury's real genius. He created the modern conception of Unionism. Unionists believed in the destiny of Britain, or England as Salisbury always called it, to rule an empire. To do so, it had to be a practical union at home. It had to govern England, Scotland, Wales, and Ireland as four divisions of the home base of the Empire. And it had to attack all attempts to loosen that union as undermining the Empire. As the Empire had become extremely popular, unionism united the Tories with their new allies after 1886, the Liberal Unionists. It divided the Liberals, and made their enforced association with the Irish Nationalists lethal to both. Members of the Primrose League had to

declare on my honour and faith that I will devote my best ability to the maintenance of religion, of the Estates of the Realm, and of the imperial ascendency [sic] of the British Empire; and that consistently with my allegiance to the Sovereign of these Realms, I will promote, with discretion and fidelity, the above objects, being those of the Primrose League (membership certificate, 1899, in Pugh 1985: 23).

But in the era of 'Disintegration', Salisbury was not yet optimistic that he could save the Tories, the Established Church, or the Empire. It took the cataclysm of 1886 to deliver the Estates of the Realm into his hands.

Facts and Counterfacts: Salisbury in 1886

In his minority administration of 1885–6, Salisbury toyed with an Irish pact. His Viceroy of Ireland, Lord Carnarvon, held a secret meeting with Parnell in August 1885, giving Parnell the (false) impression that Salisbury would condone an Irish parliament. Parnell issued a 'vote Tory manifesto' to his troops in Britain, which may have cost the Liberals several seats in the 1885 General Election (but not so many as most historians, who are too prone to take the Irish machine in Britain at its own valuation, think). The outcome was deadlock: 335 Liberals were elected, and 249 Conservatives. The disciplined Parnellite Home Rulers numbered 86, exactly the margin between the Liberals and the Conservatives. A Conservative–Parnellite coalition was a possible, but highly implausible, option. It would immediately have revealed that Salisbury had no intention of granting any autonomy to an Irish assembly. However, Salisbury was saved most of the embarrassment that his deception of Parnell could have caused by the most famous leak in British political history.

On 14 December 1885, before Parliament had met and while Salisbury was therefore still in office, Gladstone's son Herbert went down from Hawarden to London to brief selected journalists that his father had drawn up a home rule plan for Ireland. It was published on 17 December. Salisbury immediately named it the 'Hawarden kite', and the name has stuck. It was not only the most famous leak; it was the most disastrous to the leaker's interest. Salisbury's Cabinet was deeply split. Carnarvon, who had negotiated what Parnell thought was a deal, had resigned in protest at Salisbury's repudiation of it, but the resignation had not yet been publicized. Salisbury could simply grab the Hawarden kite and fly away from all these little local difficulties. On being defeated on the Queen's Speech debate, Salisbury resigned on 28 January 1886, and was in a position to see the third Gladstone government tear itself apart over Ireland. In 'an almost incoherent outpouring of protest and dismay', the Queen took Salisbury's mischievous advice, and tried to send for George Goschen in a last effort to prevent 'this half-crazy & really in many ways ridiculous old man' (Cecil 1931: 290; Buckle 1928–32: 3rd ser. i. 22–7) from becoming Prime Minister again. Goschen sensibly declined. The ridiculous old man commanded a Commons majority, and so W. E. Gladstone became Prime Minister for the third time.

The brief and tragic history of Gladstone's third ministry is well known. He did not give details of what he had planned for Ireland, in a doomed attempt to hold the Liberals together, while the Hawarden kite was in the sky for all to see. The kite had a body (a letter from Herbert Gladstone to *The Times*) and a tail (the inspired press briefings). It was the tail that most damaged Gladstone:

Mr Gladstone has definitely adopted the policy of Home Rule for Ireland and there are well-founded hopes that he will win over the chief representatives of the moderate section of the party to his views. . . . Mr Gladstone is sanguine that this policy of settling the Irish question once for all, will commend itself to the majority of his party and to the English people, when it is clearly understood that no other course can bring real peace. If he is enabled to eject the [Salisbury] Government in this issue, he will have a large majority in the House of Commons for his Irish bill, and he believes that the House of Lords, weighing the gravity of the situation, will not reject it. Should there be a sufficient defection of the moderate Liberals to encourage the Lords to throw out the bill a dissolution would be inevitable, but . . . the country would in all probability endorse Mr Gladstone's policy and give him an unmistakable mandate to carry it into law. There is reasonable expectation that both Lord Hartington and Mr Goschen will come round to Mr Gladstone's view, and Mr Chamberlain and Sir Charles Dilke, in spite of their present attitude, could not consistently oppose it. (*Pall Mall Gazette* 17.12.85, quoted in Hammond 1964: 449–50)

Here was Gladstone's heresthetic in all its naked glory. It might—just might— have worked if he had kept it secret. The median member of each house was opposed to Home Rule. But Gladstone might have persuaded enough 'moderate Liberals' that public order required Home Rule to carry it in the Commons. The Lords might then have been cowed by the threat of a 'peers v. people' dissolution. But announcing his plan to all the main parties killed it. The Marquis of Hartington (whose brother had been murdered by terrorists in Dublin in 1882) and Goschen refused to join Gladstone's government. Chamberlain did, but walked out after two months. Dilke's political career was already in ruins, so his reluctant support benefited Gladstone not a whit.

Gladstone's bill was defeated in the Commons by 341 to 311—one of the largest votes in the Commons' history—with 93 Liberals including Chamberlain, Hartington, and Goschen voting against the government. The government resigned. In the ensuing General Election, Salisbury ensured that the Conservatives did not oppose the Liberals who had voted against Gladstone—now labelled Liberal Unionists (Roberts 1999: 387–8).

The 1886 election result was, as Gladstone conceded to his diary, 'a smash' (08.07.86; in Matthew 1990: 585; cf. Jenkins 1995 ch. 32 *passim*). The Gladstonian Liberals won only 193 seats, their vote having collapsed in rural areas. The Parnellites retained their iron grip on Ireland, winning 86 seats. All other Irish seats (which were in Protestant parts of Ulster) went Unionist. The Conservatives won 316 seats, and the Liberal Unionists 73. Although there was much talk of Liberal reunion for over a year (see Hurst 1967), it was inconceivable as long as Gladstone retained his magnificent obsession and his leadership. He held the first till his death in 1898, and the second till 1894. The second Home Rule Bill (1893) passed in an unenthusiastic Commons but was trounced, 419 to 41, in the Lords. The majority included almost all the Whigs and all of the bishops who voted. Many of these—new peers and bishops—sat thanks to Gladstone. (And it is an interesting sidelight on Unionism that the bishops all thought it appropriate to vote against giving devolution to a country whose church had been disestablished in 1869.) By then, the Unionist coalition had become quite cohesive. Salisbury and Chamberlain, the political extremes of 1885, had become the political allies of Salisbury's third government. This was only possible because the new dimension of popular imperialism enabled a party realignment in two-dimensional space, to which we must now turn.

4

The Great Victorian Realignment

Seats, Votes, and Proportionality

All commentators, then and since, agree that something dramatic happened in 1886. But what, exactly? Not the fall of the Liberals—they rose again triumphantly from 1906 to 1910. Not the final triumph of Unionism—it slumped from 1903 to 1912, and the Union with Ireland was dissolved in 1921. Not the defeat of Home Rule—it was enacted in 1914. Not the confirmation of the Lords' veto power—they lost it in 1911.

Rather, 1886 marks the hinge of the great Victorian realignment. We use realignment in the standard American political science sense of a shift of large voting blocs from habitual support for one coalition to habitual support for another. In the USA, there was a Civil War realignment in 1852–60 and a New Deal realignment from 1928–36. In Britain, the great Victorian realignment did not happen at one moment—it never does. Therefore this chapter reaches back to 1867 and forward to 1918. But the events of 1886 confirmed its shape and direction. Furthermore, and most important: *It was not the realignment that all the most acute contemporary commentators expected and that too many modern ones have read back into the past.*

Table 4.1 gives the vote and seat shares of the parties in the UK General Elections from 1868 to 1910 inclusive, continuing where Table 3.2 broke off. Seats, not votes, determine the formation of governments, so we must also consider the mapping from votes to seats—the bias and responsiveness of the system.

Table 4.1 contains some remarkable numbers, which are usually overlooked. The first column shows that the Liberal share of the vote declined steadily throughout the period, consistently with the realignment hypothesis. Note in particular that the Liberals won a higher share of the vote in 1874 (when they lost) than in 1906 (when they won a landslide of seats). The second column shows that the mapping from share of the vote to share of seats fluctuated wildly during the period. In 1874, the Liberals got more votes but fewer seats than the Conservatives. In 1906, the Liberal vote advantage was narrow but their seat advantage was huge. In both 1910 elections, the votes-to-seats mapping again favoured the Liberals.

Table 4.1. Seats, votes, and proportionality: UK General Elections 1868–1910

Year	Lib Vote share, %	Lib Seat share, %	Con Vote share, %	Con Seat share, %	Irish Nationalist Vote share, %	Irish Nationalist Seat share, %	Lab Vote share, %	Lab Seat share, %	Prop/ality Index (Monroe)	Respon-siveness	Bias to:
1868	61.24	58.81	38.71	41.19					95.23	0.96	none
1874	51.95	37.12	44.27	53.68	3.66	9.20			73.05	1.29	C
1880	54.66	53.99	42.46	36.35	2.84	9.66			86.75	1.06	none
1885	49.73	50.00	43.57	37.16	6.70	12.84			86.64	0.91	none
1886	45.51	28.66	51.14	58.66	3.29	12.69			69.79	1.27	C
1892	45.41	40.60	46.96	46.87	6.77	12.09	0.34	0.45	89.08	0.94	C
1895	45.66	26.42	49.01	61.34	3.96	12.24	1.15	0.00	63.74	1.35	C
1900	44.62	27.31	50.34	60.15	2.58	12.24	1.78	0.30	67.09	0.66	C
1906	48.98	59.70	43.05	23.43	0.62	12.39	5.86	4.48	61.37	1.35	L
1910J	43.03	41.04	46.75	40.75	1.90	12.24	7.58	5.97	80.91	0.96	L
1910D	43.82	40.60	46.26	40.60	2.52	12.54	7.10	6.27	81.33	0.97	L

Sources: Summary statistics from Craig 1989: Tables 1.10 to 1.20.
Dubious cases assigned from Craig 1974, individual constituency tables; Stenton & Lees (1976–81); and *DNB* (CD-Rom version).
Monroe index: adapted from Monroe 1994 Eqn 15.
Responsiveness: as between the two main parties only, the ratio of the gaining party's seat share to its vote share.
Bias: as between the two main parties only, the one which would hold more seats if they had an equal number of votes. 'Con' columns include Liberal Unionists from 1886.

The columns for the Irish Nationalists show how much a geographically concentrated party benefits from the British electoral system. From the moment that Isaac Butt organized them as a separate party in the 1874 campaign, they won seats out of proportion to their share of the vote. From 1885 onwards, their tally of seats hardly varied. It had hardly any scope for variation. Even though Irish Nationalism was riven by internecine disputes from 1891 until after 1910, an Irish Nationalist won every seat in Catholic Ireland at every election. From 1885 onwards the Liberals disappeared in Ireland; the Unionists fought only seats in Protestant districts. The Nationalists won most seats without contests, except contests in which one Nationalist opposed another.

The anomalies in the mapping from votes to seats are measured by the column headed 'Prop[ortion]ality index (Monroe)'. If the parties' share of seats exactly mirrored their shares of votes, the index would have a value of 100. It would have a value of 0 if all the seats went to parties which won no votes. As is well known, the UK plurality ('first-past-the-post') electoral system scores fairly low on any index of proportionality. The most disproportional elections of recent years, such as those of 1983 and 1997, have proportionality indices in the low 70s. Table 4.1 shows that the range in Victorian and Edwardian elections was much wider. The General Elections of 1886, 1895, 1900, and 1906 had much more disproportional outcomes than any modern case. The first three favoured the Unionists, the last the Liberals. And the election of 1874 seems on the face of it a clear-cut case of 'the wrong side winning'—something that was almost never mentioned by contemporaries, nor by historians. So what was going on?

Bias and Responsiveness from 1868 to 1910

The mapping changed after the 1885 redistribution, as Dilke and Salisbury expected and (for their different reasons) hoped. The first election fought on new boundaries and with a new franchise was that of 1885. After that, neither boundaries nor franchise changed until 1918. Up to 1900, when there was a bias, it favoured the Conservatives and Unionists; after that, the Liberals. Bias is defined as the seat ratio between the two leading parties, when they get an equal number of votes. In 1874, and from 1886 to 1900 inclusive, the Conservatives would have won more seats than the Liberals on an equal split of their vote; from 1906 this advantage lay with the Liberals.

There are two main components of bias in this period: unequal constituency sizes, and efficient or inefficient distribution of supporters. In the electoral map in force from 1868 to 1880, there remained large numbers of small constituencies. In large boroughs, with two or more seats, the Liberals were ahead in 1874. The Conservatives got their seat majority from county seats and from small boroughs. Disraeli's calculations, although they did not save his party in 1868, were proved sound in 1874.

After 1880, the small-constituency effect dwindled, because the 1885 redistribution was the first to accept the principle of approximately equal electorates. Equality was very approximate indeed. But the main beneficiaries were now not the Conservatives but the Irish Party. In order to retain the goodwill of the Irish Party, Gladstone had refused to reduce the number of Irish seats to the proportionate amount.

The most efficient distribution of the vote is to have too many votes in one's pocket for it to be worth the opposition's time and money to fight the seat. The Conservatives (and, again, the Irish Party) usually had the edge in uncontested seats. Table 4.2 lists unopposed returns in our period.

Table 4.2 shows that as soon as the Irish Party was organized in the constituencies, the outcome was a foregone conclusion and there was no point in contesting the seats. The dip in 1892 occurs because the Irish Party had split between supporters and opponents of Parnell, who had died in 1891. Although the split endured, the pattern of uncontested seats in Ireland returned. As between Liberals and Conservatives, the elections where the Conservatives had the biggest advantage in uncontested seats are those where the outcome was most biased in their favour. In the old system, last seen in 1868, safe incumbents were equally likely to be from either party, many of them in boroughs which 'belonged' to some proprietor. This pattern crumbled for the Liberals before it did for the Conservatives. The pact that Conservatives and Liberal Unionists made not to oppose one another in 1886 gave the two parties a huge seat bonus.

The main reason for the switch of bias in the Liberals' favour in 1906 and 1910 was the way the Labour Party emerged. The Liberals made a pact with

Table 4.2. Unopposed returns, General Elections 1868–1910

Year	Lib	Con	Irish	Lab
1868	121	91		
1874	52	125	10	
1880	41	58	10	
1885	14	10	19	
1886	40	118	66	
1892	13	40	9	
1895	11	132	46	
1900	22	163	58	
1906	27	13	73	
1910J	1	19	55	
1910D	35	72	53	3

Source: Craig 1989, Table 14.10.

Labour in 1903 not to fight one another. It was observed in 1906 (except in Scotland, to which it did not apply). In 1910, both parties saw the mutual advantage in not challenging one another in the seats they had obtained by means of the pact. So the Labour (especially) and Liberal vote was now distributed more efficiently than the Conservative. This was Salisbury's nightmare of 1884, but it only occurred three times before the First World War shattered everything.

The responsiveness of the electoral system means the degree to which a change in votes is magnified (or suppressed) in terms of seats. Joseph Chamberlain's associate James Parker Smith (see Chapter 5) was the first to formulate the 'cube law', which states that in certain circumstances, such as those of 1906 in which Parker Smith had lost his own seat, the ratio of seat shares was the cube of the ratio of vote shares. An accurate calculation of the responsiveness of the 1868–80 and 1885–1910 electoral systems would require far more data than we have available.[1] The responsiveness index in Table 4.1 is a very rough and ready substitute. It is calculated only on the seats and votes going to the two main parties. For each election, it measures the ratio of the gaining party's seat share to its vote share. If the number is significantly below 1, the gaining party did not get a seat bonus. If it is significantly above 1, it did.

The noteworthy cases are therefore 1874, 1886, 1895, and 1906 on one side, and 1900 on the other. In each of the first four cases, the gaining party gained a seat bonanza as a result of the system's responsiveness. As it happens, in each case the gaining party was also the beneficiary of bias. These four landslides of power were not based on landslides of the popular vote. There should be nothing surprising about this. It is one of the known properties of the British electoral system. Some defenders of the system, indeed, elevate it from a property to a virtue—it is said to be essential to delivering stable governments. The only danger is the danger of the wrong level of analysis. Since none of these elections was an electoral landslide, we do not have to explain the movement of huge classes of voters, nor assume as contemporaries sometimes did and historians, with less excuse, sometimes still do, that these four administrations were swept to power on huge waves of popular acclamation.

The counter-case of 1900 rests on geometry. If the votes–seats ratio is plotted on a graph, the relationship is shaped like an S on its side. With few votes, a party wins no seats. As it passes an electoral threshold, it starts gaining seats very rapidly. When it is very successful already, it has to do extremely well to start winning the other side's few remaining fortresses. The Unionists had already done very well in 1895. Their vote gain in 1900 brought them few extra seats.

---

[1] Specifically, it would require up to 670 constituency results from each of eleven general elections to be entered, and the data analysed using the King–Gelman *Judgeit* program or something similar, after appropriate modifications to deal with unopposed returns. This would be a very worthwhile project for a research funding body to sponsor.

Seats and Power

The proportion of seats a party holds, say in the House of Commons, is not the same as the proportion of power it wields. A party that holds more than half of the seats in any legislature has all the power, except for proposals that need more than a simple majority of those voting to carry (there are almost none such in the procedure of the House of Commons). A party that holds fewer than half of the seats may or may not be in a bargaining position. If there are some possible coalitions that it would turn from minorities to majorities by joining them (or equivalently from winners to losers by leaving them), then it has bargaining power; if not, it has none. There are several indices, and a large literature, on power and power indices. For our purpose, it is only necessary to use the most appropriate index, which here is the *normalized Banzhaf index*. (For an explanation of why this is the right index for the present purpose see Felsenthal and Machover 1998: ch. 3.)

Table 4.3 displays the power of each of the party groups after each General Election in our period. For this purpose, we need to list the Liberal Unionists separately for the period (1886–95) during which they were clearly organizationally separate from the Conservatives. We also need to take account of the schisms of Irish nationalism. In 1891, the Irish Party split between the supporters and opponents of Parnell. Parnell died within a year but the splits continued until the demise of the Irish Party itself.

Table 4.3. Power: UK General Elections 1868–1910

Year	Seats						Bz normalized index					
	Lib	Con	LU	Irish (main faction)	Irish (minority faction)	Lab	Lib	Con	LU	Irish (main faction)	Irish (minority faction)	Lab
1868	387	271					1.00	0.00				
1874	242	350		60			0.00	1.00		0.00		
1880	352	237		63			1.00	0.00		0.00		
1885	335	249		86			0.60	0.20		0.20		
1886	192	316	77	85			0.17	0.50	0.17	0.17	0.00	0.00
1892	272	269	45	72	9	3	0.33	0.33	0.00	0.33	0.00	0.00
1895	177	340	71	70	12	0	0.00	1.00	0.00	0.00	0.00	0.00
1900	183	403		77	5	2	0.00	1.00		0.00	0.00	0.00
1906	400	157		82	1	30	1.00	0.00		0.00	0.00	0.00
1910J	275	273		72	10	40	0.33	0.33		0.33	0.00	0.00
1910D	272	272		74	10	42	0.33	0.33		0.33	0.00	0.00

Sources: Seat totals: as for Table 4.1.
Bz normalized index: Felsenthal and Machover 1998: Definition 3.2.2 and appendix A1.

What is 'power' in the legislature? It may be defined either as the opportunity to press for a share of the spoils, or the opportunity to influence the outcome of legislation. Both are relevant in our period, but the second is more general, and more appropriate to our case (the Irish Party sought to influence legislation, but did not want a share of the spoils of power). Each concept of power has an index attached to it. The Banzhaf index shown in Table 4.3 may be interpreted as follows. Immediately after each General Election, it shows the bargaining power that each party or faction had to try to get its policies implemented. For elections in which one party won half or more of the seats (1868 to 1880 inclusive, and 1895 to 1906 inclusive), it merely reflects back the truism that one party controlled the Commons, and need therefore make no policy concessions to any other party. In particular, neither the Unionists from 1895 to 1905, nor the Liberals from 1906 to 1910, need make any gestures towards Irish Home Rule.

The interesting cases in Table 4.3 are 1885, 1886, 1892, and 1910 (both). In each of these elections, parties' share in power was a very different matter to their share of seats. In 1885, the Liberals were just one seat short of an overall majority. But that one seat gave Parnell and Salisbury 20 per cent each of the bargaining power. A Salisbury–Parnell coalition to give devolution to Ireland was not inconceivable. Gladstone hoped for it. Parnell thought that Salisbury's Viceroy Carnarvon had offered a deal. Salisbury did not reveal his intentions until after the Hawarden Kite. Even if Gladstone's intention to deliver Home Rule had not been leaked, the blocking power of the Irish would have forced some concessions from any incoming Liberal government.

The numbers for 1886 show the pivotal position of the Liberal Unionists, and they show that Salisbury's position was not so secure as hindsight has made it seem. There was a possible rival Liberal–Liberal Unionist–Irish coalition. However unlikely such a coalition might seem, Salisbury had to pre-empt it by accommodating Joseph Chamberlain, who had seemed to stand for the destruction of everything Salisbury held dear ('they toil not, neither do they spin') only a year earlier. In 1892, however, the Liberal Unionists had become a dummy, and so they remained. The Liberals, Unionists, and Irish were, *ex ante*, in equal positions of power. Although a Unionist–Irish coalition was now inconceivable, the Liberals remained the prisoners of the Irish— and *vice versa*. This pattern was repeated in 1910. The Liberals must legislate for Home Rule, whether they wanted to (Gladstone in 1893) or not (Asquith in 1911).

Nowhere has the retrospectoscope been more distorting than in judging the influence of the early Labour Party. Throughout this period, it was a dummy player. There was no coalition that it could make by joining or break by leaving. Therefore, if its policies made any progress (and some of them did), this must be a result of Liberal attempts to take over Labour's issue space, not of Labour's bargaining power. The difference may seem subtle but it is utterly crucial, as we shall argue in Chapter 6.

Similarly, the bargaining power index shows that the splits in the Irish Party were irrelevant to bargaining in our period. They did not—could not—affect the total number of Commons seats held by Irish Nationalists. If the numbers had been different, the minority factions might have been in a position to bargain independently. But they never were. The main bloc of the Irish Party, however, had as much bargaining power as the two much bigger UK parties in three elections out of the ten in which they were a separate force, and some power in two more. Not bad for a party which commanded only 3 per cent of the UK vote (6 per cent when all its seats were contested).

The Realignment Everybody Expected

In summary, then, the electoral system exaggerated vote movements into legislative majorities. Almost everybody anticipated a profound shift in the balance of political power. Here are four acute contemporary observers, from left to right:

Karl Marx

The Irish question predominates here just now. . . . [I]n the long run it will benefit the English working-class itself . . . The overthrow of the established church in Ireland will mean its downfall in England and the two will be followed by the doom of landlordism—first in Ireland and then in England. . . . [O]nce the Irish Church is dead, the *Protestant* Irish tenants in the province of Ulster will make common cause with the Catholic tenants in the three other provinces of Ireland. (Karl Marx to L. Kugelmann, 06.08.68, in Marx and Engels 1962: 544–5)

John Stuart Mill

But even in this democracy [viz., a representative democracy using proportional representation], absolute power, if they chose to exercise it, would rest with the numerical majority; and these would be composed exclusively of a single class, alike in biasses, prepossessions, and general modes of thinking, and a class, to say no more, not the most highly cultivated. (Mill [1861] 1972: 276–7)

Robert Lowe (the leader of the Cave of Adullam)

This [1867 Reform] bill, so far as it has any principle at all, is founded on the principle of equality. . . . Who does not see that the necessary result of such a mode of proceeding must be that the inhabitants of counties, whom you exclude from the franchise, will not rest satisfied under that exclusion, and that you are in this way sowing the seeds of a discontent and agitation which will not terminate until the county and borough franchises are placed on the same level? . . . You cannot trust in a majority elected by men just above the *status* of paupers. . . . I believe it will be absolutely necessary that you should prevail on our future masters to learn their letters. (Speech on 3rd Reading of Representation of the People Bill, 15.07.67, *Hansard* 3s 188: 1539–49, quoted at 1540–1, 1544, 1549)

Lord Salisbury (as Lord Cranborne)

Depend upon it, if any storm arises, if there is any question of labour against capital, any question of occupation against property, it will be no protection to you that you may have men who belong to the class of proprietors or the class of capitalists in this House; it will be no more protection to you than it was to Louis Seize that a Philippe Egalité was found among the French Revolutionists. . . . [T]he Members of Parliament who will be returned under this Bill will be wealthy men with Conservative instincts, and steeped to the lips in Radical pledges. We know from the example of this Session how much Conservative instincts will avail with men who are acting under the fear that they will lose their seats. (Speech on 3rd Reading of Representation of the People Bill, 15.07.67, *Hansard* 3s 188: 1526–39, quoted at 1531)

No one at present doubts that as far as figures go, the transfer of power has been complete. . . . Few care by injudicious frankness to incur the wrath of the new masters, whose rule is inevitable now. . . . A clear majority of votes in a clear majority of constituencies has been made over to those who have no other property but the labour of their hands. The omnipotence of Parliament is theirs, wholly and without reserve [did he forget the Lords' veto?—IM]. Subject to them is a minority possessed in various degrees of a vast aggregate of accumulated wealth. If he were to set all considerations of conscience aside, each member of the poor but absolute majority would naturally desire so to use this new power as to make some portion of this wealth his own. ([Lord Cranborne], 'The Conservative surrender', *Quarterly Review* October 1867, in P. Smith 1972: 253–91, quoted at pp. 257–8).

And, from one of the founders of the modern spatial approach to political science, Anthony Downs:

T]he enfranchisement of the working class in the late nineteenth century had shifted the voter distribution far to the left of its old position. And the Liberal Party, even after it moved to the left, was to the right of the new center of gravity, although it was the more left of the two parties. The founders of the Labour Party correctly guessed that they could out-flank the Liberals. (Downs 1957: 128).

This would have been a classical single-dimensional realignment. Marx expected it enthusiastically, Mill nervously. Salisbury and Lowe were horrified, but thought it was probably inevitable. Salisbury's actions between 1880 and 1886 were largely directed to persuading Whigs, especially in the Lords, that the centre of political gravity, and the Liberal Party with it, were moving far to the left, and that they should therefore switch to his party. Many of them did, even before 1886, and almost all of them did afterwards.

But, if such a realignment had happened, it would not have helped Salisbury in the elected house. As Downs points out, if the median voter moves to the left by the addition of poor, and by presumption more left-wing, voters to the electorate, the median election-winning policy also moves left. It would help Salisbury not a whit if every Whig joined the Tories—the policy of the median legislator in the elected house would move inexorably to the left, towards Disintegration. Salisbury (Cranborne) made the point clearly in his 1867 speech—'T]he Members of Parliament who will be returned under this Bill will be wealthy men with Conservative instincts, and steeped to the lips in Radical pledges'.

What about the unelected house? Salisbury helped to ensure that the Lords were solidly in his pocket. He probably did not have to do much to achieve that, given the Liberals' move sharply leftwards in the 1880s, but the 'Disintegration' theme of protecting property and freedom of contract was just what the landed aristocracy needed to hear. However, some vetoes, like the bee's sting, would be as lethal to the stinger as to the stung. Under Salisbury, the Lords could, and did, safely veto legislation that they knew was unpopular, such as the second Home Rule Bill in 1893. But if they were to veto popular legislation, they would raise a query about their own legitimacy. They did not veto English parish councils in 1894. Salisbury's successors continued the pattern. In the 1906–10 Parliament, the Tory Lords did not veto the programme of the new, Lib–Lab, liberalism. For all Salisbury's stress on the sanctity of contract, the Lords did not veto the Trades Disputes Act 1906, which like the Irish Land Acts was a huge violation of the sanctity of contract. It gave trade unions immunity from litigation for breach of contract. Prime Minister Campbell-Bannerman withdrew the government bill, which did not give such immunity, in favour of the Labour bill on the floor of the house, to the horror of Liberal lawyers (Clegg, Fox, and Thompson 1964: 393–5). Was this not the naked expropriation of property that Lowe and Salisbury had foreseen?

Two-Dimensional Realignment

If it was, it was an isolated case. The genius of Disraeli and Salisbury was to introduce a new dimension to British politics—attitudes to the Empire. It mapped and reflected the hidden centre–periphery division in domestic politics. Much of it was accidental. For instance, the idea of the Queen becoming Empress of India was hers, not Disraeli's. But nobody else could have hammed it up so magnificently:

The Faery [Disraeli's nickname for Queen Victoria] is much excited about the doings at Delhi. They have produced great effect in India, and indeed throughout the world, and vindicate triumphantly the policy of the measure wh. was so virulently, but so fruitlessly, opposed. It has no doubt consolidated our empire there. Our poetical Viceroy is doing justice to the occasion. The Faery is so full of the great incident, and feels everything about it so keenly that she sent me an Xmas card and signed her good wishes *Victoria Regina et Imperatrix* (Disraeli to Lady Bradford, 28.12.76, in Monypenny and Buckle: ii. 826).

Unruly colonial administrators out of London's control started many of Disraeli's and Salisbury's small imperial wars. But, though they might not control the wars, they always managed to control the consequences for UK domestic politics. Winning a battle under the Conservatives seemed to benefit them:

Roberts' great victory [in the Afghan war] has taken the wind not only out of the sails, but out of the bodies of our opponents. . . . Poor Hartington is in lamentable case, and is reduced to asking my advice as to the best mode of attacking us, without hurting us. (Sir Stafford Northcote to his wife, 06.12.78, in Monypenny and Buckle: ii. 1269)

Losing a battle under the Conservatives seemed to benefit them:

A DISGRACEFUL EXHIBITION

[When the Secretary of State for War had the] very painful task of communicating to the House of Commons the disaster which had befallen Lord Methuen's Column in the Western Transvaal . . . the profound silence which . . . reigned in the Chamber . . . [was broken by] LOUD LAUGHTER AND SHOUTS OF DELIGHT FROM THE [IRISH] NATIONALIST BENCHES. THE VOCIFEROUS CHEERING LASTED FOR NEARLY A MINUTE. . . . These are the men with whom Sir Henry Campbell-Bannerman . . . hoped the Liberal party would work in 'CORDIAL COOPERATION'. Loyal Englishmen, Scotsmen, and Irishmen, always remember those cheers. (National Union of Conservative and Unionist Associations leaflet March 1902, quoted by McKenzie and Silver 1968: 59)

Winning a battle under the Liberals did not happen often, but when it did the Liberal leadership tended to make no political capital from it:

Conclave on Egypt 12 $^1/_2$–2$^1/_2$ [12.30 to 14.30]. Another flood of good news. No more blood I hope. Wolseley in Cairo: Arabi a prisoner: God be praised. (W. E. Gladstone, Diary for 15.09.82, in Matthew 1990: x. 331)

Although on that occasion Gladstone ordered church bells to be rung, to remind the electorate that Liberals, too, could have God on their side, Liberals were never as successful at playing the patriotic game as Conservatives.

Losing a battle under the Liberals was the Conservatives' ace of trumps. In 1884, Gladstone's government sent the excitable general Charles Gordon to report on the logistics of evacuating Sudan, an Anglo-Egyptian protectorate in the throes of a religious and nationalist revolt. Gordon disobeyed his orders, artfully played the then equivalent of the tabloid press, and announced he was staying to hold Khartoum for the Khedive (the British puppet in Egypt). Another expedition then had to be sent, at great peril and for no British interest, to relieve him. As is well known, it failed. Gordon had been killed two days before the relief expedition arrived. The Queen sent Gladstone a telegram *en clair* (not in cipher), which reached him at Carnforth station, saying 'These news from Khartoum are frightful, and to think that all this might have been prevented and many precious lives saved by earlier action is too fearful' (quoted in Jenkins 1958: 183). It was promptly leaked to the press. Salisbury won a vote in the Lords against the government's handling of the Gordon crisis by 189 to 68 (*Hansard* 3s 294: 1594–7; 27.02.85). Tories turned Gladstone's nickname GOM (for Grand Old Man) into MOG ('Murderer of Gordon'). Colin Matthew (1995: 149), Gladstone's most distinguished academic biographer, reported that 'Giving talks in the 1970s and 1980s on Gladstone to non-historians, I have been struck by the fact that Gladstone's part in the death of Gordon was almost always raised by a questioner.'

All the Liberals' main election victories except that of 1868 have been the subject of 'Nuffield studies' (Lloyd (1968) on 1880; Russell (1973) on 1906; Blewett (1972) on 1910). Each monograph offers a case study of how the Liberals' weakness on imperialism was not always fatal. Lloyd concludes (1968: 1–2) that

The Liberals owed their great [sic] victory of 1880 to a judicious combination of appeals to political enthusiasts over the Eastern crisis of the late seventies and other foreign policy issues with appeals to the electorate to vote against the government because it was responsible for the depression in trade.

Political activists were evenly matched between Conservative imperialists and Radical Little Englanders. In 1880 the Conservatives failed to take imperialism down from the activists to the electorate, where imperialists hugely outnumbered Little Englanders.

We consider 1906 and 1910 in later chapters. Briefly, in 1906 the Liberals turned imperialism aside by representing it as a tax on food. In 1910, the House of Lords handed Lloyd George the best campaign slogans a leader of the left has ever had in the UK.

The imperial–Little England dimension cross-cut the left–right dimension, in Parliament, among party activists, and in the country alike. In Parliament, it split the Liberals, but (after 1868) not the Conservatives. Some of the most radical Liberals, especially the Queen's twin *bêtes noires* Dilke and Chamberlain, were also fervent imperialists in 1880–5. In 1886 Chamberlain defected and Dilke was marginalized by the divorce case, but the Liberal split did not disappear. In 1905 the leading Liberal imperialists agreed, in the 'Relugas compact' named after Sir Edward Grey's shooting lodge, not to serve under the Little Englander Campbell-Bannerman (Jenkins 1964: 145–7). The pact broke up as soon as Balfour resigned, but the tensions remained. Among activists, Little England positions were very popular. Among the electorate, they were not. The forced alliance between the Liberals and the Irish gave the Conservatives an opportunity to remind the electorate every day that their opponents were far away from the electoral median position of enthusiastic support for the Empire.

What about the electorate? We have no polls, but we do have aggregate data (Pelling 1967, Wald 1983), which show large geographical variations in Unionist support. Averaging over six of the eight elections from 1885 to 1910,[2] Pelling (1967, Table 52) found that the median Unionist vote share for constituencies in each region varied from 38.6 per cent in Wales to 56.2 per cent in the south-east of England and 55.2 per cent in the West Midlands. This could just—only just—be reconciled with the Marx–Salisbury prediction of a two-party, two-class realignment, if Wales were overwhelmingly working class and the West Midlands overwhelmingly middle class, so that region was

---

[2] Pelling unfortunately excluded 1886 because he mistakenly thought that the Liberal split would reduce the information value of the data, and December 1910 because of unopposed returns and its closeness to the January 1910 results.

a surrogate for class. It was not, and Wald (1983) proves by multiple regression analysis that it was not. Wald, like Pelling, takes as the dependent variable the Unionist share of the vote in the General Elections from 1885 to 1910. 'To judge by the regression coefficients, religion had a much stronger electoral impact than social class . . . a religious predictor was more powerful than a class measure in 107 of the 144 analyses' (Wald 1983: 142; cf. his tables 6.9 to 6.11). For each election except 1900 and 1910D, the strongest predictor of Unionist vote is a measure of Nonconformity; a class measure usually comes next. The third predictor, significant in every election, is the proportion of Roman Catholic clergy. A simplified version of Wald's data is in Table 4.4.

Table 4.4 shows that Marx's realignment had not yet happened by 1910. Butler and Stokes (1969: ch. 6) showed that it was not yet complete in Britain by 1969; in Ireland, it has not yet happened. In the Salisbury–Chamberlain era, religion was the best predictor of vote. Nonconformist areas voted Liberal; Anglican areas voted Unionist. The positive association between Catholic clergy and Unionist vote is, as Wald says, 'a textbook example of fallacious ecological correlations' (1983: 91). The positive association arose not because Catholics voted Unionist, but because the presence of many (usually Irish) Catholics aroused the local population to vote against them (on which see also Matthew, McKibbin, and Kay 1977).

Wald's findings have failed to enter the mainstream. One reason is that political historians are often frightened of numbers. Another, alas, is that the class alignment perspective is so well entrenched in some quarters that it takes more than facts to shift it. A third is that his explanation of the reasons for the decline in the religious alignment does not bear the weight he puts on it. Wald (1983: ch. 8 *passim*) puts great stress on the decline of

Table 4.4. Unionist share of the vote, best predictors, GB 1885–1910

Year	Best	Next-best	Third-best	Multiple r^2
1885	Nonconformity (−)	Working class(−)	RC clergy (+)	0.52
1886	Nonconformity (−)	Working class(−)	RC clergy (+)	0.46
1892	Nonconformity (−)	Working class(−)	RC clergy (+)	0.54
1895	Nonconformity (−)	RC clergy (+)	Working class(−)	0.55
1900	Working class(−)	RC clergy (+)	none	0.50
1906	Nonconformity (−)	Working class(−)	Anglican clergy (+)	0.40
1910J	Nonconformity (−)	RC clergy (+)	Working class(−)	0.69
1910D	Working class(−)	Nonconformity (−)	RC clergy (+)	0.54

Source: Wald 1983: Table 6.11. The sign of each association shows its direction. A high proportion of Nonconformists, and of working-class (or unionized) voters, implied a low Unionist vote. A high proportion of Catholic, and of Anglican, clergy implied a high unionist vote. Wald treats the Church of Scotland as functionally equivalent to Anglican and the Scottish Free churches as functionally equivalent to Nonconformist. However dubious theologically, this is justifiable politically.

Nonconformist schooling after the 1870 Education Act, which he says ended the socialization of later citizens from Dissenting families into a specifically Dissenting world-view. But there were never enough children in Nonconformist schools for that explanation to bear weight; it also cannot apply to Scotland.

An alternative explanation is that denomination is a surrogate for centre–periphery attitudes. In the language introduced in Chapter 1, the basis of cleavage before 1886 was that of centre against periphery. The centre was not just a geographical centre, although it had a geographical concentration in the London area. It united those groups that wished to expand the power of the kingdom, within the UK and—from Disraeli's time—into the Empire. The periphery comprised those groups that resisted the expansion. The centre's weapons included an Established Church and its schools, so the periphery's resistance included resistance to those institutions. Therefore, Irish and Welsh disestablishment (achieved 1869 and 1920), Home Rule, and attempts to shake off Established Church control of education, taxation, and local government, were all parts of the periphery's political agenda, and resistance to these measures was part of the centre's agenda. In Scotland, the centre tended to operate through the established Presbyterian Church, the periphery through the Free Church created by the Disruption of 1843.

In this light, the realignment of 1886 marked not the supersession of centre–periphery politics, but their *revival*. The Liberals became more than ever the party of the periphery, the Unionists the coalition of the centre. Although periphery and centre still fought over religious issues into Edwardian years, with the Lords continuing to block the Liberals' disestablishment and education proposals, religion moved off centre stage. The lapsed Unitarian Chamberlain could become a leading figure of the centre, and the high Anglican Gladstone of the periphery. The centre found a new issue—the Empire. The Empire became a cause to appeal to the traditional periphery and to the new working- and lower middle-class electorate. It appealed to both material and non-material interests. Members of the upper and middle classes could hope for jobs governing the Empire; members of the working class could hope to emigrate there when times were bad. Although the Marxist proposition that the formal Empire served the economic interests of the ruling class has been disproved (compare Hobson 1905 and Lenin 1996 [1920] with Robinson and Gallagher 1961), it served the *political* interests of a wide range of Britons, both rulers and ruled. And people of all classes and regions could take pleasure that 'we hold a vaster Empire than has been', an Empire on which the sun never set. (A lot of it was in uninhabited Arctic Canada, which Mercator's projection on school maps made into a huge blob of pink). However, the more peripheral a voter, the less likely was he to be beguiled by the ideology of Empire. Catholic Irishmen did not wish to be part of the Empire at all, still less for it to be enlarged. People in Wales and Scotland, especially their own peripheral areas, felt too keenly the centre's relatively recent suppression of their language (Wales) and land rights (Scotland).

Meanwhile, Marx and Salisbury were not wrong about the rise of a class alignment. They were partially right. Yes, the arena of class politics was changing from the land–capital struggle it had been in the 1840s to a capital–labour struggle. Yes, organized (industrial) capital and organized industrial labour could not, and did not, subsist forever in the same Liberal coalition. But the imperial dimension meant that the old centre–periphery alignment did not give way to an equally single-dimensional class alignment. The two coexisted, to generate two-dimensional issue space. Two-dimensional politics gave all the politicians of the middle chapters of this book—Salisbury, Chamberlain, and Lloyd George—the opportunity for heresthetic.

Party Activists and Two-Dimensional Politics, 1868–95

The years from 1868 to 1891 marked the evolution of party organizations from Tadpole and Taper to their recognizably modern forms. In the early part of our period, such party organization as there was emanated from the Carlton (Tory) and Reform (Liberal) Clubs. They were involved with selecting parliamentary candidates, and with aiding the efforts of the parliamentary whips, but with little else that a modern party does. The tasks of party management in the age of Disraeli and Gladstone (Hanham 1959) were the tasks of personal management in small constituencies. Until 1883, this often involved wholesale bribery and torrents of gin and beer (O'Leary 1962). Throughout the period from 1867 to 1918, it involved substantial legal work on trying to register your supporters and to deregister the other side's.

But after 1868, things changed, and contemporaries knew they must change, further encouraged by the secret ballot (1872) and very tight constituency expenditure limits (1883). Electorates became too big to canvass personally. Connections of patronage and individual power must give way to making links with a mass electorate. Increasingly, too, local campaigning must be subordinated to national campaigning.

Peel was the first politician to issue a national platform, in his Tamworth Manifesto of 1835. But, as its name implies, this was his own election address to his constituents in Tamworth. He consulted nobody before issuing it—it would not have been in his nature. The next innovator in this area was Gladstone. His Midlothian campaign bounced the Liberals into adopting his policy on the Eastern Question, and bounced himself back into the leadership, from which he had retired in 1876. He publicized it adroitly in the newspapers and by publishing the speeches (Gladstone 1879), an example followed by Chamberlain (1885). We have already noted several cases in which national politicians 'spun' the press as adroitly as today—whether successfully (as with Salisbury's rubbishing of Randolph Churchill) or not (as with the Hawarden Kite).

'One, and not the least useful, among the duties of a Central Liberal Association' was to publicize the leader's speeches, according to the Scottish Liberals' introduction to Gladstone (1879: 1). But throughout the 1870s, 1880s, and 1890s, it was questionable who did, and who should, control the mass organization of the parties.

The National Liberal Federation, the Primrose League and the Law of Curvilinear Disparity

A number of writers (including McKenzie 1963 and Lloyd 1968) have compared the National Liberal Federation with the National Union of Conservative and Unionist Associations. Although the two organizations were formally similar in function, both of them being the peak organizations of their respective party activists, the comparison is misleading. The NLF was always ideological as well as organizational. The NUCUA was not, and when it appeared to be ideological, the ideology was a badly fitting mask for Randolph Churchill's failed leadership attempt. For spreading and voicing activists' ideology, the NLF must be compared, not with the NUCUA, but with the Primrose League.

The NLF began as the Birmingham Caucus. The Liberals there created an organization to maximize their seats under the limited vote. As already described, they divided their supporters into three segments, asking them in each segment to vote for a different pair of Liberal candidates. Thus the Liberals won all three seats in the city in 1868, 1874, and 1880. The method was extended to local politics in 1870, when the Education Act created school boards elected by the cumulative vote. The cumulative vote, like the limited vote, is a device intended to secure proportional representation for minority interests (See Hart 1992; McLean, McMillan, and Monroe 1996). As with the limited vote, the organized did better than the unorganized. The Birmingham Liberals organized a campaign to get their supporters to cumulate votes on the Nonconformist candidates for the School Board. Chamberlain, who had already come to prominence as a leader of the Nonconformist National Education Association, organized the campaign. But it came to grief because the Nonconformists nominated too many candidates. In the cumulative election game, over-nomination can be as disastrous as under-nomination. Chamberlain squeaked on to the Birmingham school board in thirteenth and last place (Garvin 1932: 122–3). He got it right at the second election in 1873.

The Nonconformist campaign against the 1870 Education Act failed, but it created the precursor of a body that was both organizational and ideological—the National Liberal Federation. In January 1877 Chamberlain closed down the National Education League, to 'transfer its remaining work to the Liberal Associations of the country' (Garvin 1932: 258). He got Gladstone to address the first meeting, in Bingley Hall, Birmingham, where Chamberlain was to launch his own Tariff Reform campaign nearly thirty years later (Chapter 5).

The conventional picture of the NLF, thus created in 1877, was forever fixed by Ostrogorski (1902). To Ostrogorski, the Caucus was a sinister instrument of undemocratic control of elected statesmen. It imposed the ideology of radical Liberalism on moderate statesmen, first in the shape of Chamberlain's Unauthorized Programme of 1885 and then in the shape of the Newcastle Programme of 1891. Home Rule was at the head of the Newcastle Programme; but the politicians who compiled it knew that there had to be other policies, and threw in a 'compendious ragbag' (Jenkins 1995: 581) of policies to appeal to the periphery. They included disestablishment in Scotland and Wales, control of the drink trade, threats to the House of Lords, and some tentative gestures to the working-class lobby. It was less radical than the Unauthorized Programme, and it was Little England where that had been imperialist.

Apart from a couple of years under Churchill, the National Union never attempted to be a policy body. The role of enthusing the Conservative rank and file was left to the Primrose League. The Primrose League was an asset to its party; the NLF mostly a liability, but not for the reasons Ostrogorski (1902) gives. There is no evidence that either was an effective election-winner, outside the special circumstances of the limited and cumulative vote (Cox 1987: 37–45). But the Primrose League swam with the tide of public opinion; the NLF against it. The former gave an ideological basis for popular imperialism, which appealed across class, and to some in the periphery as well as most in the centre. The latter articulated the ideology of the Little England (and Wales, Scotland, and Ireland) branch of radicalism, which had no hope of forming an electoral majority except with the much-resented assistance of the Irish Party. Popular unionism and popular Liberalism both occupied positions in two-dimensional issue space; but the first commanded it and the second was at the edge.

Why Did Two-Thirds of Adults not Get the Vote? And Would it Have Made any Difference if they Had?

After 1884, any further franchise extension to universal male suffrage would predictably benefit the 'progressive parties', Liberal and Labour. The political impact of female suffrage was less clear. In many countries, women voters have been traditionally seen as a conservative force because they are closer to issues of church and family, and more remote from workplace issues, than male voters. Especially in the two-dimensional politics of the great Victorian realignment, female voters could have been an asset to whichever group courted them first. Why did politicians fail to grasp these opportunities?

In the case of voteless men, through myopia. Politicians of all parties still shared a mental picture formed in the 1866–7 Reform debates. There were the safe and the unsafe working class; the labour aristocracy and the mob; the self-improving and the wastrel; those with some stake in society and those with none. Such perceptions were widely, almost universally suffused. They colour (often literally in the accompanying maps) studies of poverty (e.g. Booth 1892–7; Rowntree 1910). They marked the deep and acrimonious divide between trade unions of the 1851 'New Model Unionism' generation, and those of the 1889 'New Union' generation. The first had formed their unions, such as the Amalgamated Society of Engineers, on the basis of respectability and the veto power conferred by their members' craft skills. You cannot bring blacklegs off the street to work a lathe. The second class lacked that power. You can bring blacklegs off the street to unload a ship. So the dockers needed allies or lucky circumstances to give them veto power. In the 'Great' Dock Strike of 1889, they and the seamen's union supported one another. Once the seamen had struck, the dockers had no work anyhow, unless shipowners assembled blackleg ships' crews—in which case the seamen and the dockers had a common interest. In 1889, as in the strike waves of 1911 and 1912, the dockers' main ally was probably the summer. Not many cargoes were refrigerated; some were perishable; some perished. The summer of 1911 was the hottest in memory (Clegg, Fox, and Thompson 1964: 55–62; Bullock 1960: 33–7; Jenkins 1964: 234). But waiting for a hot summer is not a good strategy for building a permanent union. New unions fluctuated wildly. Old unions looked down on them as a threat to their own members' veto power. This threat was amplified by technical change, which led to the deskilling of some engineering jobs (McLean 1999d: chs. 1 and 9). For similar reasons, hatred of the Irish (and of the few Jewish and other immigrants who entered the UK despite the Aliens Act) was fiercest among those just above the bottom of the heap.

Therefore even the Labour Party, which on the face of it had most to gain from universal male suffrage, did not press for it. As late as 1915 we find Labour's best organizer in Glasgow, the home of 'Red Clydeside', writing,

Neither the bar-tender's pest nor the Sauchiehall Street dude ever spend a penny on the *Forward* [the Glasgow socialist weekly]. . . . In the slum areas few socialist periodicals are purchased but many copies of *Red Welcome*, *Daily Record*, *Sporting Tit-bits*, *Weekly Mail*, and *John Bull*. . . . Look at your slum wards—not a Socialist representative in the Town Council from [them]. . . . Capitalism represents these wards. On the other hand, the better paid, and more comfortably circumstanced, and better read [wards] . . . , look to them! Socialism represents these wards. And the reason is obvious. A man requires to reach a certain level of culture before he can understand Socialism. (Tom Johnston in *Forward* 28.08.15. A longer extract is in McLean 1999d: 177)

The Liberals, further away from the working class, also failed to recognize the potential—or, probably, even the size—of the bloc of voteless men. Through the Edwardian years, progressive (Liberal or Labour) politicians often gave the impression that they thought the battle for manhood suffrage was won. Keir

Hardie, no less, often said so (see e.g. W. Stewart 1921: 241—'Now [1907] . . . the working class is the dominant power', when much less than half the UK electorate was working class. For other instances see Matthew, McKibbin and Kay 1976: 724–6). Only about 65 per cent of men had the vote in 1910. But the Labour Party seemed practically unaware of the fact, and it 'proved to be a negligible factor in the passage of the [1918] Reform Bill' (Pugh 1978: 107).

As for the failure of the Edwardians to grant female suffrage, traditional explanations rely on anecdotes. Asquith was personally opposed; Keir Hardie was infatuated with Sylvia Pankhurst, one of the leaders of the militant suffragettes, whose campaigns were counter-productive. True but unsatisfying. Franchise extension was a classically two-dimensional issue and it had to get through a bicameral Parliament, of which the upper house had an absolute veto until 1911 and a suspensory veto thereafter.

Note, first, the numbers in the elected house of the legislature. The anti-suffrage Conservatives could simply sit on their hands and ignore any arguments of principle in favour of continuing to benefit from the status quo. Therefore, we should expect no change during the Unionist years 1886–92 and 1895–1905. There was no time to consider the franchise in the short session of 1886, which was dominated by Ireland. In the years 1892–5, the Liberals depended on Irish votes. In what follows, the Irish Party is modelled as one uninterested in franchise extension (because it already controlled all the seats it ever would; it had no self-interest in franchise extension). It might be prepared to log-roll and support franchise extension in exchange for something it did want; but no politicians found any such opportunity. Therefore the Liberals had only an unpredictable majority in the elected house. They had a clear majority without the Irish 1906–10, and a contingent majority again from 1910 to 1914, once again dependent on the Irish. If (and only if) the Irish abstained, then Labour was pivotal after 1910; otherwise Labour was a dummy player.

Now consider the unelected house. The Conservatives controlled the House of Lords throughout the period. Therefore, from 1885 to 1911 the median peer, a Conservative, was a veto player. If franchise extension damaged the interests (and/or offended the ideology) of the median peer, then there was no reason for him to vote for it unless either there was a trade-off for some other policy or an overriding threat to public order. The direct action of the militant suffragettes (the WSPU) was aimed at targets that mattered most to those whose interests and ideology resembled those of the median peer (Emily Davison throwing herself under the King's horse in the 1912 Derby; arson in country churches). Perhaps the WSPU strategy can be read as a rational attempt to persuade the median veto player that the threat to public order warranted his vote in favour of *restricted* female suffrage (the WSPU demand). The WSPU wanted a short bill to enfranchise women on the same terms as men. Their opponents (and some of its Conservative supporters) argued that this would merely enfranchise a socially restricted group of women who might be predominantly Conservative.

From August 1911, when the Parliament Act was enacted, it was common knowledge that anything a Commons majority was willing to devote parliamentary time to in three consecutive sessions could become law in 1914. The Irish Party was in a position to insist that Home Rule must be the first call on this scarce Commons time. Social and labour relations legislation seemed almost equally pressing. If, however, the Commons could agree a position on suffrage extension, it was common knowledge from 1911 on that, so long as it was first presented at latest in the 1913 session, the Commons would get its way in time for the 1915 General Election. (Note that the Parliament Act also reduced the maximum length of a parliament from seven years to five.)

Why then could the Commons not agree a position either during the Liberal hegemony of 1906–10 or when they were in a position to overcome the Lords veto after August 1911? Because the issue was classically two-dimensional and parliamentary procedures are binary. The franchise could be extended in either or both of two directions: to women and/or to men who did not yet have the vote. This yields the matrix of Table 4.5.

Both male and female politicians were divided. Female politicians, as is well known, were divided between the 'militant' WSPU and the 'moderate' National Union of Women's Suffrage Societies. The labels 'militant' and 'moderate' are traditional but singularly unhelpful. Both wings of the movement, of course, preferred any outcome with women's suffrage to any outcome without. Therefore both preferred the set {B, D} to the set {A, C}. For the WSPU leaders, their campaign was a single-issue one. The easiest goal in their dimension was to achieve female suffrage without changing the male suffrage (the latter requiring a lot of parliamentary time and, before 1911, likely to face a Lords veto even if not accompanied by female suffrage). Therefore, they preferred B to D. The NUWSS was linked to the radical (Lloyd George) wing of the Liberals. Less of a single-issue group than the WSPU, they agreed with the radical Liberals that, as option B would enfranchise the relatively prosperous women who would qualify for the franchise under the existing 1885 rules, it carried the risk of putting in place a Conservative Commons majority who could block other social reforms. Therefore, they preferred D to B. Their male allies could rationally prefer C to B as well, for the same reason.

So far, we have not considered strategic position-taking. But the two-dimensional matrix gave a wonderful strategic opportunity to Conservatives.

Table 4.5. Franchise extension 1906–14: 2 × 2 matrix

| | | Give women the vote? | |
		No	Yes
Extend male	No	*A*	*B*
franchise?	Yes	*C*	*D*

They could pretend to back D over B on the grounds that, if B were carried, 'the present measure would block the way for a far more sweeping reform' (Cornford [1908] 1994: 108. It is quite likely that this manoeuvre is one of those that Cornford had in mind.) In a binary vote between B and the status quo A, this gave them a ground for supporting their true preference A without being exposed to the charge of misanthropy.

A gross, but robust, oversimplification of the parliamentary position between 1906 and 1910 appears in Table 4.6. An explanation of the cell entries follows.

Any parliamentary voting game before August 1911 is a simple *mutual veto game*. Each house has a veto on all non-financial legislation. (For financial legislation, it had been believed since the English Civil War in the seventeenth century that the House of Lords did not have a veto. In 1909, when the Lords used the veto that others thought they did not have in order to block the 1909 Budget, the result was that the rules were rewritten to make it quite clear that they did not have it.) Although, formally, the game is tricameral, with the monarch also a veto player, this was not so in practice by 1906. William IV had tried to cast a veto by dissolving Parliament in 1834. It had exploded in his face—the side he disliked emerged stronger than before. Queen Victoria had fulminated against some of her governments (especially those led by Gladstone), but (luckily for her) her fulminations did not become public.

A non-finance bill passed the pre-1911 Parliament if, and only if, it was carried in both the House of Commons (670 seats) and the House of Lords (about 1,000 seats, but an unknown number in practice, since many peers never turned up). The indeterminate size of the Lords is unimportant for our model, because as it happens the Lords in this period shared the values of the Conservative Party in the Commons. Therefore we can simplify the Lords into the median peer, who was a Conservative. The decision rule for Table 4.6 is that any winning coalition must include the median peer and a majority of the Commons. Then the outcome can be read off very simply, without further ado. No parliamentary majority can defeat the status quo A. If Conservative

Table 4.6. Preference orderings on female suffrage 1906–10

	Median peer	Cons MPs	Lib MPs (Asquith faction)	Lib MPs (Ll G faction)	Lab MPs
N in class	1	157	200	200	30
Best	A	A	C	D	B
	B	B	D	C	D
	C	C	A	B	C
Worst	D	D	B	A	A

peers had been strategically minded, they could have juggled their preferences among B, C, and D. But it would only have been sophisticated fun. Although the divisions of opinion among MPs did not help the cause of female suffrage, Table 4.6 suggests that they did not hinder it either as it was doomed—unless, indeed, the WPSU could convince the median peer that the threat to public order was so dire that he would put B above A. They failed. Equally, the Liberals, despite their huge Commons majority, did not even propose a manhood suffrage bill (option C) to the Lords during the 1906 Parliament. The detailed orderings of the parties in Table 4.6, therefore, are irrelevant. The Irish Party is not included in Table 4.6, because they did not care and were not pivotal in the Commons. The Labour Party suffered huge internal strains. Keir Hardie, its leader, was infatuated with Sylvia Pankhurst, one of the leaders of the WSPU. He therefore pressed for option B (the WSPU demand) whilst most of his colleagues, and the extra-parliamentary party, would have preferred option D. This led to the Labour Party's first constitutional crisis. In 1907 Hardie threatened to resign as leader (and even as a member of the parliamentary party) rather than carry out an instruction to push for D (W. Stewart 1921: 237; Morgan 1975: 162–70). This was of great importance for the Labour Party, then and since, because it defined for all time the relationship between the parliamentary party and the party conference. But it was of no importance for the issue of suffrage. It explains why the Labour Party's preferences were as given in Table 4.6. But the median peer's veto is sufficient to explain why the Labour Party could never have been decisive before 1911.

Table 4.7 gives the Commons position after the General Election of December 1910. (This is again a gross oversimplification: Pugh 2000, not seen till this section was complete in draft, suggests that there were more pro-franchise Conservatives than Table 4.7 shows. This merely strengthens our conclusion that option D was a frustrated majority winner—see below.) Female suffrage was impossible before August 1911, for the reasons just given. From then on, it could be introduced with a two-year delay, providing that in each session Home Rule passed first. To see that the Irish were in a posi-

Table 4.7. Preference orderings on female suffrage 1910–14

	Cons MPs	Lib MPs (Asquith faction)	LG Libs & Lab (1/2)	LG Libs & Lab (1/2)	Irish MPs
N in class	272	136	89	89	84
Best	A	C	D	C	
	B	D	C	D	ABCD
	D	A	B	B	
Worst	C	B	A	A	

tion to impose this condition, note that they held eighty-four seats. *Ex hypothesi*, they could not give a damn about franchise extension. They held all the seats they ever would in the Commons, whether the franchise was extended or not. They wanted to sit, not there, but in the Irish Home Rule parliament. Any interest they had in non-Home Rule legislation was therefore purely tactical. If any of B, C, or D were proposed in the Commons without their consent, they could block it in coalition with the Conservatives, as their eighty-four seats plus the Conservatives' 272 comprised a majority. As this was common knowledge, nobody tried to push suffrage extension ahead of Home Rule in the Commons timetable. The government Whips calculated that the latest date for the first introduction of a franchise bill (C, with the option of a free Commons vote to convert it to D) was 15 March 1912. Any later, and it would not get through the Parliament Act procedure of two Lords rejections and three Commons re-presentations in time to affect the 1915 General Election.

The position of the Irish, and the rational foresight of MPs, explain the contrasting fate of two private members' Conciliation Bills (that is, bills to enact option B) in 1911 and 1912. Sir George Kemp's bill of 1911 was carried on Second Reading by 255 to 88; Sir John Agg-Gardener's bill of 1912 was defeated on Second Reading by 222 to 208. This swing had everything to do with tactics and little or nothing to do with changes of opinion. The suffragist MP W. H. Dickinson later recalled,

From time to time the House protested its undying devotion by voting in favour of the second reading of Bills that it knew could make no further progress; but if you asked me to name a dozen members who would have gone through fire and water for the cause of Women's Suffrage I could not do it (26.3.18, quoted by Pugh 1978: 35).

But the promoters of the 1911 bill secured a promise from the reluctant Asquith that he would give them parliamentary time for a future bill. This so enraged the Irish that they changed sides, voting against the 1912 bill on the grounds that

As the maintenance of his [Asquith's] personal credit and authority were vital to the prospects of Home Rule, it was clearly to their interest to rescue him from his difficulties (C. P. Scott, diary for 15.1.13. Scott 1970: 65).

Home Rule consumed a huge amount of parliamentary time and ministerial energy, as Unionist opposition to it was so bitter, extending to the spectre (and in July 1914 the near reality) of civil war in Ulster. So franchise extension was pushed to the margins. There, it fell victim to the two-dimensionality of the issue. A government bill was promoted in 1912 to abolish plural voting and introduce manhood suffrage. The government signalled that it was open to private members to amend it to permit any desired degree of female suffrage. In January 1913, four different amendments, permitting different extents of female suffrage, had been tabled. Then the Conservative leader, Bonar Law, went to the Speaker to object that the female suffrage amendments 'would completely alter the intention and character of the Bill'. After some days' thought, the Speaker (a former junior Conservative minister) agreed, and refused to accept any female suffrage amendments. The government then withdrew the entire bill, thus losing the prospect of any electoral advantage to itself in time for the 1915 General Election. This sequence of events is analysed further below.

How and why did the factions come to rank the options in the order they did?

Things were simplest for the *Conservatives*. The further an option was from the status quo, the less they liked it. Option B was, for them, a relatively minor change for the worse. It might bring new issues into the political domain which Conservatives, as Conservatives, wished to keep out. However, as the women it enfranchised would have similar economic characteristics to the men already in the electorate, they had least to fear from it. They had most to fear, economically, from the extension of the franchise to voteless men (C). Although they might extend their campaign of imperialism and xenophobia to cater for this class, it would cost them resources that would be saved if there were no change in the franchise. Finally, they perceived—at least their leaders did—that universal suffrage (D) could not be quite as bad for them as universal male suffrage—the women would temper the rampant progressivism of the enlarged male electorate (Pugh 1978: 26).

All the non-Conservatives had to balance the strategic with the tactical, the short-term with the long-term. Those *Liberals* who followed *Asquith's* lead saw female suffrage as a distraction to the Liberal programme of constitutional and social reform. The electorate that would give that programme most support was a universal male suffrage electorate (C). Universal suffrage (D) could dilute that programme by introducing new subjects in which women were interested and men—at least Asquith—not. By the same reasoning, option B was the worst of all worlds because it introduced the distraction with no compensating electoral advantage.

The *Lloyd George* wing of the Liberals and *Labour* were divided. Hardie was no longer Labour leader, and therefore unable to press his distinctive preference for B. But there were good reasons for a progressive to put C above D, and equally good reasons to put D above C. In the absence of more detailed evidence, we have assigned half to each camp. The *Irish Party*, as before, were indifferent among all four options.

The next step is to calculate how each option would have fared against each other if they had been put head-to-head in a direct pairwise vote (Table 4.8). Parliamentary procedures are binary. All votes are on propositions. The proposition is either carried or not; if not, the status quo (here A) remains. Votes may be queued, with amendments and substantive proposals being taken in a preordained order. The general rules, which ultimately derive from eighteenth-century parliamentary practice, are in Robert (1991) and Citrine (1952).

Table 4.8. Pairwise comparison, Copeland and Borda scores for preferences in Table 4.7. (Dodgson matrix)

		Votes for:				Copeland score	Borda score
		A	B	C	D		
Votes against:	A		408	272	272	1	952
	B	178		272	272	0	722
	C	314	314		225	2	853
	D	314	314	361		3	989

Table 4.8 may be called a *Dodgson matrix* after C. L. Dodgson (Lewis Carroll), who first proposed counting in this way (see McLean and Urken 1995: 294). It works as follows. The votes for option *i* against option *j* are in row *i* column *j*. For example, from Table 4.7, we calculate that in a pairwise contest between A and B, 408 would have voted for A and 178 for B. So we enter 408 in the first row, second column, of Table 4.8, and 178 in the second row, first column. All the pairwise comparison cells are filled in the same way. The cells for each option against itself are blank of course, as that comparison is meaningless.

The rightmost two columns of Table 4.8 then present two different ways of calculating the 'winner' among the four options. The column marked *Copeland score* identifies the *Condorcet winner* if there is one. The column marked *Borda score* identifies the *Borda winner*. The Condorcet winner is the option which could beat each of its rivals in a set of pairwise votes. The Borda winner is the option which gets the highest score on average. These two winners are not always the same; and sometimes no Condorcet winner exists—that is what generates a cycle. Neither complication arises in this case. Option D—universal adult franchise—is the winner on both scores.

Why then did it not occur? Because of Speaker Lowther and the Irish. Speaker Lowther's veto is the only instance of a fourth veto player besides those introduced in Chapter 1 to feature in our story. He says of his veto:

My decision was based upon a ruling . . . of Mr Speaker Peel's in a somewhat similar case, and I am satisfied that, however unexpected, I was correct. (Ullswater 1925: ii. 137)

His ruling was that any amendment to the male suffrage bill (option C) which introduced any degree of female suffrage 'would completely alter the intention and character of the Bill'. As it had already passed its Second Reading, the Speaker held this to be improper. Most commentators disagree. (e.g. Jenkins 1964: 249.) We need only recall the story of Disraeli and the Hodgkinson amendment (Chapter 2) to see that on earlier suffrage bills amendments which altered the intention and character of the bill far more completely had been accepted without cavil by the Speaker.

To overrule a Speaker's ruling would have required more than a simple majority of those voting. At the very least it would have required the active participation of the Irish. But, as stated above, the Irish Party had no interest in the matter unless they could use it as a bargaining counter with the other parties. That was no longer so by 1913.

The loss of the 1912 bill need not have been the end of the matter. But the leader of the government, who had to implement any future decision to introduce another government bill, wrote in January 1913, 'The Speaker's *coup d'état* has bowled over the Women for this session—a great relief.' (Asquith to Venetia Stanley, 27.01.13 in Jenkins 1964: 250)

Therefore a combination of myopia and veto players explains the failure of the progressive majority parties to widen the franchise between 1906 and 1918. If they had widened it, then the class dimension would have come to dominate the centre–periphery dimension somewhat earlier than it did. Lloyd George's manoeuvres (Chapter 6) to establish the Liberals—or whatever the party he tried to create would have called itself—as the hegemonic class party controlling the median voter in the class dimension—would have had more chance of success. In the next two chapters, we look first at those who tried to exploit the second dimension (Chamberlain and Powell) and then at the man who tried to shut it down (Lloyd George). As the heresthetic of Enoch Powell cries out for comparison with that of Joseph Chamberlain, we take them together even at the expense of violating chronology.

5

The Failure of Imperialism: Joseph Chamberlain and Enoch Powell

Introduction

'All political lives, unless they are cut off in midstream at a happy juncture, end in failure, because that is the nature of politics and of human affairs. The career of Joseph Chamberlain was not an exception' (Powell 1977: 151). So wrote one of the subjects of this chapter about the other. When he wrote it, he knew that it was true of himself as well. It is one of the sayings for which Enoch Powell is anthologized. The other is less elegiac:

Those whom the gods wish to destroy, they first make mad. We must be mad, literally mad, as a nation to be permitting the annual inflow of some 50,000 dependants, who are for the most part the material of the future growth of the immigrant-descended population. It is like watching a nation busily engaged in heaping its own funeral pyre. . . . As I look ahead, I am filled with foreboding. I seem to see 'the River Tiber foaming with much blood'. (E. Powell, Speech to the Annual General Meeting of the West Midlands Area Conservative Political Centre, 20 April 1968)

Chamberlain and Powell shared a common failure. They both identified race and empire as an issue (or a pair of issues) with the potential to reconstruct British politics on an entirely new alignment. They both tried to realign politics, seriously damaging their own parties. Chamberlain did it twice, to different parties. They both failed, although they were correct about the power of race and empire. It was a truly potent issue, full of foreboding for the left-wing parties and of dangerous excitement for the Conservatives. In the 1960s and 1970s, for which we have opinion poll evidence, it was an issue on which the public were far out of line with the leadership of both big parties. The public were overwhelmingly in favour of restricting the immigration of non-white British subjects and their dependants to the UK (Table 5.1). Small wonder that Enoch Powell, the only leading politician who enthusiastically backed them, was the most popular figure in British politics for some years. In polls asking 'Who would make the best prime minister?', he regularly outpolled the actual Prime Minister (see Table 5.2).

Table 5.1. 'Do you think that too many immigrants
have been let into this country or not?'

	1963	1964	1966
Too many (%)	84	81	81
Not too many (%)	12	13	14
Don't know (%)	4	6	5
	100	100	100

Source: British Election Survey, 1963, 1964, and 1966 waves. Butler
and Stokes 1969: 350, Table 15.7.

There are no opinion poll data for Chamberlain's front-bench career from
1880 to 1906. But he became one of the most popular and best-known politicians of his day. He outshone his leader, A. J. Balfour, when the latter succeeded his uncle Salisbury as Conservative leader and Prime Minister in 1902.
Salisbury chose to retire unexpectedly when Chamberlain was temporarily
out of action after an accident in a hansom cab. As Marx wrote of Napoleon
I and Napoleon III, the Nephew succeeded the Uncle. Salisbury did nothing
by accident.

Imperialism was hugely popular. We have seen in earlier chapters how Disraeli, the Queen, and Salisbury encouraged it, in different ways, to their
mutual advantage and to Gladstone's and the Liberals' disadvantage. Popular
imperialism was powerful and dangerous for left and right. Its power is
obvious from the way that the Conservatives and the Liberal Unionists tapped
it again and again in their popular appeals. Here are a few samples, from the
wonderful collection used by McKenzie and Silver (1968).

The only policy of the
   Radical Party is Destruction—
The neglect and betrayal of British interest abroad; at home, attacks upon ancient and
beneficent institutions, which have grown up with the greatness and prosperity of
England.
   Our Imperial greatness deeply concerns the English people.
The World-wide trade of England depends almost entirely upon the strength and pros-
perity of the Empire, and upon the security of our Imperial commerce. Let the electors
of Great Britain ask themselves one simple question:—

Why is it that our Imperial and commercial interests are now being threatened in every
quarter abroad . . . ? [a list of six outrages follows, including *that France has been and is
attacking British interests*, that *the French have killed three British officers and six Native
Police*, that *Russia has sent an expedition into the Pamirs*, and that *a desperate War has
broken out between Japan and China*—the last, it might seem, rather hard to blame on
the British Liberal government]

THERE CAN BE BUT ONE ANSWER—

Because every enemy of England abroad realises that there is now in office in Great
Britain *a weak, vacillating, craven Ministry*, which has no foresight and no resolve, which

dares not defend British interests effectively, and which will *submit to being kicked and kicked and kicked* until at last the spirit of the English people is aroused in its majesty. (National Union leaflet no. 231, Jan. 1895, in McKenzie and Silver 1968: 52–3)

Shortly afterwards, the spirit of the English people was aroused in its majesty; at least the Conservative–Liberal Unionist coalition convincingly won the 1895 General Election. Joseph Chamberlain became Colonial Secretary, the post he retained until he resigned in 1903 over tariff reform.

Being in government did not inhibit the Unionist spin-doctors. The 'LET 'EM ALL COME!' leaflet of 1904 (quoted above, Chapter 1) echoes down the twentieth century. In 1904, it paid to denounce 'The Radicals, by their obstruction to the Aliens Bill' for 'fill[ing] our streets with profligacy and disorder'; in the shape of 'foreigners who are criminals; who suffer from loath-some diseases; who are turned out in disgrace by their fellow countrymen; who are paupers'. In 2000, the Labour and Conservative Parties are engaged in a bidding-down war to persuade the electorate that they are tough on bogus asylum seekers. In 2000, as in 1904, the presumption is that all foreign asylum seekers are bogus.

That popular imperialism was dangerous for the left needs no further illus-tration. But it was dangerous for the right as well. It threatened to unleash a power beyond Disraeli's, or Salisbury's, or Chamberlain's control. It brought to the forefront those best able to exploit it, who were not necessarily from the traditional governing classes, and who therefore did not seek to conserve whatever Conservatives thought needed conserving in the social order or the Church.

Like Disraeli, Chamberlain was an outsider. Unlike Disraeli, he did not seek the symbols of traditional social order. He never bought a country estate nor joined the Church of England. He lived in unfashionable Birmingham throughout his life, and he was buried according to the rites (such as they are) of the Unitarian church. Enoch Powell was also a West Midlander, whose striking Black Country accent was quite unmistakable. Unlike Chamberlain, he was a devout Anglican, who merited a controversial memorial service in Westminster Abbey. But he was no closer than his great predecessor to the heart of Conservatism (nor of Christianity).

Chamberlain and Home Rule

There is no need to repeat the facts of the 1886 Home Rule crisis. But the actions and motives of Gladstone's unexpected defector in 1886 need to be explained.

Joseph Chamberlain came into prominence as a pressure-group lobbyist and electoral organizer. Born in 1836, he was by 1869 the manager of Nettlefold & Chamberlain, screw manufacturers of Birmingham and Smeth-wick. (The firm survives as GKN, where the N stands for Nettlefold.) In that year he was elected to Birmingham City Council, and in 1870 to the Birmingham School Board. School Boards were the first elected bodies to control state schooling. Chamberlain became chairman of the National Education League in 1870. This was a body set up to campaign against Anglican privileges in state education. The Nonconformists were bitterly disappointed by the Gladstone government's Education Act of 1870. Once it was passed, however, Chamberlain concentrated for a while on city politics. He became mayor of Birmingham for three successive years, 1873–6. He was an active executive mayor. Under him and his followers, Birmingham became a showpiece of municipal socialism. The city took over and invested in its gas and water supplies, developed the commercial centre using the Tory government's Artisans' Dwellings Act (but provided few artisans with dwellings), patronized the arts, and controlled the licensed trade. Chamberlain's Birmingham is still visible in its civic buildings, in its late nineteenth-century commercial district centred on Corporation Street—what a Chamberlainite street-name that is! and in its few but large pubs—the product of a long-term policy of restricting the number of licences in the city.

Both the education campaign and Birmingham politics spurred Chamberlain's interest in electoral organization. The School Board was elected by the cumulative vote, and Birmingham's MPs by the limited vote. These are games in the technical sense of game theory; there is an optimal nomination strategy for each party or faction.

The person who understood these strategy games the best was Lewis Carroll (C. L. Dodgson). His feat was the more remarkable as he analysed optimal strategy using game-theoretic tools, half a century before game theory was invented. Joseph Chamberlain followed close behind. He helped to operate the notorious Birmingham Liberal scheme to frustrate the intentions of Lord Cairns, the originator of the limited vote clause in the 1867 Act. The Liberals divided the city into three zones. In each zone, Liberal voters were asked to vote for a different pair of the Liberal candidates (Garvin 1932: 95). As a result the Liberals won all three seats in Birmingham in each of the three General Elections (1868, 1874, and 1880) for which the limited vote operated in Birmingham. Elsewhere, using Lewis Carroll's methodology, we have proved that Chamberlain's strategy was optimal (McLean, McMillan, and Monroe 1996: xxvi–ii. For background, see also Hart 1992: 20–1, 77–8, 119–21, and 126–9). Fittingly, Chamberlain was himself elected an MP for Birmingham at a by-election in 1876.

In 1877, he folded the National Education League into a new National Federation of Liberal Associations, with its headquarters in Birmingham. Chamberlain was to control the 'Birmingham caucus' for the rest of his life, carrying it, and all the city's MPs, bodily from the Liberal to the Unionist ranks in 1886. In 1880, he was regarded as the electoral architect of the Liberal victory.

On entering Parliament, Chamberlain formed a close alliance with his fellow radical Charles Dilke. So inseparable were they that they forced

Gladstone to include either both or neither when he formed his second government in 1880. He chose both, 'looking as I seek to do all along to the selection of the fittest', as he said in curiously Darwinian language to Chamberlain (Gladstone to Chamberlain, 27.04.80, in Joseph Chamberlain Papers, University of Birmingham Library, JC5/34/1. Henceforth cited as JCP). He did not like their advanced radicalism, and the elevation of Dilke caused endless trouble with the Queen, who did not like his views about the cost of her household. Dilke finally became Secretary of the Local Government Board, with a Cabinet seat, in 1882. Chamberlain served as President of the Board of Trade throughout Gladstone's second government. Chamberlain and Dilke were radical outliers in the Cabinet. Dilke put it in terms that show the potential for political realignment:

the holding of strongly patriotic and national opinions in foreign affairs, combined with extreme radical opinions upon internal matters, made it difficult to act with anybody for long without being attacked by some section with which it was necessary to act at other times, and made it difficult to form a solid party. (quoted in [Egerton] 1927)

Chamberlain, too, had already signalled that he was a radical at home and an imperialist abroad (see e.g. Powell 1977: 33). His term as President of the Board of Trade was marked by an attempt to regulate shipping in order to protect seamen's safety against unscrupulous owners of 'coffin ships' and, ironically, by a defence of free trade in the face of a protectionist resolution by the Conservative C. T. Ritchie, whom we meet later in this chapter. In 1885, he pioneered a device he was to use again in 1903. While still a member of the Cabinet, he tried to move the home agenda leftwards with a series of speeches in which he outlined what became known as the Unauthorized Programme. The Unauthorized Programme called for progressive taxation and manhood suffrage (Garvin 1932: 548–54). Addressed to the 'toilers and spinners', it excited the young Lloyd George, who in 1909 was to repossess that biblical phrase and turn it against the House of Lords. Chamberlain's independence annoyed Gladstone, who frequently urged him to speak 'with as much reserve on pending and proximate subjects as your conscience will allow' (Gladstone to Chamberlain, 02.12.83, JCP 5/34/20; cf also same to same 6.12.83, 10.12.83 and 05.02.85, all in JCP 5/34; Garvin 1932: 548–68).

Chamberlain was to repeat the tactic of freelance speech-making, while claiming to be a loyal follower of his party, in 1903. So was Enoch Powell in 1968. It was always dangerous. In 1903, Ritchie, who had by now switched sides with Chamberlain, complained furiously to their leader Balfour that

[Chamberlain] seems to have set himself to the task of making it impossible for any one who does not share his views to remain a member of the Government. . . . I don't see how we [the Unionist free traders] can openly express our disagreement with him and he and we remain members of the Cabinet (Ritchie to Balfour, 30.05.03, in Sandars MSS, Bodleian Library, Oxford, MS Eng. Hist c.739 ff 30–1).

In the 1880–5 government, Chamberlain was also the Commons spokesman on the Colonies, as the Colonial Secretary was in the Lords. Here he developed his imperialist ideas, although not until the Irish crisis did they start taking on a federal form. Chamberlain's views on Ireland have puzzled many. He seemed to be a great promoter of Irish devolution, and in Parnell's early years in the Commons allied with him. Yet he resigned from Gladstone's third government in March 1886 over Home Rule, and remained implacably opposed to Home Rule thereafter. What was the huge difference between Chamberlain and Gladstone?

Gladstone's Home Rule Bill of 1886 initially proposed that there should be no Irish representation at Westminster after Home Rule, and that the Home Rule Parliament should have power over all matters not specifically reserved to Westminster. Chamberlain's model was based on local government, and he tried to introduce some form of democratic local government in Ireland during both ministries. 'I am not in favour of any system which would go further than this, and which would separate the Imperial relation between the two countries', he said as early as 1874 (quoted in Powell 1977: 21). Chamberlain held out for Home Rule all round, or a parliament for each of Ireland (perhaps including a separate one for Ulster), Wales, Scotland, and England, with an imperial parliament over all. In his resignation speech he suggested that the idea might be extended to the colonies—'to draw tighter the bonds which unite us and to bring the whole Empire into one federation' (Hansard, 3s: 304, 9 April 1886, col. 1203).

One ground of Chamberlain's opposition to the Home Rule Bill was its unpopularity. On hearing of the 'Hawarden Kite' (Chapter 3), Chamberlain wrote to Gladstone:

If there were a dissolution on this question, and the Liberal party or its leaders were thought to be pledged to a separate Parliament in Dublin, it is my belief that we should sustain a tremendous defeat. The English working classes . . . are distinctly hostile to Home Rule carried to this extent. . . . I fear that with the expectations now raised in Ireland, it will not be possible to satisfy the Irish Party with any proposals that are likely to receive the general support of English Liberals (Chamberlain to Gladstone 19.12.85, JCP 5/34/83).

Chamberlain was a unionist and an imperialist, and he knew that both causes had the power to attract the working classes. He also had reason to believe that Gladstone's crusade would not get in the way of realignment for long. Gladstone had summoned him to his house at Hawarden in October 1885. They had talked past one another about Ireland. But Gladstone explicitly told Chamberlain, according to the latter's memorandum written afterwards, that 'in a very few months, I propose to hand over the leadership to Hartington' (Chamberlain Memorandum, in Garvin 1933: 109). Hartington (who by 1903 had become the Duke of Devonshire) was the leader of the Whigs, and Chamberlain must have thought he had a good chance of supplanting him.

But Gladstone did not retire after the failure of the Home Rule Bill. By 1887 both Irish federation and Liberal reunion were dead. Chamberlain admitted that the future of the Liberal Unionists lay with the Tories. 'At least our allies will be English gentlemen', he said in a phrase that Powell (1977: 78), with his sensitive antennae for English nationalism, saw as highly significant. From then on, if there were to be any federations in Chamberlain's scheme of things, they would be Anglo-Saxon federations. Even within the Empire, the Irish, the French Canadians, the South African Dutch, and—the great hole in Chamberlain's schemes—the Indians were not truly part of the picture. The Empire really meant Australia, New Zealand, English Canada, and the English settlements in South Africa.

Chamberlain, Imperial Preference, and Tariff Reform

As this is not a life of Chamberlain, we cavalierly jump over fifteen years of great importance in his career and pick up the story at the unexpected resignation of Salisbury in July 1902. As noted above, Chamberlain was in-capacitated and unable to make a bid for the premiership. What is more surprising is that he stayed with the Colonial Secretaryship in Balfour's new administration. He seems not to have seen the importance of controlling any of the financial departments if the idea of colonial preference were to become a reality. His absence had weakened his bargaining power in any case; upper-class Unionists, even in South Africa, still did not regard him as one of them.

In 1902, Chamberlain presided over his second Colonial Conference, intended to coincide with the coronation of Edward VII as the first, in 1897, had coincided with the Diamond Jubilee of Queen Victoria. Three ideas—imperial federation, imperial defence, and an imperial tariff area—dominated both Conferences. They opened up problems that were already a century old and (in the shape of devolution within the UK and relations with the European Union) still loom over British politics.

Imperial federation implied an imperial parliament, an imperial executive, and perhaps an imperial judiciary. The last of these was actually the least con-troversial. Chamberlain insisted that a right of appeal to the Judicial Com-mittee of the Privy Council (JCPC) should remain in the constitution of the Commonwealth of Australia (ch. III s. 74) when the UK government approved it in 1900. The Australians were reluctant, but the JCPC survives as the last functioning remnant of empire. It hears New Zealand and Caribbean appeals and links the common law countries of the former empire. The Blair gov-ernment has revived its constitutional function with the provision that it is to settle intergovernmental disputes between the Scottish and UK govern-ments that may arise under the Scotland Act 1998.

An imperial judiciary was logistically possible—Australian appeals could be heard in London, although the Australian parties would have to be very patient. An imperial executive or legislature was not. As it would take weeks or months for Dominion members to travel between London and their Dominion, they could in no sense be responsible from day to day to either their local government or their people. Consequently they would have no legitimacy. An Imperial War Cabinet did indeed function during the First World War, but even then its representation from the Dominions comprised those who got on well with Lloyd George.

If there were no imperial parliament, how could there be imperial taxation? Any direct taxation would be taxation without representation—the issue that led to American independence. And as with the USA a century earlier, the UK government was bearing most of the costs of imperial defence. It saw the Dominion governments as free riders (as Lord North and his administration had seen the American colonists, who had benefited from the British Army's defence of them against the French and the native Americans without paying for it). The Royal Navy patrolled the seven seas, but the British taxpayer paid for about 6.95 of them. This perception was particularly unfair to the Indians, who had to pay not only for the Indian Army but also for its excursions into neighbouring colonial wars. But on this as on other things, Chamberlain's blind spot was his ignorance of India. His attempts to get the Dominions to pay more for imperial defence failed.

But there was huge imperial sentiment and some common interest between the British government and those of the white English-speaking colonies. Chamberlain, like all other imperialists, was impressed by the fact that Canada, Australia, and New Zealand had all voluntarily sent troops to fight alongside the British in the Boer War. The Empire was popular in Britain for reasons of pure nationalism and the prospect of emigration. The Mother Country was popular in the white dominions, though more sentimentally and less practically than Chamberlain realized. How might Chamberlain and the Dominion governments take advantage of the huge wash of popular imperialism?

It was the Canadians who first handed him an answer. In 1897 Canada, which had a high tariff, offered the UK preferential rates for UK exports to Canada. The UK, as a free trade country, could not reciprocate, nor did it offer any special favours. But in the 1902 Budget, Salisbury's Chancellor Hicks-Beach had imposed a duty on imported corn. This gave Sir Wilfrid Laurier, the Canadian Prime Minister, the opportunity to suggest reciprocity, an offer Chamberlain eagerly seized. An imperial *Zollverein*, as Chamberlain called it after the nineteenth-century German example, suddenly seemed possible. The Empire would be a free trade area with high external tariff walls—something like the European Union in its early years. This could get round the impracticality of an imperial executive and imperial direct taxation. For instance, the proceeds of a British tariff against non-Empire imports could be put in part towards the cost of the Royal Navy. Chamberlain put this suggestion to Beach but was rebuffed (Amery 1969: 15–45).

This was where the effect of Chamberlain's failure to seize any of the financial ministries became apparent. When Salisbury resigned, so did Beach. But

C. T. Ritchie, whom we last met as a protectionist in the 1880s, succeeded him. As Chancellor, Ritchie 'had fallen entirely under the influence of Sir Francis Mowatt, Permanent Under-Secretary of the Treasury, a fanatical free-trader' (Austen Chamberlain to Mrs Blanche Dugdale, Balfour's biographer, 04.03.31; JCP 18/18/22). He rejected all Chamberlain's ideas more brusquely than Beach. In November 1902 the Cabinet agreed that there could be an imperial remission from the Beach corn duty. Ritchie noted his dissent. In March 1903, Ritchie persuaded the Cabinet to let him abolish the duty, thus undercutting all Chamberlain's efforts. Chamberlain extracted only the right to raise the issue again. Another department he failed to control was the India Office. Chamberlain's Colonial Office was not responsible for India. India was a free-trading country and the Secretary of State for India, Lord George Hamilton, believed (or repeated his officials' brief) that it should stay that way. Faced with an upcoming question in the House of Lords on how any imperial preference scheme would affect India, the free-trader Devonshire appealed to Chamberlain who said

My own feeling is . . . that India does not do nearly enough, and that neither in connection with the Army, the Navy, nor with Commerce does she give us the assistance for which we are entitled to ask (to Devonshire 5.7.03, quoted by Amery 1969: 271)

This, if it had been factually correct, might have made a good argument for an imperial tax on India. It did not make an argument for India and/or Britain to introduce an entire tariff system for the sole purpose of exempting one another from it.

The background to Chamberlain's launch of his campaign was therefore inauspicious. He launched it at a meeting in Bingley Hall, Birmingham, on May 15, 1903. He made explicit that the proposed scheme for imperial preference was not to involve 'those hundreds of millions of our Indian and native fellow subjects' but 'our own kinsfolk, . . . that white British population that constitutes the majority in all the great self-governing Colonies of the Empire'. They numbered 10 million (compared to the British population of 40 million) but their numbers would grow rapidly through emigration from Britain and exploitation of their virgin resources. He mentioned the shortfall of colonial military spending; explained that he could not rebate the corn duty to the Canadians because it was not his decision; and concluded, 'I desire that a discussion on this subject should be opened. The time has not yet come to settle it' (Chamberlain 1903: 6–18).

One potential weakness was as evident to him as to everybody else. As agricultural products were a high proportion of exports from the white Empire to Britain, any tariff on those imports from the rest of the world would be a tax on food. When Beach had introduced the corn duty, Chamberlain wrote to his agent that 'I do not believe in the argument . . . that the new Tax will cost the working class nothing' (Chamberlain to Vince (his agent), 26.04.02, quoted in Amery 1969: 15). But in due course he and the Tariff Reformers were forced more and more into the corner of proclaiming that it would cost them nothing, or nothing perceptible. Other Tories were terrified of being accused of taxing food. Ritchie wrote in his Cabinet memorandum objecting to an imperial preference scheme,

I am told that the Corn Duty tells heavily against us in the constituencies; Middleton [chief Conservative agent] tells me that it is the one thing he is afraid of at an election.

On his copy, against the reference to Middleton, Chamberlain annotated 'He is an ass' (Ritchie memo of 15.11.02, Chamberlain's copy; Amery 1969: 119). Chamberlain faced the issue head-on.

If you are to give a preference to the Colonies—I do not say that you are—you must put a tax on food (*Opposition cheers*). I make hon. Gentlemen opposite a present of that. (Hansard 4s vol. 123 col. 185, 28.05.03)

Chamberlain's insouciance is remarkable, but it is consistent with his belief that the Tariff Reform campaign would be long. More than once, he said that it might require more than one General Election before it succeeded. He said so when first outlining the scheme to his ally Lord Milner in Johannesburg. In the recollection of the only other person present, Milner thought that Chamberlain 'was too sanguine, and underrated the fanatical devotion to so-called Free Trade . . . It will take years. He is too old to undertake the task, and complete it' (Memo by Sir Percy Fitzpatrick, 28.11.23, quoted by Amery 1969: 128–9).

In 1903, Chamberlain was a very fit 67. As the campaign progressed, it became clear that Balfour could not hold his Cabinet together. Three ministers including Ritchie and Hamilton were hardline Free Traders. Balfour was not sorry to see them go when they resigned in mid-September—indeed, he virtually sacked them. Chamberlain resigned amicably at the same time. Having stayed in the Cabinet when he should have resigned (when Ritchie abolished the Hicks–Beach duty), he now resigned when he should have stayed, as the Free Trade Ministers would have gone in any event.

From then on, Chamberlain concentrated on converting the country and the party to Tariff Reform. He succeeded with the party and failed with the country. He insisted that 'Without preferential tariffs you will not keep the Empire.' He went round a series of towns hit by import competition, pointing out which industries were losing to imports (such as watches in Prescot and glass in St Helens—Chamberlain 1903: 92, 156–7). Later, his Tariff Commission collected much more of the same self-selected evidence. Industries that were suffering from import competition gave evidence to the Tariff Commission. Those that were not did not.

The loss of some of his ablest ministers, from both wings, severely damaged Balfour and his government. The Tory war on tariff reform continued, with Balfour ineffectually holding the ring. Finally he resigned in December 1905—the last instance of British political history of a voluntary government resignation that was not accompanied by an immediate dissolution of Parliament.

The incoming minority Liberals did dissolve immediately, and cruised to the greatest left-wing victory between 1832 and 1997.

In the General Election of 1906, the Liberals won 400 seats, an absolute majority of the Commons. Labour, with whom the Liberals had agreed a pact in 1903 when things were not going so well for them, won 30 seats, mostly uncontested by the Liberals. The Irish Party maintained its iron grip on Catholic Ireland, winning 83 seats, 74 of them unopposed. The Liberal landslide seems a very rare instance of an election won on, and for, free trade. If so, it would be indeed remarkable. Free trade is good for all, but protection is good for each, in the industry in which each works. Chamberlain's Tariff Commission was busy going round pointing out who lost from free trade. The idea of retaliation was undoubtedly popular. But the free trade forces took decisive advantage of Chamberlain's great weakness. They campaigned on 'the Big Loaf versus the Little Loaf'—'if you want your loaf, you must shut up Joe' (Liberal leaflet, December 1905, quoted by Russell 1973: 67). They even, for the only time in British electoral history, turned racism into a winner for the left. The Lib-Lab campaign against Chinese indentured labour ('slavery') in South Africa seems an odd one for a British General Election. It was raised by high-minded liberals but took on a life of its own. Graham Wallas, the first academic political psychologist, wrote:

[W]hen an . . . agitation was proposed, an important personage said that 'there was not a vote in it'. Any one, however, who saw much of politics in the winter of 1905–6 must have noticed that the pictures of Chinamen on the hoardings aroused among very many of the voters an immediate hatred of the Mongolian racial type. This hatred was transferred to the Conservative party. (Wallas [1908] 1962: 126–7)

The Conservative wipe-out in votes was much less total than in seats. The Conservatives achieved 43.6 per cent of the vote in their contested seats. The Liberals had only 49.0 per cent, or 54.9 per cent if the Labour and Liberal votes are counted together. The responsiveness of the system—the exaggeration of the vote margin into the seat margin—was at its highest ever in the twentieth century. It was after this election that James Parker Smith, a Cambridge mathematics graduate who had been Chamberlain's parliamentary private secretary, first proposed what has become known as the 'cube law'. The cube law states that when votes are in the ratio $a:b$, seats will be in the ratio $a^3:b^3$. (Royal Commission on the Electoral System, Minutes of Evidence; PP 1910 vol. xxvi: 443). In fact, Parker Smith, no doubt sore at losing his own seat in the 1906 wipe-out, pointed out that the exaggerative effect was greater than cubic for the two landslides of 1886 and 1906. As the uninformed and confused examination of his evidence should have warned him, Parker Smith's insight failed to illuminate the Report of the Royal Commission, which in any case led nowhere.

Undaunted by the election result ('We are not downhearted—the only trouble is we cannot understand what is happening to our neighbours'— speech at Smethwick, 18.01.06) Chamberlain pressed on, as he had always said he would. He persuaded the reluctant Balfour to hold a party meeting of Conservative MPs, although Balfour professed that he did not know how it should proceed (the letters are in JCP 30/7/9; Balfour's has been published in McKenzie 1963: 71). This enabled the Tariff Reformers to seize control of the parliamentary party, as they had already seized control of the mass organizations of both the Conservatives and the Liberal Unionists. But on 11 July 1906, Chamberlain suffered a disabling stroke, which made him unable to write or to speak clearly. He would not admit for many months how badly disabled he was. In January 1907, Balfour commissioned a doctor to study a photograph of Chamberlain in order to tell him how badly affected Chamberlain was. Not for another year would Chamberlain admit that he could not take his seat in Parliament (Amery 1969: 910, 922). He was returned in both 1910 elections, but his only appearance was to take the oath in January 1911, carried in by his son Austen and a friend, after all the other members had departed.

Without Chamberlain, the Tariff Reform campaign drifted in circles, trapped in its own contradictions. The details need not concern us (see Sykes 1979; 1998). The final blows were Laurier's proposal for a free trade treaty with the USA (although that was lost with Laurier's defeat at a General Election) and the abandonment of Tariff Reform by the new Tory leader, Bonar Law, in 1913. Austen wrote to his stepmother:

I have prepared you and Father for what this letter has to tell, yet I find it a very difficult one to write. I have done my best, but the game is up. We are beaten and the cause for which Father sacrificed more than life itself is abandoned! (Austen Chamberlain to Mary Chamberlain, 7.1.13, in Amery 1969: 981)

Of all the Tory leaders at the time, Chamberlain was the only heresthetician. He outmanoeuvred the Unionist Free Traders and took complete control of both the Conservative and (what was left of) the Liberal Unionist party machines. He successfully linked a set of issues, each of which had wide popular appeal. Tariff Reform, as put forward by the Unionists between 1903 and 1913, had at least eleven main components, all of them attractive to large swathes of the British electorate:

1. The Empire is good and must be protected, for mutual defence and to protect emigration opportunities for white Britons.
2. A link between the Union of the British Isles (including Ireland) and the white Empire strengthens both.
3. The UK is in relative economic decline, especially in agriculture and (some) old industries, e.g. iron and steel, watchmaking, glassmaking.
4. The UK is failing to develop new industry.
5. We need an imperial *Zollverein* to do for the Empire what the original *Zollverein* did for Germany.
6. We need to protect UK agriculture.
7. We need to protect UK industry.

8. We need to protect UK jobs.
9. The fairness (and/or bargaining counter) argument for retaliation:—if foreigners levy tariffs against us, it is pointlessly magnanimous not to levy tariffs against them.
10. We can use tariff revenue to pay for social reform.
11. We can make the foreigner pay. To keep his market share in the UK, he will reduce his pre-tax price.

The combination looked powerful—why did it fall apart?

Propositions 1 and 2 already worked in the Salisbury era. Proposition 3 was necessarily true when anybody else industrialized. Relative decline was therefore not necessarily a bad thing (and if it is inevitable anyhow, there is no point in trying to remedy it). But contemporaries did not realize that. Perceptions matter, therefore perception of decline did help shape policy. Proposition 4 was true, as is more obvious now than then. One respectable argument for tariffs is the 'infant industry' argument. But almost by definition, infant industries have no lobby. The infant industry argument is usually used by senile industries, as it was in 1903. Proposition 5 was a good one, but faced the problem that the original *Zollverein* was a union of small states which, to begin with, had high and expensive tariffs against one another. Britain had no tariffs, and neither did India. A *Zollverein* would harm, not help, agriculture in the UK (proposition 6), because Canada and Australia were cheaper producers. Propositions 3 and 6 jointly implied food taxes, the killer of the Conservatives in the 1906 election. Chamberlain saw the problem coming. In his resignation letter to Balfour he conceded that 'a preferential agreement with our colonies involving any new duty, however small, on articles of food hitherto untaxed is . . . unacceptable to the majority in the constituencies'. To Lord Halsbury he added, 'The part of our programme which has strong popular support is retaliation and reciprocity. The part which is weak, is Preference to the Colonies with its attendant tax on corn' (Chamberlain to Balfour, 09.09.03, JCP 30/4/198; to Halsbury, 15.09.03, 30/4/202).

As to proposition 7, only import-vulnerable industry benefited from protection, and then only if it did not have to increase its input prices (including the price of labour, itself affected by the price of food) by more than it gained. Of large industries at the time, that applied to iron and steel, but not to coal, cotton, or finance, whose leaders refused to co-operate with Chamberlain's Tariff Commission. Proposition 8 looked like a good argument at times of high unemployment (such as 1907–9), but its force faded at other times. Proposition 9 also looked like a good argument. Balfour seized on it, in his *Economic Notes on Insular Free Trade* (Balfour 1903), in the vain hope of uniting the Unionists behind it. Most professional economists rejected the case for retaliation, but the economic argument the other way is too subtle for politicians or voters. Proposition 10 was the most important, but also the worst argument. It was important because it made the heresthetic link between imperialism and social reform, potentially undercutting the left-wing parties and forming a new coalition of support for Chamberlain and the Unionists. But Ritchie (1903) dealt the fatal blow in his parting shot to the Cabinet in September 1903, probably written by Sir Francis Mowatt

But, of course, the object of preference is to reduce the proportion of the supplies from foreign countries, and the more the policy succeeds, the less will be the Exchequer share (Ritchie [1903] 1997: 330).

The protectionists had been impaled on the same dilemma in 1846. Chamberlain's copy of Ritchie's Cabinet memorandum survives in the Chamberlain Papers. It is silently eloquent on how one-sided the economic argument was. Chamberlain scribbled objections to some of Ritchie's points, notably this one. His annotation to this point is unfortunately illegible. But none of his others, made at what was both his and Ritchie's last Cabinet meeting, begins to cope with the Treasury's fusillade (JCP 18/16/2). He did not submit a counter-memorandum.

Proposition 11 was, as A. C. Pigou called it, 'frankly a national one. It is admitted that the world at large would suffer . . . , but it is claimed that in certain cases the direct loss experienced by this country would be less than its indirect gain through the tribute levied upon other nations' (Pigou 1904: 243). That made it bad economics, but it could be excellent politics. 'Make the foreigner pay' is a powerful xenophobic slogan. Many incoherent programmes have gone far in politics—think of Joseph McCarthy's witch-hunts, which swept US politics for six years although he could never name the communists in the State Department who were supposed to be corrupting national politics. Or think of the Social Credit movements in Canada and New Zealand, equally incoherent economics but for several decades successful politics. The Tariff Reformer George Wyndham reported as follows in 1905, about his constituents in Dover:

They do not distinguish between Retaliation, High Protection, Low Protection, Preference to Colonies, Tariff for Revenue etc etc. But they want a change. They talk of the Imperial Idea; want to 'pal' with the Colonies; are annoyed—this above all—with Foreign countries for taxing our goods unfairly. (Mackail and Wyndham [1925], ii. 521–2)

The Tariff Reform was witheringly criticized by the leading economists of the day. A. C. Pigou, for instance, pointed out that there was no evidence that foreign companies dumped goods on the UK at below cost price, nor any motive for doing so unless they were world monopolists. However, domestic dumping was known to exist:

A Birmingham concern, for example, engaged in the manufacture of screws is popularly supposed, at one period, to have succeeded in dumping other English screw-makers out of existence (Pigou 1904: 243.)

Whether or not Pigou knew it, Chamberlain's business practices as managing partner of Nettlefold & Chamberlain in the 1870s give some support to that jibe (E. Jones 1987: 152–7).

The Tariff Reform economists recruited by Chamberlain (W. J. Ashley and W. A. S. Hewins) were no match for Pigou and Alfred Marshall. Chamberlain supplied Ashley with the prospectus for his *The Tariff Problem* (Ashley 1903), but admitted his own lack of background in economics, writing to Hewins, 'I do not pretend to be an economic expert. I once read Mill and tried to read Marshall. You must supply the economic arguments' (Amery 1969: 288, 290; cf. Chamberlain's similar letters to Ashley 19.05.03 and 19.08.03 in JCP 30/4/176 and 190). The economist and statistician Sir Robert Giffen wrote sorrowfully to Chamberlain, 'But would you let me urge you as an old friend always to give references when quoting *new* figures?' before going on to demolish his economic arguments (Giffen to Chamberlain 26.10.03, in JCP 18/18/64).

Losing the argument did not matter intellectually. George Wyndham's constituents did not read Pigou or Marshall. But it mattered fatally in the departmental politics of the Balfour Cabinet. In the Cabinet papers from 1903 are to be found:

- a withering memorandum from Alfred Marshall, fatally undercutting Balfour's *Economic Notes on Insular Free Trade* before they were written;
- the memorandum already quoted, signed by Ritchie but presumably written by a senior Treasury official; and
- a Cabinet paper from the Treasury or the Board of Trade, on 'Most-favoured-nation treaties v. retaliation', stating that the 'wide-spread belief in the existence of a settled policy of active hostility on the part of foreign nations against British trade' was 'quite at variance with the facts'
- a Cabinet paper from E. W. Hamilton, joint Permanent Secretary at the Treasury, stating that 'the Preferential system, grand though it may be in idea, seems to be fraught with danger to the Empire' (All in Schonhardt-Bailey 1997. Marshall, PRO CAB T168/54; Ritchie, CAB 37/66/58, and JCP 18/16/2; BoT paper CAB 37/66/56; Hamilton, BM Add MSS 49780 (Balfour Papers)

Departmental politics were very departmental in 1903—much more so than today. Chamberlain controlled neither of the key economic departments—the Treasury and the Board of Trade—nor the India Office. Balfour could sack Ritchie and George Hamilton (Secretary of State for India), but could not prevent their departments from remaining bastions of free trade ideology.

There is an instructive contrast between Chamberlain and Lloyd George. The Treasury was as horrified by Lloyd George's 1909 Budget as it was by Chamberlain's tariff campaign. It ruthlessly briefed opposition politicians against its own minister (see Murray 1980: 78). But Lloyd George, unlike Chamberlain, carried the Cabinet. Both politicians were great populist orators, but in other heresthetic arts they were opposites. Lloyd George controlled the government machine but lost his party; Chamberlain did the opposite.

Enoch Powell, the Last Unionist

The facts of John Enoch Powell's political career are well known and recorded by more biographers than those of any other modern British politician (see especially Utley 1968; Foot 1969; Roth 1970; Berkeley 1977; Shepherd 1996; Heffer 1998. On race and immigration see in particular Schoen 1977; Hansen 1999; Hansen 2000). Appointed in 1937 at the age of 25 as Professor of Greek at the University of Sydney, he resigned the chair on the outbreak of war to volunteer for the British forces as a private in the Royal Warwickshires. He ended the war as a Brigadier in the Indian Army, becoming the only person in the British forces to enter the war as a private and end it as a brigadier. He wrote a report suggesting that the Indian Army would continue to need British officers for the next twenty-five years. On his return to the UK after the war, Brigadier Powell entered politics via the Conservative Parliamentary Secretariat. He found a seat at Wolverhampton South-West, which he first fought and won in 1950. He was a prickly candidate, who threatened to resign later in 1950. However, it was the constituency Tories who realized the appeal of his second name. Enoch is a common personal name in the Black Country but nowhere else in the UK. The name; his unmistakable accent, which seemed to move from the Birmingham of his birth to the Black Country of his constituency; and his equally distinctive piercing blue eyes, formal clothes and black hat, made an unforgettable combination. The inimitable accent added further force to his doom-laden speeches.

The parliamentary leaders recognized him as a talented but eccentric back-bencher. He was slower to reach the front bench than the other intellectuals of the 1950 intake, almost certainly because of his prickly independence, which emerged early on. Having refused a junior post dealing with Welsh affairs in 1952, he first achieved office as a junior housing minister in 1955. He was promoted to the Treasury in 1957, but a year later resigned with the other Treasury ministers in protest against Harold Macmillan's rejection of their austerity programme: a programme that has often been seen as a precursor to Margaret Thatcher's. In 1959 he turned down a junior post in education, and this time his persistence was rewarded, because Macmillan appointed him as Minister of Health from July 1960, and admitted him to the Cabinet in 1962. After little more than a year, he refused to serve under Macmillan's successor Sir Alec Douglas-Home, in protest at the way that Home was selected to succeed Macmillan—Powell believed it unconstitutional.

On Labour's victory in 1964, Powell became shadow spokesman on transport and later on defence. In April 1968 Edward Heath dismissed him from the Shadow Cabinet because of his 'rivers of blood' speech. He became one of the most popular, and simultaneously one of the most loathed, politicians in the country. On most estimates, the popularity of Powell's views on race gave the Conservatives the extra percentage points in the popular vote that brought them their unexpected victory in the 1970 General Election. Their margin in seats was enough that Heath did not need to bargain with Powell, despite the latter's huge popularity. He became one of the most persistent rebels against the Heath government, on both matters of immigration and race, and the accession of the UK to the European Economic Community, which Powell consistently denounced as a betrayal of British sovereignty. In February 1974 he resigned his seat, at the same time encouraging the electorate to vote Labour in the hope of preserving British sovereignty. His view on Unionism and parliamentary sovereignty brought him closer to the Ulster Unionists. In the October 1974 general election he re-entered the Commons as Unionist MP for South Down. Although he sat for a further thirteen years, his influence never returned. His uncompromising Unionism led him to support the full integration of Ulster in the UK. The other Unionist MPs wished to restore the devolved institutions of Protestant supremacy that Craig had found so useful in the about-turn of 1921. He lost his seat in 1987, but remained an active controversialist to the end, publishing a commentary on the Gospel according to St Matthew in which he sought to show that Christianity is not a social gospel (Powell 1994). He died on 8 February 1998. Capable of causing controversy to the last, his body lay in Westminster Abbey[1] before he was buried in the Royal Warwickshires' regimental plot in Warwick, in his army uniform.

Powell will be forever remembered for the speech that led Heath to dismiss him. Speaking to the Conservative Political Centre in Birmingham on April 20 1968, Powell opened by saying that 'The supreme function of statesmanship is to provide against preventable evils'. He went on to quote a constituent who had told Powell that he and his family planned to emigrate because

'in this country in fifteen or twenty years time the black man will have the whip hand over the white man'. I can already hear the chorus of execration. How dare I say such a horrible thing? How dare I stir up trouble and inflame feelings by repeating such a conversation? . . . I do not have the right not to do so

Powell stated that his constituent was voicing the sentiments of 'thousands and hundreds of thousands' of others about the 'areas that are already undergoing the total transformation to which there is no parallel in a thousand years of *English* history' (our emphasis). He went on to quote another story, this time in doubly indirect speech—he stated that it was in a letter to him from a lady in Northumberland, describing the experiences of a second lady in Wolverhampton.

Eight years ago in a respectable street in Wolverhampton a house was sold to a Negro. Now only one white (a woman old-age pensioner) lives there. This is her story. She lost her husband and both her sons in the war. So she turned her seven-roomed house, her only asset, into a boarding-house. She worked hard and did well, paid off her mortgage and began to put something by for her old age. Then the immigrants moved in. With

---

[1] In October 1966, Prime Minister Harold Wilson's private office advised him to resist calls for a Westminster Abbey memorial service for the 144 victims of the colliery tip disaster in Aberfan on the grounds, among others, that 'the Welsh Church is disestablished and has no claim on Westminster Abbey'. Public Record Office PREM 13/1280.

growing fear, she saw one house after another taken over. The quiet street became a place of noise and confusion. Regretfully, her white tenants moved out.

The day after the last one left, she was awakened at seven am by two Negroes who wanted to use her phone to contact their employer. When she refused, as she would have refused any stranger at such an hour, she was abused and feared she would have been attacked but for the chain on her door. . . .

She is becoming afraid to go out. Windows are broken. She finds excreta pushed through her letter-box. When she goes to the shops, she is followed by children, charming, wide-grinning piccaninnies. They cannot speak English, but one word they know. 'Racialist', they chant. When the new Race Relations bill is passed, this woman is convinced she will go to prison . . .

As I look ahead, I am filled with foreboding. Like the Roman, I seem to see 'the River Tiber foaming with much blood'. The tragic and intractable phenomenon which we watch with horror on the other side of the Atlantic but which is there interwoven with the history and existence of the States itself, is coming upon us here by our own volition and our own neglect. (Powell 1991: 373–9)

Afterwards, Powell expressed regret that he had not checked the quotation from Virgil which he translated as 'the River Tiber foaming with much blood', nor given it in Latin (*Et Thybrim multo spumantem sanguine cerno*; Virgil, *Aeneid* vi. 87). 'I can't find the Roman', he told his friend John Biffen shortly afterwards, and was agitated to find that Virgil attributes the words to the Sybil, a prophet, and not to a Roman (Shepherd 1996: 359–60).

We shall discuss Powell's heresthetic in the next section. Here, his rhetoric calls for some comment. Powell's enemies have always said that the Rivers of Blood speech shows conclusively that Powell was a racialist. The Wolverhampton *Express and Star* searched long and hard for the widow with the boarding-house and the excreta through her letter box. Neither it, nor any other investigator, has ever found her. 'Piccaninnies' in Wolverhampton, by whom Powell's correspondent presumably meant Afro-Caribbean rather than Asian children, would have either been born there or have migrated from English-speaking colonies in the Caribbean. Wolverhampton piccaninnies were native English speakers.

Powell's friends have equally hotly denied the charge of racialism. Some of them seek to distinguish 'racism'—the ethically neutral view, as it is claimed, that it is good policy to separate people of different races—from 'racialism', defined as contempt for people of other races (e.g. Shepherd 1996: 364). They point out that Powell made principled stands against racialism at least twice in his life, once in India and once in his speech denouncing the British treatment of detainees in Hola Camp in Kenya (27 July 1959: in Powell 1991: 203–7).

Neither of these characterizations lays enough stress on Powell's key narrative device. Like any great novelist, he distances himself from the protagonists. There is Enoch Powell, the austere doomladen classicist who writes in sentences that might have emanated from Abraham Lincoln or from Powell's revered teacher A. E. Housman. 'I do not have the right not to do so' is a ten-word sentence constructed by the rules of Latin grammar, but containing only one-syllable words of Anglo-Saxon origin, the longest of them five letters long. (Compare Housman's desolate poem of lost love, 'He would not stay for me, and who can wonder?'—Housman 1988, *Additional Poems* vii). And then there is the Greek chorus of witnesses who speak of whip hands, of grinning piccaninnies, and of excreta through the letterbox. The subtleties of Powell are lost on some of his followers, as he may (or may not) have intended:

N[eil] A[court]: It makes you sick doesn't it. I reckon that every nigger should be chopped up, mate, and they should be left with nothing but stumps.
L[uke] K[night]: Do you remember that Enoch Powell—that geezer he knew straight away. He went over to Africa and all that.
NA: Is that what happened?
LK: Yeah, he knew it was a slum. He came back saying they're uncivilised and all that and then they started coming over here and he knew, he knew straight away. He was saying no, I don't want them here. No f—— niggers—they'll ruin the gaff. And he was right.
NA: Is he still alive?
LK: I seen him on a programme the other day.
NA: I wanna write him a letter saying Enoch Powell mate: you are the greatest. You are the don of dons. Get back into Parliament mate and show these ——s what it's all about. All these arrogant, big mouthed, shouting their mouths off, flash dirty rapists.
   (Transcript of tape from police bug, December 1994, planted during unsuccessful attempt to gather evidence against NA, LK, and three others for the murder of the black teenager Stephen Lawrence. 'Secret camera recorded racist sneers', *Daily Telegraph*, electronic edition, 26.4.1996)

Powell's Heresthetic

In a speech explicitly comparing himself with Joseph Chamberlain, Powell said in 1973:

The political earthquakes which alter the physical geography of politics for a long period afterwards can only occur when . . . the outer wing of one party finds that some single object, which for the time being seem to it more important than all the rest, is procurable not from its political allies and comrades but from its enemies. (quoted in Shepherd 1996: 436)

Powell had a clear sense of the potential multidimensionality of British politics. Like the other subjects of this book, he consciously exploited it. Like Chamberlain, he tapped one of the most powerful emotions in the British electorate. Like Chamberlain (and perhaps Disraeli and/or Salisbury), he saw that the outer, imperialist and/or racist, wing of the Conservative party might be able to procure support from a section of the electorate which otherwise would vote for the parties of the left. Powell's appeal on race issues was always strongest among low-income, poorly-educated voters, who would normally

Table 5.2. 'Who would make the best Prime Minister?', 1968–74

Date	Polling company	% for Powell	% for Heath	% for Wilson	Other or DK	Total	Note
09.68	NOP	37	41	n/a	22	100	1
11.68	ORC	30	49	n/a	21	100	1
01.69	NOP	34	49	n/a	17	100	1
06.70	NOP	11	25	20	34	100	2
09.70	NOP	9	30	25	36	100	2
02.73	MORI	20	16	25	(39)	100	2
06.73	NOP	18	18	19	(45)	100	2
06.74	ORC	14	14	30	(42)	100	2

Notes:
1. Binary choice offered: Heath v. Powell
2. Open choice offered

Source: Schoen (1977), various tables. MORI: Market & Opinion Research International. NOP: National Opinion Polls. ORC: Opinion Research Centre.

have been natural clients of the Labour Party (Studlar 1975, Table III-5; Schoen 1977 ch. 8).

Between 1968 and 1974, Powell's popularity rivalled that of his leader, Edward Heath. It is infuriatingly difficult to get a time series of poll data on this, because pollsters kept asking different questions so that their results cannot be compared directly. Table 5.2 attempts a summary. Other questions showed the strength and depth of Powell's popular support. After Heath sacked him over the 'Rivers of Blood' speech, 74 per cent of respondents said that they agreed with Powell's views on race, and 69 per cent that they disagreed with Heath's decision to sack him. Agreement with his views on immigration declined to 58 per cent in December 1968 (after he had failed to electrify the 1968 Conservative Party conference) and to 48 per cent in January 1970. In June 1970, 36 per cent of respondents agreed with the proposition 'Powell is the only politician I admire'; in October 1972, 40 per cent of respondents did (Schoen 1977: 190, 191, 97).

Powell therefore raised a set of issues which the elites of both parties very much wanted not to be raised. He linked it with other parts of his ideology (see next section). It could have been the basis for a new winning coalition. His failure was a practical one.

Powell's Ideology

Powell's ideology was a unique mixture. There were three main elements. Two of them were closely related, although with some internal tensions. The third was orthogonal to the other two, and the tensions between it and the others weakened Powell. Those who liked the first two were nonplussed by the third and vice versa.

The three components were:

• Diceyan Unionism
• English nationalism
• Neoclassical economics

Diceyan Unionism

Like A. V. Dicey (Dicey 1905, 1911, 1959), Powell had a mystical respect for the Crown in Parliament, and parliamentary sovereignty, unless it did something which he thought destroyed the nation (Irish Home Rule for Dicey; immigration and accession to the European Economic Community, for Powell). In those cases, the Ultra defenders of parliamentary sovereignty both called for referenda to overrule Parliament.

This ideology links apparently disparate campaigns of Powell's. One of his first revolts was against the Royal Titles Bill of 1953. Powell's argument was that the formula 'Head of the Commonwealth' for the Queen was 'essentially a sham'. He poured scorn on the argument that the Republic of India recognized her as that, adding that he recognized Clement Attlee as the leader of the Opposition, but that did not make him a member of the Opposition. 'Thank God' interrupted Frederick Messer (Lab., Tottenham: *Hansard* 5s. 512 col. 246; 3 March 1953).

On similar grounds he objected to the Life Peerages Act 1958, and never received one himself. He joined forces with the Labour left to defeat the reform of the House of Lords as proposed by the Wilson government in 1969. Like Dicey, he fiercely defended the Union of the United Kingdom of Great Britain and (what was left of) Ireland. Therefore he became one of the awkward leaders of the Ulster Unionists between 1974 and 1987. The awkwardness extended to his own group. Powell's ideology led him to demand full integration for Northern Ireland into the UK, whereas the other Unionist leaders wanted their local institutions of Protestant supremacy back. However, they recognized him as their best parliamentary tactician. So deferential was Powell's leader, James Molyneaux, to him that during the Falklands War of 1982 Molyneaux surrendered to Powell the right of the Ulster Unionist leader to be briefed by Margaret Thatcher on 'Privy Council terms' about the military secrets of the war as it progressed.

The Falklands War was the last moment of unity for Thatcher and Powell, nationalists and unionists both. Thatcher told journalists that they must 'Rejoice, rejoice!' at the recapture of the islands and made known her displeasure with the churchmen who called for remembrance of the victims on both sides. Powell was moved by the Falklands victory parade in London:

one band came down and started to play Rule Britannia and the entire crowd, right as far as one could see or hear, took it up. That was what it was about. And England had known itself, it had recognized itself. The England which tolerated the British Nationality Act of 1948, the England which thought it could reoccupy the Suez canal, was an England which had not recognized itself. (In *Enoch: a life in politics*, TV documentary 1987. Quoted in Shepherd 1996: 487)

Their unity was shattered by two actions of Thatcher's which Powell thought destroyed parliamentary sovereignty: the Anglo-Irish Agreement of 1985, and the ratification of the Single European Act in 1986. 'Does the Prime Minister understand—if she does not understand, she soon will—that the penalty for treachery is to fall into public contempt?' asked Powell. Unsurprisingly, Thatcher found his remarks 'deeply offensive' (14.11.85; *Hansard* 6s vol. 85, col. 682.).

It was his war service in India that made Powell a romantic imperialist. However, once Britain not only ceased trying to rule India, but allowed India to become a Republic within the Commonwealth, Powell was outraged. For him, the Commonwealth was a sham, and the British advance on Suez was the self-delusion of a government that did not realize that it no longer had an empire. The Empire had been bound together by the common status of its members as subjects of the Crown, expressed at its finest during the two World Wars. Powell often said that he wished that he had died in the war ('a remark, incidentally, which his widow once remarked with good humour was a little insulting to her'—Utley 1998).

Powell's remarks about the British Nationality Act need more decoding, and a careful look at the contemporary record. No recent piece of legislation has been more misunderstood. Analysts on the right (including the later Powell) say that it opened the floodgates to immigration by coloured people from the Caribbean and the Indian subcontinent, to whom the Act granted the status of citizen of the UK and Colonies. Analysts on the left can point to contemporary statements by both Labour and Conservative politicians to show that they were surprised by and hostile to the first small waves of migration from the West Indies at the time (see examples in Hansen 1999: 67–9). Both analyses miss the point that the Act was not intended to be about immigration at all. The Canadian Citizenship Act 1946 defined Canadian citizenship and stated that 'a Canadian citizen is a British subject' (s.26). This sounds innocuous, but it struck at the concept of subjecthood on which the British Empire had been founded. Subjecthood was a medieval concept, imputing a direct link from the subject to the sovereign without intermediation by parliament or by statute. It was extended from England to Scotland after the union of crowns in 1603 (not after the parliamentary union of 1707). It was extended to Ireland, America, and all the colonies, as the British Empire grew. Self-government by the white dominions and Ireland put it under severe strain. The strain helped to cause civil war in Ireland in 1922–3 between those who were prepared to accept some Irish allegiance to the Crown and those who were not. But until 1946 it caused no real trouble in Britain itself. As in Chamberlain's day, British legislators were slow to see that the white dominions had their own policies and priorities, and would not legislate with the interests of the British Empire first. One of the things they naturally wanted to do was to control their own immigration and emigration policies. The rebellious Irish were the first to do this, after the party that had lost the Civil War came to power in 1933. In 1935, De Valera's government, led by the man who had fought vainly for 'external association' rather than membership of the Empire (Chapter 7), defined Irish citizens, and classed British subjects who were not Irish citizens as aliens. Perhaps because of the potential for bloodletting in Northern Ireland, this did not provoke the British government. To this day, (and to Powell's fury), British law accords full voting and civil rights to Irish citizens in the UK, although Ireland left the Commonwealth altogether in 1949. British and Irish accession to the European Union has not smoothed out the anomaly. Irish citizens, but not the citizens of the remaining thirteen member states of the EU, may vote in UK domestic elections.

Canada was different, precisely because it was a loyal member of the Commonwealth. Where Canada led, the others must be expected to follow. The Canadian Act entailed the possibility of some people being British subjects in some parts of the world and not British subjects in others. If one Commonwealth country defined citizenship, then, the ministers responsible in Britain reasoned, all must. Hence the British Nationality Act (BNA) 1948, which divided those who had previously been British subjects into two main categories: Citizens of Independent Commonwealth Countries (CICCs), and Citizens of the UK and Colonies (CUKCs). There were transitional provisions to cover those Commonwealth countries that had not yet drafted a citizenship law but were expected to. CICCs, CUKCs, and those covered by the transitional arrangements all retained the right, which they had always had, to move to the UK without immigration control.

Powell, then at the Conservative Parliamentary Secretariat, drafted notes for Conservative speakers on the bill, deploring the demise of the undifferentiated status of British subject. The Conservatives succeeded in reinstating 'subject' for 'citizen' in the Lords, but the Lords accepted the Commons' rejection of these changes. This cannot have been because of the *force majeure* threat of the Parliament Act, *because the bill was first introduced in the Lords, and the Parliament Acts do not apply to such bills.* This shows that the bill was expected to be uncontroversial as between the two front benches. Governments would be unwise to introduce bills they expect to be controversial in the Lords, precisely because they cannot then use or threaten the Parliament Acts in the event of trouble.

Thus it is true that Powell saw from the outset that the BNA fatally undermined the concept of British subject, which was important to his romantic Diceyan Unionism. It is untrue that he, or anybody else, foresaw that thousands of non-white CUKCs from the Caribbean and CICCs from the Indian subcontinent would use their right of free entry to the UK. The politicians' awakening came within only days of the bipartisan passage of the BNA. A troopship, the *Empire Windrush*, which had taken demobilized Jamaican servicemen home, arrived in London with a return load of Jamaican CUKCs, who came to look for work in the UK. They were immediately categorized (inaccurately) as 'immigrants', and Labour ministers immediately tried to see how the influx could be controlled. They realized that, in terms of the legislation they had just passed, it could not be. So did their Conservative successors, who looked into the matter several times before the first control legislation in 1962 (Hansen 1999: 90–3).

From 1958 onwards, it became increasingly clear that coloured Commonwealth citizens were unpopular with some of their white fellows. Before Powell's speeches, the starkest reminder of this was the defeat, against the nationwide swing, of the Labour frontbencher Patrick Gordon Walker in neighbouring Smethwick in the 1964 General Election. His conqueror, Peter Griffiths, had allegedly campaigned on the slogan 'If you want a nigger neighbour, vote Liberal or Labour'. Shortly after the election, Harold Wilson attacked Griffiths violently in the Commons as a 'Parliamentary leper' who would make no mark until speedily despatched by the electorate. Griffiths was ousted from Smethwick in 1966, but returned as MP for Portsmouth North in 1979, and sat until 1997.

Throughout this time, Powell sat tight. He did not respond to requests to speak or act against coloured citizens in his constituency (Foot 1969: 43–65). His grasping of the issue in 1967–8 was heresthetic. Although he said in 1968 that he did not have the right not to pass on his constituent's racialist views, he had been exercising that right vigorously for ten years before that. Not until after Griffiths' victory in 1964 did Powell raise his head above the parapet (Foot 1969: 78–9). Even then, there was a lull after the 1966 election, where coloured migration did not seem to be an issue. Powell's heresthetic manoeuvre coincided with the threat by the newly independent government of Kenya to expel Asians who had not taken out Kenyan citizenship. Many of them were in the residual category of CUKC, who therefore had a right to enter Britain. British governments had been content to leave that loose end untied, lest there be a threat to the white settlers in Kenya. They had not anticipated a threat to the Asians. To repeal that right would have been to make them stateless.

English Nationalism

All of Powell's biographers agree that, between 1948 and 1953, he underwent a great transformation, which one of the unsympathetic ones labels 'Grand Imperialist to Little Englander' (Foot 1969: 11). Another, writing in 1977, said, 'Enoch Powell has lost an Empire and has not found a role' (Berkeley 1977: 62). Like other grand imperialists, Powell was intoxicated by India. His early plans made proposals for the continuation of British rule there. When the British abruptly left India in 1947, and still more when India declared itself a republic in 1949, Powell's imperialist dream was shattered. He ruthlessly and unsentimentally opposed any pretence that the Empire continued, even in the form of the Commonwealth, which he regarded as humbug. His core objection to the Royal Titles Bill 1953 was that it created the empty title 'Head of the Commonwealth' for the Queen. Empty for Powell, but not for others. If the British Government could have conceded something similar to de Valera in 1921, the Irish Civil War might have been avoided.

Likewise, he took a lonely line on defence policy. He saw no point in Britain having a defence role east of (or indeed at) Suez. That was for him a pointless imperial hangover. This made his tenure as Conservative defence spokesman from 1964 to 1968 interesting. Furthermore, he never believed that nuclear weapons prevented war, only that they prevented nuclear war. This led him to be a European in just this one policy domain. Britain's defence should be tied to that of her closest neighbours, not to that of the United States nor of the vanished Empire.

One can learn a lot about Powell's English nationalism by studying his attitude to religion, and in particular his last, extraordinary book *The Evolution of the Gospel* (Powell 1994). Neither Powell's political friends nor his enemies seem to have read this carefully. Heffer (1998: 134–7) gets what seems to me the central point, but without exploring just how explosive Powell (1994) is. It is a mixture of Nietzsche, Housman, and Hobbes. From Housman, Powell gets both his method of close textual analysis and (with Nietzsche thrown in) his style of invective. The Sermon on the Mount is 'a verbose exercise in rhetorical bombast, characterized by lavish use of pleonasm'; Jesus' missionary charge to his apostles 'comprises a mass of absurdities . . . an extraordinary concoction' (Powell 1994: 70, 109). A less obvious, but closer, ancestor is Thomas Hobbes. Hobbes uses the same method of textual analysis to show, in Books III and IV of *Leviathan*, that many of the statements in the Bible are on the face of it nonsensical and contradictory. Some of them do not mean what they obviously seem to mean, but the critic produces an alternative meaning that fits his political philosophy. For Powell, the statements in St Matthew's Gospel about the rich, the poor, and the kingdom of heaven mean not, as everybody else thinks, that it is harder for the rich than for the poor to enter it. *Rich* and *poor* 'denote those who respectively claim, or do not claim, merit accumulated by observance of the Law'. Therefore Powell's gospel is not a social gospel. It is a message that Christianity is for non-Jews (Powell 1994: xxv, commenting on Gospel According to St Matthew 19: 16–26). The last clergyman who ministered to Powell stated that 'He was not prepared to give up on Christianity' (Revd. D. Gray quoted by Heffer 1998: 137). The same was said of Hobbes on *his* deathbed.

But if you read either Hobbes or Powell in the way that they read the Bible, you cannot possibly believe that either was a Christian. (Compare Hobbes's 'It is with the mysteries of our Religion, as with wholesome pills for the sick, which swallowed whole, have the vertue to cure; but chewed, are for the most part cast up again without effect'—*Leviathan* ch. 32). They are both political philosophers, who need to tame the church and make it part of their political philosophy. Therefore they both make the church an arm of the state. The role of the Established Church is nation-building— neither Hobbes nor Powell would use the phrase, but they both use the concept. The Church of England, with the Queen at its head, is part of what defines the nation. In a frequently cited exchange, John Mortimer (1983: 48) asked Powell,

Does that [EP's Toryism] mean you're a Christian? 'I am an Anglican', said Mr Powell carefully.[2]

But this speaks to the key weakness of Powell's nationalist Unionism (see especially his speech to the Royal Society of St George, in Powell 1969: 337–41). What does it have to say to the Scots, the Welsh, the Irish, to English Nonconformists, Catholics, atheists, Hindus, Moslems, Sikhs, or Jews, not to mention Canadians, South Africans, Indians or Pakistanis? In early Powell the Queen's Realm is a thing to be venerated in, of, and for itself. In middleperiod Powell England, and in late Powell the United Kingdom, take on that role. But why? *Because it is there.* There is no external argument to persuade an Indian Nationalist, a Canadian Liberal, or an Irish Catholic that it is admirable. It is just there, and they are part of it. Like Chamberlain, the early (imperialist) Powell did not know what the Mother Country should do when another member of the Empire showed its independence by legislating in its own interests. Just as Chamberlain's scheme for imperial preference was fatally weakened by the failure of the Dominions to arrange their tariff policy in a way that suited Chamberlain, so was Powell's early dream of a unified realm in which British subjects obeyed the King destroyed by the Canadian Citizenship Act 1946.

   This came back to haunt the late Powell. He always said that the BNA was nonsensical. He always denied that Commonwealth immigration, incling the Kenyan and Ugandan Asian crises of 1968 and 1972, had anything to do with Britain's status as the former imperial power. But it did. Commonwealth citizens came to Britain from the 1950s on because before 1948 they had been British subjects. If there had been no Canadian problem and no 1948 Act, they could all have entered Britain freely as British subjects. The 1948 Act and its successors failed to define British citizens in a way that satisfied Powell because they could not, without creating large classes of stateless people. And the 1948 Act was inevitable once the Canadians had gone their own way, as the Dominions were bound to do at some time.

---

[2] Cf. an almost identical exchange with Terry Coleman, *Guardian*, 27.8.94, quoted by Shepherd (1996: 500). Berkeley (1977: 29) quotes Powell as having described himself during the war as 'an Anglican atheist', but this is hearsay.

Neoclassical Economics

Powell held office during the high corporatist era 1955–63. But signs of his revolt against corporatism in favour of (what might now be called) monetarist neoclassicism go back to his first ministerial post, as a junior housing minister in 1956. He helped to draft what became the 1957 Rent Act, the first post-war attempt to decontrol house rentals. Then came the resignation of all three Treasury ministers in January 1958—which Harold Macmillan called a 'little local difficulty'. Powell was the driving force, pushing his monetarist conviction that any increase in public spending would be inflationary because the government would print money to cover it. It was Harold Macmillan's little joke that, when he readmitted Powell to office, it was in one of the biggest spending departments of all, the Ministry of Health. None of the free-market interventions in the health service that have been tried since 1979 can be traced back to Powell.

Except on health, Powell was a fervent deregulator. He enjoyed rubbing the noses of trade associations in the uncomfortable consequences of their incorporation. He would read out immensely detailed Whitehall questionnaires about the number of staff employed in making Béchamel sauce or preparing Dover sole in front of customers. He would also read out examples of what he claimed were bluffing attempts by ministers or civil servants to get information on pay or prices which they had no legal right to demand. Powell called this the 'replacement of the rule of law by the Rule of the Threat of Law' (Powell 1969: 60–71; 99). He was equally at home telling a trade union meeting that in aggregate trade unions could only harm the interests of trade unionists (see e.g. Shepherd 1998: 420–1). He poured scorn on the idea that government could plan resources. He was as happy pouring the scorn on the heads of his fellow Conservatives as of Labour ministers. Before Powellism came to mean racialist nationalism, it meant a passion for deregulation, privatization, and control of inflation by controlling only the money supply. The *Oxford English Dictionary* defines *Powellism* as 'The political and economic policies advocated by J. Enoch Powell; *spec.* one of restricting or terminating the immigration of coloured people into the United Kingdom', and *Powellite* analogously. But neither of the articles which contain the *OED*'s first source quotations for each word (from *The Economist*, 17.7.65 and 5.6.65 respectively) contains any mention of race or immigration.

Without question it was Enoch Powell, not Edward Heath, nor Sir Keith Joseph, nor Margaret Thatcher, who fathered what we now call 'Thatcherism'. Why did he have to wait until his Ulster exile and beyond before seeing his ideas enter the mainstream of political discussion? Partly it was a matter of personality. Powell's self-image as lonely crusader blinded him to Thatcher. She admired him (until he started to attack her over issues of sovereignty); he seems to have despised her. But, more profoundly, it was a matter of the tension between the two main wings of Powell's ideology.

Even Powell's friends felt the strain, and sometimes pointed it out to him (e.g. William Rees-Mogg in 1965; Ralph Harris in 1968; Heffer 1998: 381, 445). Powell, it seemed, was in favour of free trade in every market except one— the labour market. Powell retorted that, when the two principles clashed, he put the principle of nationalism ahead of the principle of the market. But it left his support badly divided. The politician with the most similar pairing of ideologies was Margaret Thatcher. But personality kept Powell and Thatcher apart. And something more than personality. Whereas Thatcher said, 'there is no such thing as Society. There are individual men and women, and there are families', Powell said, 'There is no such animal as an individual who exists without society' (to Mortimer 1983: 49). Arguably, Powell was the truer Tory.

Strengths and Weaknesses of Powell's Heresthetic

Powell's strength was his popular appeal—while he was talking about race. No other insurgent politician in the history of polling in the UK has achieved the popularity scores that Powell did between 1968 and 1974.

Powell's main weakness was the opposite of Chamberlain's. Chamberlain was brilliant at converting his party, and failed totally to convert the electorate. Powell brilliantly picked up a latent issue and made himself hugely popular with the electorate. But he could not or would not get involved in party management. As even he was aware, his frequent resignations and refusals to take office made his leaders distrust him, however much his intellect awed them. When he ran for leader against Heath and Reginald Maudling in 1965, he got only fifteen votes. If he made strategic calculations about the outcome of elections, he got them wrong. He expected (as, to be fair, did everybody else) that Heath would lose the 1970 election. If he had, then Heath would surely have resigned or been forced out of the Conservative leadership. A reduced cohort of Conservative MPs with a higher proportion of Powellites among them might then have elected Powell rather than the lacklustre Maudling or the erratic Hogg to succeed Heath. Another obvious successor, Iain Macleod, died suddenly a month after the General Election. But Powell's campaign gained the Tories more votes than it lost them (see the Appendix to this chapter). It ensured that a party whose MPs would not elect him as their leader was returned with a large enough majority of seats (30 over all other parties combined; 43 over Labour) that the small band of devoted Powellites could not form a swing coalition to defeat the government. Powell put his deadly enemy Heath into office.

In the 1970–4 Parliament, Powell was the Conservatives' most frequent and most prominent rebel. The nearest he came to success was on 17 February 1972, when Heath's majority on the European Communities Bill was reduced to 8 in spite of (or perhaps because of) Heath's threat to make the vote an

issue of confidence. The European Communities Bill provoked Powell's terrifying fury because he saw it as an abdication of parliamentary sovereignty
from the UK Parliament to the EEC. On a simple reading of the numbers,
Powell was bound to fail, because there were more Labour pro-European rebels
than Conservative anti-European rebels. In the mirror image of Powell's
revolt, 69 Labour MPs had defied their whip to vote in favour of the bill in
October 1971 (and a further 20 abstained). Thus the median member of the
Commons was in favour of entry. That is not to say that Powell could not
have constructed a heresthetical winning coalition, as Disraeli did in 1846.
Indeed, he came within 8 votes of doing so. February 17 marked the Pickett's
Charge of Powellism.

On 18 April 1972, Powell did what Dicey had urged Unionists to do over
Home Rule. He supported a proposal by his fellow Conservative anti-EEC rebel
Neil Marten that entry to the EEC should not be confirmed unless it was ratified in a referendum. The Marten amendment failed, but it threw a lifeline
to the equally divided Labour Party. There, the parliamentary majority was
pro-EEC; the National Executive and the majority of those who had a vote in
the party's internal policy process were anti. Powell's counterpart Tony Benn
therefore aligned most of the Labour Party behind a referendum. This gave
Harold Wilson the exit he needed. He promised that, should Labour win the
next election, it would renegotiate the terms of entry that Heath had achieved
and put the revised terms before the electorate in a referendum.

In February 1974, Powell issued what has been widely labelled his 'Vote
Labour' manifesto after refusing to stand as a Conservative. It did not explicitly ask for a Labour vote. But both of the other parties had supported
the 1972 Act and entry on the terms already negotiated. Powell stated that
at the 1972 Paris EEC summit, Heath had accepted a commitment to
'economic and monetary union' with the rest of the Community by 1980.
He thundered:

So here we have the most far-reaching and revolutionary act of policy that can be imagined—and the Conservative Party does not think it necessary to tell the electorate,
let alone seek the electorate's approval. . . . There is one reason and one reason
alone why the most important fact about Britain and the Common Market was
suppressed in the Conservative Party's appeal to the voters. It was suppressed because
everybody knew that the electors would detest it if they were allowed to know about
it. (Powell 1991: 455)

As he had been downcast by the Conservative victory in 1970, so Powell was
upcast by the Conservative defeat in February 1974. He told his friends that on
hearing of Heath's defeat he went upstairs and sang the 'Te Deum' ['We praise
thee O God; we acknowledge thee to be the Lord'] (Heffer 1998: 710). In the
Appendix to this chapter we show that, although the evidence that Powell won
the February 1974 election for Labour is less conclusive than that for the claim
that he won the 1970 election for the Conservatives, the 1974 contest was on
such a knife-edge that even a tiny 'Powell effect' may have been decisive.

So here is paradox indeed. Chamberlain cost his own side heavily in the General Elections of 1906 and 1910. On a robust set of assumptions, Powell was responsible for the victory of the Conservatives in 1970 and of Labour in February 1974. But in 1970 he would certainly have done better if the Conservatives had lost. If the Conservatives had won in February 1974, Heath would have remained Conservative leader for longer, and the spread of Powellite ideas through Margaret Thatcher might have been delayed (or might never have happened at all). But on the issue Powell most cared about at the time, namely the loss of UK sovereignty consequent on joining the Common Market, his triumph was short-lived. As recounted above, Wilson took the device of the referendum, which Powell had backed, to save him from the divisions in *his* party.

Powell's objections to the UK's loss of sovereignty, and particularly to European economic and monetary union, strike a chord that has resonated through UK politics ever since. But the promised referendum did not go Powell's way. For most of the period from 1967 to 1974 inclusive, including the period when Britain was joining the EEC, the polls showed that the balance of public opinion was against it (Butler and Kitzinger 1976: 247, Table 1). As the date fixed for the referendum drew nearer, the pros first passed the antis, then roared ahead. The referendum vote, on June 5 1975, was *Yes* by a margin of 67.2 to 32.8 per cent. Apart from a lower than average *Yes* vote in rural Scotland, there was no regional variation—the level of *Yes* vote in each county was almost entirely a function of party support there in the previous general election. Most of the defeated *No* campaigners accepted their defeat with good grace. Powell, however, having lost the referendum, reverted immediately to orthodox Diceyanism:

It is no more than provisional. . . . This will be so as long as one Parliament can alter or undo whatever that or any other Parliament has done (quoted in Butler and Kitzinger 1976: 274).

Why did the *No*s lose, when they had been so far ahead for so long? In increasing order of importance:

- The media were overwhelmingly on the *Yes* side. Every voter got three statements, two of which (from the government, and from the *Yes* campaign) favoured staying in, and one of which, from the *No* campaign, favoured leaving. This would not have mattered, except that:
- 'support for membership was wide but it did not run deep. . . . It was a vote for the *status quo*. . . . The public is usually slow to authorise change . . . Before entry, a vote for going in would have been to vote radically. But after entry, it was at least as radical and unsettling to vote for leaving' (Butler and Kitzinger 1976: 280).
- Normally, on a non-salient issue like Europe, voters take their cue from their party. The leadership of both parties, in 1975, was pro. Both parties, of course, were divided. So the fallback was to take one's cue from the leaders

Table 5.3. Attitudes to leading politicians, April 1975

	Net respect (%)
Pro EEC	
Harold Wilson	+19
Edward Heath	+21
Jeremy Thorpe	+29
William Whitelaw	+25
Roy Jenkins	+25
Anti EEC	
Enoch Powell	+2
Ian Paisley	−62
Tony Benn	−15

Source: Harris Poll, 1–6 Apr. 1975, reported in Butler and Kitzinger 1976: 236, Table 9. Rows are politicians who had at least 80% name recognition. Column entries are (% 'respect and like'—% 'Don't like').

one trusted. Table 5.3 shows the net respect for the leaders on each side in April 1975.

Powell was still intensely liked. He was also intensely loathed. But, unlike in the Wolverhampton period, the numbers of his lovers and haters were roughly equal. His fellow *No* campaigners were also intensely liked and intensely loathed. Unfortunately for Powell, their net balance was negative. Also, only 7 per cent of voters said that British independence was the issue that 'affected their own vote most' (NOP poll for National Referendum Campaign 20.05.75, cited by Butler and Kitzinger 1976: 259). This led the anti campaign to switch its emphasis from constitutional to economic issues.

Chamberlain and Powell, a Comparison

A successful heresthetician must fight for hearts and minds in many places—in the electorate, among party members, among party leaders, and in the executive. To win (or coerce) all of these is demanding. Chamberlain succeeded with party members, but failed among both the electorate and the executive. Powell succeeded with the electorate and ordinary Conservative Party members, but failed among Conservative elites and in the executive.

Both Chamberlain and Powell saw that nationalism and imperialism had a close family relationship. But as in other close families, the concepts of nation and of empire did not get on well together. Unlike Chamberlain, Powell did not ignore India. But neither politician could make India fit into his imperial dream. For Chamberlain, it was a free-trading colony for which he was not responsible. For Powell, the Indian subcontinent provided the largest number of the British subjects who threatened his conception of English nationhood.

Neither politician could quite make nationalism into the dimension-busting issue that successful heresthetic required. Chamberlain's nationalism ran into the sand over the contradictions of Tariff Reform. Powell failed to sell his mixture of nationalism and neoclassical economics to anybody except Margaret Thatcher. English nationalism remains a potent subterranean force in the electorate (Heath *et al.* 1999). But, despite the urgings of Tory pamphleteers for a century, the spirit of the English people has not yet been aroused in its majesty.

Both Chamberlain and Powell showed, too, that English nationalism divides the Conservative Party. In 1903 and since 1988 (as also in 1846), the Tories have been deeply divided between English nationalists and free trade internationalists. This division underlay Heath's sacking of Powell, demanded by the internationalist Tory elites and resisted by their nationalist grass roots. One striking parallel unites the plight of the Conservative Party in 1906 and 1997. One might expect that catastrophic defeat leads people to abandon the policies on which they have just been defeated. It did not, nor did it for Labour after 1979. Although I have no systematic evidence, I suspect a safe seat effect. The Tories left in Parliament in 1906 and 1997, like the Labour members left in 1979 and 1983, were by definition the holders of safe seats. If the Chicago political economy of trade policy is correct, then the safest seats for a protectionist party, or a party with a protectionist wing, are those whose local industry is most vulnerable to international trade. This fits the position of the protectionists reasonably well in 1846 (Schonhardt-Bailey 1994) and in 1906 (Marrison 1983; Irwin 1994). The true believers are left as uncomprehending as Chamberlain in 1906. They cannot see how and why their message has failed elsewhere.

APPENDIX 5.1

Did Enoch Powell Win the 1970 General Election for the Conservatives? Did He Win the February 1974 General Election for Labour?

The Problem

Here is a tantalizing piece of counterfactual history. In 1970, Enoch Powell was hugely popular and hugely prominent, thanks to his speeches on immigration and race. Although he had been dismissed from the Conservative Shadow Cabinet, he urged people to vote Conservative. Because of Powell (and only because of Powell), the Conservatives were perceived as the party most likely to restrict coloured immigration—a position supported by the large majority of the electorate. The Conservatives won. In February 1974, Powell was still very popular (not quite so popular as in 1970). He had broken with the Conservatives over the UK's entry to the European Economic Community. He urged people to vote Labour. Labour won. Did Powell cause either or both of these outcomes?

Seats and Votes

Appendix Table 5.1 gives the UK share of seats and votes won by Labour and the Conservatives in the two elections in question. The first point to note is that the Ulster Unionists were part of the Conservative coalition in 1970, but not in 1974 (or since). The coalition between the two parties, which dated back to 1922, was broken when

Appendix Table 5.1. Votes and seats, General elections of 1970 and February 1974

	1970			F1974		
	Seats (n)	Seats (%)	Votes (%)	Seats (n)	Seats (%)	Votes (%)
Cons less UU	322	51.11	45.1	297	46.77	37.8
UU	8	1.27	1.3	11	1.73	1.4
Total Cons	330	52.38	46.4	297	46.77	37.8
Lab	287	45.56	43.0	301	47.4	37.1
All others	13	2.06	10.6	26	4.09	23.7

Source: Butler and Pinto-Duschinsky 1970 and Butler and Kavanagh 1974, Appendix 1 in each case. 1970 Northern Ireland figures: our disaggregation. UU = Ulster Unionist (1970); Anti-Assembly Unionist (1974).

the Heath government abolished the devolved Stormont parliament in 1972, after the Northern Ireland government had refused to give control over the security forces to the British government. Enoch Powell had no direct influence on these events. (His involvement with the Ulster Unionists began after the abolition of Stormont and the Conservative–Unionist split.) The Conservative loss in 1974 can therefore be split into two components, which did not interact: a Unionist loss of known size (eleven seats), and a Powell effect of unknown size (the sum of any pro-Conservative Powell effect in 1970 and any pro-Labour Powell effect in 1974).

To separate any Powell effect from the Unionist effect, therefore, we have to treat the Conservative Party in 1970 as if it did not include the (then eight) Ulster Unionists. Note that without the Unionists, the Conservatives still held more than half of the seats in the UK. If the split had happened before 1970, it would not have prevented Heath from forming a government then. At the 1974 dissolution, the Conservatives had lost six seats at by-elections and through one unfilled vacancy, leaving them with still the barest overall majority possible—316 seats—not counting the Ulster Unionists.

What if the split had not happened by February 1974? Then the coalition would have held 308 seats. This is a difficult counterfactual to take far, because a world in which the Conservatives and Ulster Unionists had not split (but nothing else had turned out differently) is difficult to envisage. But probably, nothing would have happened differently to the actual outcome. In the actual world, Heath still had the first move, being the incumbent Prime Minister, after the election result was known. The Queen did not (and could not) send for Wilson until Heath reported that he had failed to come to an agreement with the Liberals to form either a coalition or a minority government. A counterfactual Heath with eleven more seats would have had the moral advantage of heading the largest single party. But it would have conferred no constitutional advantage. Had no party leader been an incumbent, it would have done, as the Queen would have sent for him first as the leader of the largest party. But as he was the incumbent, this is irrelevant. His hypothetical 308 seats, plus the Liberals' fourteen, would have constituted a bare majority 322. But the ideological distance in such a coalition between the Liberals and the Ulster Unionists would have been vast. Jeremy Thorpe, the Liberal leader, would almost certainly been unable to carry his party into such a coalition. He *would* have been in a stronger position to bargain with Wilson than he actually was. When Heath resigned, Wilson formed a minority government, ignoring the Liberals. He could not have done that in our counterfactual world, given that the Liberals could have voted with the hypothetical Conservative–Unionist coalition against a Wilson Queen's Speech. So the unexpected conclusion of our 1974 counterfactual is that the position of the Conservatives would have been no stronger, but the Liberals would have been able to extract formal concessions from Wilson. Holding the position of Powell constant and altering that of the Unionists does not change the conclusions of this appendix.

As Appendix Table 5.1 shows, the Conservatives got more votes, but fewer seats, than Labour in February 1974. This resulted from the biases in the system of mapping from seats to votes. This is discussed at the end of this Appendix. One consequence of it is that Powell need only have influenced a very small proportion of the voters towards Labour for his influence to have been crucial.

Aggregate Analysis

In principle, two sorts of data are relevant. Aggregate data (here, election statistics) reveal information about groups of people, but not about individuals. In the UK, election results are not published for any unit smaller than the parliamentary constituency. It is an offence to reveal how any individual voted. Individual-level data can only come from instruments such as surveys, which ask a representative sample of the population political questions such as 'how did you vote?', 'how do you rank Enoch Powell?', and 'what do you think are the most important issues facing the country today?' Both aggregate and individual data can be brought to bear. Each suffers from some methodological problems, to be discussed below.

The best-known aggregate-level analysis of the 1970 election results is that by Steed (1971) in his regular appendix to the Nuffield election study of the 1970 General Election (Butler and Pinto-Duschinsky 1971). He did not see any 'Powell effect' in the Conservatives' favour, although he did note an exceptionally high swing to Conservative in the seats around Wolverhampton SW and also in Leicester. He did say that 'the evidence that Mr Powell helped the Labour party by mobilising support for it from coloured immigrants is extremely strong', pointing out that some constituencies with many coloured immigrants swung less to the Conservatives than the mean (Steed 1971: 393–407, quoted at p. 406). Furthermore the swing where the Conservative candidate was a Powellite was no different to the swing where the Conservative candidate was not a Powellite (Deakin and Bourne 1970).

Steed (1974) implicitly conceded that he had been wrong in 1970 to ignore a pro-Conservative local Powell effect. He pointed to the unusually high swing in the Black Country to Labour in the February 1974 General Election, and attributed it to a return to normal after what he now called the 'Powell swing' in that area to the Conservatives in 1970 (Steed 1974: 331–2, quoted at p. 315). In another appendix to the 1970 Nuffield election study, Crewe and Payne (1971) examined the residuals from a regression of the percentage of manual workers on the percentage of Labour vote (the latter, dependent, variable being expressed as the Labour proportion of the combined Labour and Conservative vote). They examined and classified the outliers—the cases where the Labour vote was furthest above, and below, the level predicted by the regression. In the high outliers they find no trace of 'extremely strong' pro-Labour Powell effect found by Steed and Deakin/Bourne. If there was a pro-Labour Powell effect due to immigrants voting Labour, it must have been countered in those seats by a pro-Conservative Powell effect from whites voting Conservative. In the low outliers, however, they do note a cluster of nine seats in the West Midlands, including Powell's, where the Labour share of the two-party vote was around 20 per cent below the level predicted by the regression. However, when they later fitted a multivariate model (Crewe and Payne 1976), they were surprised to find that proportion of New Commonwealth population was not a significant predictor.

So there were net local Powell effects in 1970, and they favoured the Conservatives. But any local effects are a small part of the story. If Powell induced a proportion of the voters all over the country to lean towards the Conservatives, such an effect will be even in all constituencies, and will not show up in the analyses discussed in the previous paragraph. We need to move from aggregate to individual-level analysis to capture any countrywide effects.

Individual Analysis

The most detailed study of these was Studlar (1975, 1978). As Studlar rightly says, to argue that an issue affected an election result one must first show at least two things: that the issue was salient, and that voters perceived a difference between the parties on it. The British Election Study (Butler and Stokes 1969, 1974) shows that for all three General Elections from 1964 to 1970 the answer to the first question was *Yes*. People cared deeply about immigration and race. Furthermore, there was potential for one party to make big gains from the issue, as opinion was very skewed. In the three waves of the British Election Study from 1964 to 1970, the proportion of respondents agreeing with the statement that 'too many immigrants have been let into this country' never dropped below 81.5 per cent. However, in 1964 and 1966, the answer to the second question was *No*. Voters perceived no real difference between the Conservative and Labour parties' approaches to immigration. By 1970, the second condition had changed. Most voters perceived the Conservative Party as the more restrictionist. This was due, not to either of the party leaders, but to Powell. In fact, the signals sent out by the party leaders were in the opposite direction. Labour sent out restrictionist signals with a White Paper in 1965, followed by the Commonwealth Immigration Act 1968. Heath sent out an anti-restrictionist signal by sacking Powell for the 'rivers of blood' speech. Yet so powerful was Powell's appeal that the electorate took his approach for the Conservatives'.

Like Crewe and Payne, Studlar estimates a multivariate regression model for the probability of voting Labour in 1970, but based on individual rather than aggregate data. He starts by dividing the sample into those who thought that Labour was 'more likely to keep immigrants out' ($n \approx 76$); those who saw no difference between the parties ($n \approx 350$), and those who saw the Conservatives as 'more likely to keep immigrants out' ($n \approx 576$; all ns calculated by regrouping figures in Studlar 1978: Table 5.) Running a regression model for the last group only, he found that 'the total net increment to the Conservatives on the basis of the immigration issue alone was 6.7 percent' (Studlar 1978: 61). The number thinking that Labour was more likely to keep immigrants out was too small for any valid inference to be made about any increased propensity for them to vote Labour (Studlar 1975: 320). But the very smallness of this group means that Studlar's estimate of a 6.7 per cent gain to the Conservatives among those who perceived them as the restrictionist need not be offset much by the opposite mechanism. Therefore, the net Conservative increment in the whole sample was around 3.8 per cent. A 3.8 per cent gain to the Conservatives implies something like a 3.8 per cent loss to Labour, and therefore (to be conservative) something like a 3.5 per cent swing from Labour to Conservative on account of the Powell effect. If this estimate is correct, the Powell effect was huge. But for Powell, the Conservatives would not have been perceived as the more restrictionist party. Instead of winning the 1970 election by 3 percentage points, they would have trailed by between 0.5 and 1 percentage point. Studlar's data covers England only, but with immigration being less of an issue in the non-English parts of the UK, that is unlikely to distort our results very much. If it does distort them, it is in the direction of *under*-estimating the Powell effect.

Studlar's dataset does not cover 1974, but Schoen (1977) gives alternative data from which estimates of the Powell effect in both 1970 and 1974 can be derived by a different methodology. Appendix Table 5.2 gives the data. Talk is cheap. We have no way of knowing how many of NOP's respondents translated their 'more likely to vote' for one party into the act of actually voting for it. In any case, many of them were probably already supporters of the party in question. The following calculations therefore assume that only a small proportion of respondents translated talk into doing something different in the election than, but for Powell, they would have done. Three sorts of action are relevant:

Appendix Table 5.2. Powell's impact on partisan choice, 1970 and February 1974

	June 1970	Feb. 1974
More likely to vote Cons.	37	2
Less likely to vote Cons	23	N/a
More likely to vote Lab	N/a	6
Neither/no effect	40	87
Net gain to Cons	14	
Net gain to Lab		4
DK	–(see note)	5
	100	100

Source: *NOP Political Bulletin*, June/July 1970 and Feb. 1974, reported in Schoen (1977: Tables 3.3. and 6.4). Of the two differences between the ways the questions were asked, one is immaterial. In 1970 respondents were asked to contrast 'more likely to vote Conservative' with 'less likely to vote Conservative'. In 1974, the same first option was paired with 'more likely to vote Labour'. However, the variables of interest are the net figures for 'more likely to vote Conservative' in 1970 and for 'more likely to vote Labour' in 1974. By subtraction, these are unambiguously 14 and 4 percent respectively. The second difference is that in 1974 the question was asked of all respondents. In 1970 it was asked only after a filter question on whether the respondent thought Powell had played a role in the national campaign. This filter accounts for the absence of Don't Knows in the reported 1970 figures. However, other evidence shows that the level of Don't Knows about any question relating to Powell at the time was unprecedentedly low.

1. Switching from Lab to Cons (1970); from Cons to Lab (1974).
2. Moving from the perceived anti-Powell party to abstention.
3. Moving from abstention to the perceived pro-Powell party.

The first action results in a switch of two votes (the losing party getting one fewer, and the gaining party getting one more). The other two each result in a switch of one vote.

The counterfactual calculation needs three steps. First, we calculate how many votes each party would have got but for Powell. Then, we translate that hypothetical vote total into a seat total. Finally, we test the sensitivity (robustness) of our results to sampling error and to alternative assumptions about how many people might have translated talk (to NOP) into action (at the polling booth).

The first step is easy once one has taken a figure for the last unknown. To get going, let us assume that 10 per cent of the net 14 per cent (1970) and net 4 per cent (1974) of respondents who said that Powell swayed them actually acted on it. This implies 1.4 per cent of all voters (1970); 0.4 per cent of all voters (1974). Of these numbers, let us next assume that half switched parties, and half moved to or from abstention. These assumptions translate into the following vote shares demonstrated in Table 5.3. Next, we apply these numbers to Steed's (1971: Table 10; 1974: Table 12) tables of the vote/seat mapping for the uniform swing they imply, viz. a swing of 1.05 per cent to Labour in 1970 and a swing of 0.3 per cent to Conservative in 1974. After interpola-

Appendix Table 5.3. Hypothetical vote shares, in absence of Powell effect

	1970		F1974	
	Actual votes (%)	Hypothetical votes (%)	Actual votes (%)	Hypothetical votes (%)
Cons excl. UU	45.1	44.05	37.8	38.1
Lab	43.0	44.15	37.1	36.8
All others inc UU	10.6	10.6	23.7	23.7

Appendix Table 5.4. Hypothetical seat shares, in absence of Powell effect

	1970		F1974	
	Hypothetical votes (%)	Hypothetical seats (n)	Hypothetical votes (%)	Hypothetical seats (n)
Cons excl. UU	44.05	304	38.1	304
Lab	44.15	308	36.8	294
All others inc. UU	10.6	18	23.7	37

tion, and exclusion of the Ulster Unionist seats from the Conservative total in 1970, we derive Appendix Table 5.4.

Bias, Proportionality, and Confidence Intervals

In any plurality electoral system, the mapping from vote shares to seat shares has two distinct properties, its *bias* and its *responsiveness* (Gelman and King 1994). The *bias* of the system, as between the two leading parties, is the seat advantage that one of them would have if their vote shares were equal. The *responsiveness* of the system is, roughly, the proportion of seats that change hands for every unit change in votes. In both 1970 and 1974, the net bias in the UK electoral system favoured Labour. Most contemporaries expected it to decline between the two elections because a redistribution of seats took place. Redistributions always tend to reduce a bias towards Labour that builds up gradually as an apportionment of seats ages. But in 1974 this effect was more than outweighed by effects in the other direction (essentially, that the Conservatives lost more seats than did Labour to the insurgent Liberals and Nationalists). The pro-Labour bias in 1974 is most easily seen in the fact that Labour won fewer votes but more seats than the Conservatives.

A more exact definition of bias and responsiveness can be derived from the following equation:

$$\frac{S_{con}}{S_{lab}} = \alpha + \left(\frac{V_{con}}{V_{lab}}\right)^{\beta}$$
(1)

where

	S_{con}	=	Conservative share of seats
	S_{lab}	=	Labour share of seats
	V_{con}	=	Conservative share of votes cast
	V_{lab}	=	Labour share of votes cast
	α	=	bias term
	β	=	responsiveness exponent

In a system with exactly even sized districts, uniform turnout in each district, and no movements to or from third parties, the bias term α would be 0. In 1970 it was −0.013 approximately (negative signs meaning biases to Labour, positive signs meaning biases to the Conservatives). In other words, if the Conservative and Labour parties had had identical votes, Labour would have held 4 more than the Conservatives out of the 612 that they held between them. In 1974 the pro-Labour bias had widened to −0.052 approximately. With even vote shares at that election, Labour would have held 16 seats more than the Conservatives out of the 598 that they jointly controlled.

In a system with pure proportional representation, the value of the exponent β would be 1. Then the distribution of seats would be an exact microcosm of the distribution of votes. It is well known that the plurality electoral system usually exaggerates the lead of the winning party. In Britain this relationship has been commonly, but wrongly, called the 'cube law', meaning that β had the value 3. The cube law is not a law; it is a special case of the more general relationship captured in Equation (1). The cube law requires certain assumptions to be true about the geographical dispersion of support for each of the two parties in the equation, and for there to be no serious third parties. As neither of these applied in 1970–4, the value of β was not 3 but approximately 2.

On the basis of both the British Election Study data analysed by Studlar, and the NOP data presented by Schoen and analysed here, our answer to both title questions is *Yes. Powell did win the 1970 General Election for the Conservatives. And he did win the February 1974 General Election for Labour.* How confident can we be of these conclusions? There are two elements to consider—the confidence intervals directly attaching to the survey responses reported, and the effect of changing the arbitrarily chosen proportion of Powellites who may have turned preference into action.

The Studlar data come replete with significance tests. The crucial finding quoted above is statistically significant (Studlar 1975: Table VII-5). The NOP/Schoen data are more speculative than the BES/Studlar data, but they are all we have for 1974. One reliability check on them for 1970 is that Gallup asked a very similar question in June 1970 to NOP's, and got a very similar answer, with a net 11 per cent of respondents saying that Powell's speeches made them 'more inclined' to vote Conservative (Gallup 1975: ii. 1100). Another is that the Schoen data, on our methodology, gives a very similar result for 1970 to the more comprehensive Studlar data. However, we can use Equation 1 and/or the tables in Steed (1971: Table 10; 1974: Table 12) to assess the minimum proportion of the voters who need to have been swayed by Powell for him to have been decisive. There are two thresholds: an overall majority of seats (316 in 1970, 318 in 1974), and the status of largest single party.

The Conservatives (minus the Ulster Unionists, as throughout this analysis) would have fallen below the threshold of 316 in 1970 on a 0.3 per cent swing against them. This would be achieved in a no-Powell-effect world if 0.3 per cent of the total vote, which would but for Powell have gone Labour, went Conservative (or if a total of 0.6 per cent of the total vote moved either from Labour to abstention or from abstention to Conservative). This would require only about 2.14 per cent of the Powellites to switch, or double that proportion to move to or from abstention. In 1974 it would have taken a swing of about 1 per cent to give the Conservatives an overall majority. That is beyond the upper bound of the Powell effect according to the NOP/Schoen data.

The Conservatives would have ceased to be the largest single party in 1970 on a 0.9 per cent swing against them. Therefore all the numbers for 1970 in the previous paragraph need to be multiplied by 3 to get the lower bound for the Powell effect. These are still modest requirements. In 1974, the Conservatives were behind Labour in terms of seats. If the Powell effect led to a swing of only 0.15 per cent, it delivered what would have been the Conservatives' two most marginal seats to Labour, and therefore made Labour and not the Conservatives the largest party.

Finally (as the Unionist split had not in fact happened in 1970), can we say that the 1970 Powell effect was so large that without it, Labour would have been the largest party, or held a majority of seats before the Unionist complication is brought in? On the Studlar model, yes. On the Schoen model, Labour would have needed a 1 per cent swing to become largest party over a united Conservative and Unionist phalanx. It would have needed a 1.5 per cent swing to gain an absolute majority of seats. These are well within the range of possibilities on the NOP/Schoen figures.

Conclusion

Therefore the conclusion that Powell delivered the 1970 election to the Conservatives is robust. The evidence that he delivered the 1974 election to Labour is less robust. But, because that result in terms of seats was so close, any Powell effect at all contributed to the fatal weakness of Edward Heath after that election.

6

Lloyd George: Supreme Tactician and Ambitious Strategist

Lloyd George—a Thumbnail Sketch

David Lloyd George was born in 1863. He was brought up in a fiercely Dissenting and Welsh-speaking household in north Wales. The man who was closest to him as Prime Minister wrote, 'Hostility to privilege and to English domination was early sown in his arrogant and sensitive nature alongside an intense pride in a national heritage ignored by the local ruling caste.'[1] He became a solicitor in Porthmadog, the intensely Welsh slate-exporting port at the top of Cardigan Bay.

The first County Council elections took place in 1889 under Salisbury's Act of 1888. They gave Welsh nationalist liberals their biggest electoral opportunity to date, and drew Lloyd George into politics. A year later, he was adopted as Liberal candidate for Caernarvon Boroughs, which he won (fairly narrowly) in a by-election and held for the rest of his Commons life. From 1890 to 1899 his main campaigns were on Welsh Nonconformist issues, fighting guerrilla raids on the power of the Anglican Church in Wales under the leadership of Tom Ellis (on whom see Masterman 1972). With Ellis's premature death in 1899, Lloyd George ceased to be primarily a Welsh politician and became primarily a British politician. But those who said, and still say, that he turned his back on Wales misunderstand him profoundly.

One of the sources of Lloyd George's strength was that he was a clear-eyed outsider tao the British establishment. He was not interested in its blandishments and did not care about hurting it. The parallel with Parnell is striking; that with Chamberlain is also fairly close. The House of Lords obstructed the Nonconformists of Wales in his early career. Very well, he could provoke them into ever more counter-productive extremism in 1909, in order to weaken their position. He could lead the campaign to restrict

---

[1] Tom Jones, biography of Ll.G in *Dictionary of National Biography* (CD-Rom version).

their powers in 1910–11. And, once he found out that there was a market in political honours, he could exploit it to the fullest possible extent. If people were stupid enough to spend good money in becoming peers, there were gains from trade all round. The purchaser of honours got the piece of ermine that he wanted; Lloyd George got the party funding that he wanted.

Similarly, he could make surprising alliances with others who were not from the traditional ruling class—various labour leaders; Arthur Griffith; Bonar Law. It did not always work. One failure was on Christmas Day 1915 (McLean 1999d: 49–62); another was with De Valera in July 1921, as described below. But Lloyd George was one of the most successful of all British politicians at seeing the world from the other party's viewpoint, at least well enough to strike a deal where others could not.

Third, from his background he got outstanding rhetorical skills—in two languages. Though Lloyd George was never religious, he learnt the skills of oratory from the uncle who brought him up, a fiery Welsh preacher. One of the rhetorical arts is to make the same words mean different things to different hearers. Lloyd George was a master of this, as we shall see when we discuss his Irish negotiations in detail. And one who speaks two languages where most of those he speaks to speak only one has a double advantage. At least once, he used this skill to effect in the Irish negotiations.

Lloyd George rose rapidly through the Liberal ranks after he emerged from the shadow of Tom Ellis. A leading 'pro-Boer' and then campaigner against the Unionist government's education acts, he went straight into the Cabinet, as President of the Board of Trade, in the 1905 Liberal administration. In 1908 he became Chancellor of the Exchequer, in 1915 Minister of Munitions, in July 1916 Minister of War, and in December 1916 Prime Minister. He stayed in that post until October 1922, when he and the rest of his Coalition ministry were toppled by a backbench Conservative revolt (hence the title '1922 Committee' for the executive committee of the backbench Conservatives in the Commons). He never held office again. In January 1945, with only three months to live, he was appointed to the House of Lords—as much to avoid an embarrassing election contest in Caernarvon Boroughs as for any other reason.

The heresthetic of Lloyd George involved reducing, not increasing, the dimensionality of politics. Although himself very much part of centre–periphery politics, he succeeded in getting the biggest such issue—Ireland—off the political agenda for fifty years. As politics reduced itself to the class dimension, the Liberal Party would be vulnerable unless it could establish itself as a hegemonic party, controlling a large coalition including the median voter. This Lloyd George failed to do in the end. But it was an interesting failure, which came closer to success than most historians seem willing to concede.

Liberals, Labour, and Irish

Consider the strategic position in British politics when Lloyd George took office in December 1905. The Unionist government had resigned in disarray and exhaustion. Joseph Chamberlain's campaign for Tariff Reform and imperialism had captured the Conservative Party in the country but not the whole of the government nor, as the 1906 General Election was to show, the electorate. The Liberals swept to power with 400 seats. Their allies in the Labour Representation Committee (LRC) added a further thirty. The two parties had concluded a pact not to oppose one another in most seats. The LRC promptly renamed itself the Labour Party. The Liberals' more awkward and strictly contingent allies, the Irish Party, contributed yet a further eighty-three seats, seventy-four of them unopposed—the Irish Party's dominance over Catholic Ireland was total, although it was beset by internal strains. So the 'progressive alliance', as some contemporaries called it, controlled 513 out of the 670 seats in the Commons (76.57 per cent). The Conservatives were reduced to 157, their worst performance since 1832, not to be matched until 1997.

A Liberal triumph, then? Not exactly; and not only because we now know what happened to it. The danger signs were already there, and all leading politicians including Lloyd George must have been able to see them. First of all, the electoral system performed its usual trick of exaggerating a narrow majority in votes to a huge majority in seats. The Liberals won only 49 per cent of the votes cast, while the Conservatives got 43.6 per cent (compare their 30.7 per cent in 1997). Furthermore, the bias in the system, which up to then had favoured the Unionists, swung over to benefit the Liberals (see Chapter 4). If the Labour vote is counted in with the Liberal vote, the allied share rises to 54.9 per cent. The Irish share is almost impossible to calculate, because of all the unopposed returns. But the danger from the Irish Party was not that their share of the Irish vote was at risk. Rather, it was that their demands put intolerable strain on British politics. The election had been lost by the Conservatives, not won by the Liberals. Conservative unity would return, at some time. And the House of Lords, unapologetically Conservative, still held a veto over legislation.

What should a rational Liberal politician do, then? We cannot avoid the advantage of hindsight. But an *a priori* list for an intelligent politician in December 1905 would have been:

- Widen the social and intellectual base of Liberalism
- Incorporate the Labour Party and its voters into an unbreakable hegemonic progressive party
- Curb the power of the House of Lords
- Get rid of the Irish question

Lloyd George tried all four. When all due allowance is made to the role of Campbell-Bannerman, Asquith, Winston Churchill, and a few other politicians, Lloyd George stands out by far as the politician who did most to turn the Liberals into a hegemonic party. He nearly pulled it off.

The fact that the Conservatives lost the election rather than the Liberals winning it, together with the huge Liberal majority of seats, gave them breathing space. The Conservatives lost through their sheer disunity. Had they been united, they might have presented an electorally popular package of imperialism, xenophobia, and protection—the last packaged as 'Empire Free Trade'. Never had they so powerfully corralled imperialism and xenophobia to their cause as they had done during and immediately after the Boer War. For instance, consider the leaflet 'A Disgraceful Exhibition' (March 1902) (above: p. 97) and its telling reference to

LOUD LAUGHTER AND SHOUTS OF DELIGHT FROM THE NATIONALIST BENCHES. THE VOCIFEROUS CHEERING LASTED FOR NEARLY A MINUTE. . . . These are the men with whom Sir Henry Campbell-Bannerman . . . hoped the Liberal Party would work in 'CORDIAL COOPERATION'. Loyal Englishmen, Scotsmen, and Irishmen, always remember those cheers.

The charge that Liberals were unpatriotic had been devastating before and would be devastating again, as soon as the Conservatives could reunite. (No prudent Liberal could have calculated, in 1905, that the Conservatives would not be reunited until 1912.) Lloyd George knew well what it was to be a 'proBoer'. However popular his stance had been within the Liberal Party, he had had to escape one of his meetings disguised as a policeman to avoid the wrath of the crowd. The Liberals had won in 1906 on free trade and Chinese labour. The latter was a strictly short-term issue, and free trade was unlikely to retain its mass appeal. The Liberals needed a new electoral and social base.

Widening the Social and Intellectual Base of Liberalism; Curbing the Power of the House of Lords

The Liberals in 1905 faced the same problem as Disraeli's Tories in 1846: their social base was too narrow. The classic Liberal coalition forged by Gladstone involved urban capital, the non-English and remote parts of the geographical periphery, and those who were not of the established religion. The coalition had intellectual coherence: it could argue for free trade and freedom of religion, and against established institutions that impeded the one or the other. Lloyd George was himself part of that social base as a Welsh Nonconformist. But urban capitalists had been deserting the Liberals since before the Home Rule crisis of 1886, and that event speeded up the decline. Many of them had become Liberal Unionists. They entered the Conservative coalition when the Liberal Unionists and Conservatives coalesced. Gladstone had been able to keep (some of) the leaders of capital and of labour in the same party;

his successors could not. Politics brought up more and more issues that divided urban labour from urban capital, including the issues that the Labour Representation Committee was founded in 1900 to pursue (see next subsection). Meanwhile, the old issues of land and religion, which united capital and labour, were declining. Although religion remained the best determinant of voting as late as 1910, a prescient politician could see that class was taking its place. Free trade, which in 1846 had united capital and labour, was by 1905 much more ambiguous. Both capital and labour were divided between exporting sectors of the economy, which benefited, and import-competing sectors, which suffered. Disraeli and Salisbury had created a potent second dimension—imperialism and xenophobia—which helped to preserve the Conservatives. Although Chamberlain had just signally failed to win with that coalition, the second dimension would certainly recur in the shape of the Irish question, and an intelligent Liberal could see that in the long run the Liberals must get rid of the fateful Irish alliance that crippled both parties.

The Liberal Party went into government with an agenda of Gladstonian measures: education reform; temperance reform; licensing reform; disestablishment of the Anglican Church in Wales. All of these failed, mauled in the Lords. If Liberal politicians, including Lloyd George, had still thought of these measures as their core agenda, they would have used them as the ground for the constitutional attack on the Lords which finally came between 1909–11. The issues seemed clearcut. A government that had won a clear majority in the elected house proposed all of these measures. None of them was a surprise. The unelected Lords could not say in their own defence that these were unprecedented or new ideas that needed the caution and sagacity of a revising chamber. They threw them out because they did not like them. But when the attack on the Lords came, it was not on education, nor licensing, nor Welsh disestablishment. It was on Lloyd George's 'People's Budget' of 1909. Lloyd George and Asquith had chosen on which ground to fight and on which ground not to.

Demography was inexorably moving the majority of the population to the cities and suburbs. Electoral change lagged behind population change, and change in the composition of the median parliamentary constituency lagged still further. The growing population centres had a smaller proportion of their population on the electoral register than did the declining population centres. And, although the 1885 redistribution of parliamentary seats was the first to aim for something like population equality between constituencies, it allowed many anomalies to stand and—more important—contained no mechanism for boundary revision to keep the constituency pattern in line with the pattern of population change. Therefore the median constituency was more rural than the median voter, who was more rural than the median adult male. But no foreseeable change would ever restore rural dominance. Every change, whether in the franchise or in constituency boundaries, would move the median constituency closer to the median adult. Although, for the reasons we have already examined, no franchise bill succeeded between 1905 and 1918, Lloyd George knew that one must come.

Incorporating the Labour Party into a Hegemonic Progressive Party

Lloyd George did not create the progressive alliance between Liberals and Labour. That was initiated by Herbert Gladstone (Liberal chief whip, son of W. E. Gladstone, flier of the calamitous Hawarden Kite in 1885) and Ramsay MacDonald (rhetorical but pragmatic secretary of the Labour Representation Committee). During 1903 MacDonald made numerous approaches, through an intermediary, to Gladstone, and impressed him with the fact that if Labour and the Liberals fought one another at a General Election, they would both lose. The MacDonald–Gladstone Pact was concluded in Leicester Isolation Hospital in September 1903. It gave the Labour Party (as the LRC renamed itself after the 1906 election) a clear run in twenty-four seats, many of them two-member boroughs where the parties put up one candidate each. Both parties somehow managed to persuade their local activists not to put up candidates in seats that had been assigned to the other party, without revealing that there was a pact between them (Marquand 1977: 72–93).

Lloyd George's first known intervention in a labour dispute was on behalf of fifty railwaymen who had been sacked because they would not or could not speak English (Wrigley 1976: 11). Labour and nationality were entwined in the longest and bitterest industrial dispute of the era, which took place in and around Lloyd George's constituency. This was the lock-out of slate quarrymen by Lord Penrhyn in 1897 and again from 1900 to 1903. The quarrymen had a strong, solidaristic, entirely Welsh culture that enabled them to survive the dispute (R. M. Jones 1982: 175–266). Passions ran deep. The row of houses near Bethesda that Lord Penrhyn built for his imported employees is still known locally as 'Traitors' Row'. But the quarrymen were radicals, not socialists. So was Lloyd George. His speech to the 1902 Trades Union Congress (TUC 1902: 61) attacked Lord Penrhyn as 'feudal' but did not propose any socialist solution to the conflict. As he had written ten years before:

I cannot understand why there should be any necessity for a separate Labour Party at all. . . . Inasmuch as those interested in Labour questions compose the overwhelming majority of the electorate of the United Kingdom, they have only to . . . take the simple course of joining Liberal Associations and then select candidates who fairly represent their views. . . The danger of the labour movement at the present moment seems to be to confine itself to one or two questions of what I cannot but help thinking [sic] to be of secondary importance. . . . I consider the land question, the temperance question and the question of Disestablishment to be equally matters of interest to labourers as an Eight Hours Bill (October 1892; quoted in Wrigley 1976: 24).

The idea that 'labour questions' were somehow subordinate to the real political issues of the day was commonplace; indeed it was shared by Keir Hardie,
the founder of the Labour Party (see McLean 1975: 87–8). The main division
in what Edwardians called the 'progressive movement' was not between
liberals and socialists. It was between those who thought labour interests
should be promoted in a separate party and those who thought they should
form an interest group in the Liberal Party. From 1908 until around 1921,
Lloyd George led the latter group. He thought that 'the greatest danger to the
Liberals will arise from a split between Liberalism and Labour, such as
destroyed Liberalism in Germany and elsewhere' (1909; quoted in Murray
(1980: 207); cf. also Wrigley (1976: 26) for the same sentiment in 1904). Once
he became Chancellor of the Exchequer in 1908, he was in a position to do
something about it. The 1908 Budget (prepared and introduced by his predecessor Asquith, although Lloyd George had already become Chancellor)
introduced non-contributory old-age pensions. The Budget of 1909 had to
raise money to pay for the pensions (and also for rearmament). To begin with,
Lloyd George did not intend the 1909 Budget to be an election weapon. But
it was bitterly attacked by landowners. The Duke of Buccleuch refused to pay
a guinea subscription to his local football club because of the swingeing duties
proposed by the Budget (Jenkins 1968: 88–9). Lloyd George eagerly grasped
the opportunity. He told his brother in August,

There is undoubtedly a popular rising such as has not been witnessed over a generation. What will happen if they throw it out I can conjecture and I rejoice at the prospect.
Many a rotten institution, system and law will be submerged by the deluge. I wonder
whether they will be such fools. I am almost wishing they should be stricken with
blindness (LG to William George, 17.08.09, in George 1958: 230).

They were and they were. Lloyd George provoked them at Limehouse in July
and in Newcastle-upon-Tyne in October:

The question will be asked 'Should 500 men, ordinary men, chosen accidentally from
among the unemployed, override the judgment—the deliberate judgment—of millions
of people who are engaged in the industry which makes the wealth of the country?'
That is one question. Another will be, who ordained that a few should have the land
of Britain as a perquisite; who made 10,000 people owners of the soil, and the rest of
us trespassers in the land of our birth[?] (At Newcastle, 09.10.09; Jenkins 1968: 94)

A fully-equipped duke costs as much to keep up as two Dreadnoughts; and dukes are
just as great a terror and they last longer. (At Newcastle, 09.10.09; *The Times* 11.10.09)

The anti-Lords campaign helped the Liberals to win the January 1910 election, which on the evidence of by-elections they would otherwise have lost.
Furthermore, the Unionist leaders knew that they were likely to lose. They
were trapped by numerous forces—Tariff Reform, Joseph Chamberlain dic-
tating messages from his bed, their own unstoppable backwoodsmen—into
the most disastrous tactical mistake the Conservatives have ever made, at least
since 1832. Labour and the Irish Nationalists were trapped too, rather more
subtly. The Irish hated the spirit duties in the Budget, but they hated the

Lords' veto even more. As Home Rule was paramount, they must get rid of the Lords' veto. Therefore they must not vote against the Budget. As for Labour, they were out-orated and outclassed. Lloyd George was at pains to revive the MacDonald–Gladstone pact. He was able to persuade both MacDonald and Keir Hardie that it was in the interests of both parties that they should not stand against one another in winnable seats, so as to ensure that there would be a majority for the Budget in the new Parliament (Murray 1980: 206–7). This corralled Labour. In the January 1910 election, their seat total rose from the thirty of 1906 to forty, but this concealed an underlying decline. The miners' MPs had rebadged themselves from Liberal to Labour in 1908. Labour actually suffered a net loss of seats in the January 1910 election. Crippled by the 1909 Osborne judgment, which outlawed union contributions to political funds until the law was changed in 1913, Labour fought only seventy-eight seats in January and only fifty-six in December, where it improved its net position by only two.

As we know, the 1909 Budget led to the constitutional crisis, in which Lloyd George continued to irritate the peers and the successive kings, while Asquith stood his ground. By 1911 the Liberals were confirmed in power and the Lords' absolute veto had gone. Since, before 1909, nobody had believed that the Lords' veto applied to financial matters anyhow, the constitutional change had less effect on financial policy than on Home Rule and the rest. The crisis did lead to Lloyd George's first attempt to reshape the party system (see below). But here we continue with financial policy, putting topical coherence ahead of chronology.

Lloyd George's next great play for the working-class vote was the National Insurance Bill of 1911. He saw this as a way to free the working class from the clutches of the 'industrial' insurance companies such as the Prudential, who collected small weekly subscriptions half of which, he alleged, were swallowed up in administration costs ('Criccieth Memorandum', 17.08.10, in Scally 1975: 379. Lloyd George Papers C/6/5/1). His enemies saw it as a gigantic bribe—'ninepence for fourpence'—involving a massive cash transfer from taxpayers and employers to the working class. For every 4d (fourpence) paid into the National Insurance fund by each employee it covered, the employer was to pay 3d and the state 2d.

Braithwaite (1957) is the essential record of Lloyd George's manoeuvres. Its only peers are Peel's *Memoir* (Peel 1856–7) and the parts of Tom Jones' diary describing Lloyd George's Irish negotiations (T. Jones 1971). All three are contemporary narratives of heresthetic politicians at the height of their powers. W. J. Braithwaite was a civil servant from the Inland Revenue who found himself the principal draftsman of the sickness part of the National Insurance scheme. His qualifications seem to have been that his father, a clergyman, ran the Stoke and Melford Friendly Society, which gave sickness benefit to Suffolk farm labourers (Braithwaite 1957: 79–80); and that he was endlessly patient and would work on Lloyd George's impossible demands for days and nights on end without sleep. He provides a wonderful picture of Lloyd George making it up as he went along—for instance, decid-ing to add golf caddies to the list of those covered while he and Braith-waite were out golfing. At the same time, Lloyd George's overall political purpose was never in doubt.

The political need was to outflank the Webbs. The Fabian socialist intel-lectuals Sidney and Beatrice Webb had been the moving spirits behind the *Minority Report* (1909) *of the Royal Commission on the Poor Laws* (P. P. 1909 xxxii). The Minority Report argued for a non-contributory scheme of social insurance financed out of general taxation. This would have involved huge redistribution from the healthy and wealthy to the poor and sick. It could have been a rallying-point for the socialists, and one from which an organ-ized socialist party could outbid the contributory scheme that Lloyd George produced as a riposte. Lloyd George could not have got Cabinet approval for a non-contributory scheme, as the non-contributory Old Age Pension scheme was proving much more costly than ministers had anticipated (and had pro-voked the 1909 Budget tax increases). He probably had the same long-term aim as the Webbs. In 1911, he told his private secretary:

Insurance [is] necessarily [a] temporary expedient. At no distant date hope state will acknowledge a full responsibility in the matter of making provision for sickness, break-down and unemployment. It really does so now, through Poor Law; but conditions under which this system had hitherto worked have been so harsh and humiliating that working-class pride revolts against accepting so degrading and doubtful a boon. (LG to R. G. Hawtrey, 07.03.11, in Braithwaite 1957: 24).

If this is to be believed, then the National Insurance scheme of 1911 was a second-best. Yet Lloyd George managed to outflank Labour, incorporate the Conservatives and the Irish, navigate around the vested interests, and produce a scheme that, although unpopular in the short term, was his biggest single contribution to making the Liberals the natural party of the working class.

He outflanked Labour because Labour was itself divided. Some Labour members shared the Webbs' preference for a non-contributory scheme. But the majority were sufficiently close to the Victorian idea of self-help, which was a powerful strand in trade union ideology, that they were captured by the scheme. Under Braithwaite's and Lloyd George's scheme, National Insur-ance would be compulsory for employees earning less than £160 a year. It would be administered not by the state but by approved societies, which must be financially sound and be in some way answerable to their members. Trade unions could fulfil this role—and have a valuable recruiting tool into the bargain. They would be distributing the something for nothing—or at any rate ninepence for fourpence—that Lloyd George seemed to promise. Of course, as any economist would point out, the employer's contribution is really a tax on labour just as much as the employee's contribution. It raised the cost of labour to an employer and the true incidence fell as it always does on labour, not capital. Nevertheless, this is hidden and therefore politically palatable.

Incorporating the trade unions also helped Lloyd George with the other vested interests. It weakened the power of the industrial companies, who had to accept a clause empowering the Insurance Commissioners to decide what constitutional arrangements were acceptable measures of democratic control. In a typical Lloyd Georgian move, he picked up this idea very late on from a friendly society delegate at a conference and within weeks it was in the Act (Braithwaite 1957: 211–12). He faced down the doctors, in a way strikingly similar to that Aneurin Bevan was to employ at the birth of the National Health Service in 1948. On both occasions, the British Medical Association held pledges from the majority of its members that they would not participate in the scheme. Both times, the BMA's bluff was called—successfully (Braithwaite 1957: 38–40; Gilbert 1992: 27–31; for Bevan, see Campbell 1987: 171–8).

Lloyd George had to concede a separate Irish Commission to placate the Irish Party. This infuriated Braithwaite, but was the salvation of the scheme in 1912. The Irish demand was matched by the Scots and Welsh, and Lloyd George could then play off the three non-English commissions—known to the civil servants as the 'Celts'—against the English commission in order to get the scheme up and running in 1912.

He incorporated the Unionist front bench, proposing 'conferences with the Unionist leaders on terms that if they can propose improvements they shall have the credit of moving them later' (Braithwaite 1957: 158)—a proposal thoroughly in the spirit of Lloyd George's coalitionism. The Unionist leaders were inclined to agree, but could not persuade their back-benchers with links to the interests affected.

Most important, he initiated the pretence that the National Insurance fund was a fund. An actuarially sound insurance policy would be unable to pay out in full from day one of the scheme, because it would have to admit older workers (who were worse health risks) at the same time as younger ones, who were better. Lloyd George's aim was always for a 'pay as you go' scheme, in which present benefits were paid out of present contributions, so that today's young and healthy would be paying out to relieve today's old and sick. He provided ingenious arguments for this stance ('the proper course for the Chancellor of he Exchequer was to let money fructify in the pockets of the people, and take it only when he wanted it'—Braithwaite 1957: 88). But he knew he was unlikely to get away with it, and in the end 'he went upstairs to dress for dinner, saying over the banisters, "I am inclined after all to be virtuous"' (Braithwaite 1957: 126–7). Set up so cynically, the National Insurance Fund has never been a fund and the scheme remains as it was from the beginning a form of taxation.

Lloyd George's policies in this era had two consistent features. First, they were poised between the old Liberalism and the new; second, despite this ambiguity, they utterly overshadowed the Labour Party. The first feature is reflected in the prominent place which Drink and The Land still had, e.g. in his coalition memorandum of August 1910 (Morgan 1971: 150–5) and in his

Land Campaign of 1912–14. In the National Insurance legislation, he had wanted to give the Insurance Commissioners the power to shut down pubs in areas of very poor public health. And in 1915 as Minister of Munitions, Lloyd George nationalised the brewery serving the pubs in the munitions district around Carlisle, and introduced the restricted opening hours that survived until very recently (McLean 1999*d*: 13, 19).

The Land Campaign of 1912–14 was intended, in the words of one recent biographer, to be 'the culmination, or a joining together, of all previous Liberal reforms' (Gilbert 1992: 57). It had antecedents in Chamberlain's Unauthorized Programme and the 1891 Newcastle Programme; and it was an understandable revenge on the landed interest, possible only after the great defeat of 1911. Lloyd George launched and ran it in a way very similar to Chamberlain's tariff campaign in 1903. Unfortunately, it had not resulted in any proposals fit to put in legislative form by 1913, which was the deadline beyond which the Lords could veto any land reform until after the 1915 General Election. So Lloyd George determined to put land reform in the only place where the Lords could not touch it, namely his 1914 Budget. There, he proposed to make all land subject to rates (local authority property taxes) on its site value. As in 1911, his detailed proposals were not ready. Unlike in 1911, he was unable to improvise them on the hoof. In June 1914, the Government had to withdraw the land tax proposals, because they could not all be shoehorned into the untouchable Finance Bill. On a wider stage, Lloyd George had failed because he had not managed to make urban land a political issue. His outlook was still that of rural Wales. Land campaigns have not faded away. They have some urban appeal, as witness for instance the mass trespasses in the Peak District in the 1930s, and the Scottish Parliament's taking of land reform as its first issue in 1998. But they are insufficiently central to form a maker or breaker of alignments.

Despite this failure, the Labour Party was hopelessly outclassed. After its one great triumph—the Trade Disputes Act 1906—Labour had contributed nothing to the programme of legislation, was not pivotal in Parliament, and depended on the goodwill of the Liberals for holding almost all of its parliamentary (but not local council) seats. The credit for incorporating Labour by taking over its trade union bill belongs to Campbell-Bannerman. He retired in 1908, to be succeeded by Asquith, who appointed Lloyd George Chancellor of the Exchequer. Lloyd George carried over from the old post to the new one his enthusiasm for fixing labour disputes. He was very good at it; his leader equally bad.

Lloyd George first put his special talents to use on the railway unions, who threatened a national strike in autumn 1907. Railway rates were controlled by law. This reduced the returns to both labour and capital below those obtainable in other industries. Capital got a compensating protection from competition, as each railway company was more or less a local monopoly. Labour got no such compensation. In November 1907, the members of the main rail union, the Amalgamated Society of Railway Servants, voted by a huge majority for a national strike. Lloyd George gave his first virtuoso display. According to one of them, the company representatives went into their meeting with him after

A preliminary meeting at Euston Station, where it was unanimously resolved that we would not yield in the slightest degree. . . . Lloyd George . . . displayed such a thorough acquaintance with all the ins and outs of the subject; . . . dwelt so forcibly on the disastrous consequence to the country of a prolonged strike on the railways . . . that our opposition melted away and we left the conference having consented to the appointment of conciliation boards or committees (Maxwell [1932]: 305–6; quoted in Wrigley 1976: 56)

Lloyd George told his brother, 'Conciliation at first but, failing that, the steam roller' (LG to William George, 21.10.7, in George 1958: 212). Both with the employers and the union, he introduced his characteristic device— the sudden ultimatum. He told each side, in separate meetings, that he needed an immediate decision, or else (Wrigley 1976: 56 (employers); 57 (union).) He infuriated his civil servants with his interventions, as he was later to do at the Treasury (Du Parcq 1912: iii. 495–6; Askwith 1920: 100–30 *passim*).

Or else what? Lloyd George's tactical genius was to persuade people that dire alternatives would follow their failure to agree on the spot, when it is not obvious in hindsight what the dire alternatives were, nor what Lloyd George's real bargaining power was. He most resembles one of these salesmen who advertise heavily in American flight magazines that they can teach you how to close a deal.

Lloyd George pulled it off again in 1911, after his leader Asquith stormed out of a meeting with the rail union leaders saying 'Then your blood be on your head' (17.08.11; in Wrigley 1976: 63). Asquith had not mastered the unspecified 'or else'. A national rail strike began. Lloyd George told friends, 'I could have stopped it if I had been there.' Two days later, he did. According to his colleague R. B. Haldane, quoted seven months later in a letter from Austen Chamberlain to his stepmother, written to keep the invalid Joe informed:

'Suddenly Lloyd George burst into our room exclaiming "A bottle of champagne! I've done it! Don't ask me how, but I've done it! The strike is settled". And', concluded Haldane, 'from that day to this I have never known and none of his colleagues have ever known how it was done' (A. Chamberlain to M. E. Chamberlain 01.03.12, in Chamberlain 1936: 437)

At fourth hand, this may be inadmissible evidence. But it shows what Chamberlain, a Unionist front-bencher, thought of the Welsh wizard whom he was to serve loyally in the Irish negotiations ten years later. Another witness, Rufus Isaacs, told W. J. Braithwaite that 'no other man in the country *could have settled it*' (Braithwaite 1957: 201; stress in original).

As of 4 August 1914, Lloyd George's attempt to turn the Liberals into the working-class party was looking pretty successful. Labour stood to be almost eliminated outside the coalfields in the General Election of 1915 or 1916. The main threat was to the Liberals' activist base. Lloyd George's manoeuvres had alienated many rich Liberals, and as a result the constituency parties were starved of funds and badly organized. The grass-roots activist was, and remained, Lloyd George's greatest unsolved problem.

War led to corporatism. Lloyd George remained Chancellor of the Exchequer until the First Coalition of 1915–16, when he became Minister of Munitions; in the Second Coalition of 1916–18 he was Prime Minister. In all three posts he actively incorporated representatives of capital and labour in the wartime production process. The many businessmen he brought into government, some of whom remained after 1918, represented capital. Labour first entered through the Treasury Agreement of March 1915. Lloyd George made the craft trade unions promise to give up their restrictive practices. In return he promised that they could have them back at the end of the war offered them incorporation in government by consultative committees. (See McLean 1999d: 10, 32–3). This built on foundations laid for the National Insurance Act, which unions were eligible to administer, and paved the way for political as well as industrial incorporation when Arthur Henderson and other Labour ministers were brought into the government in 1915. The promise to let unions restore pre-war trade practices was kept in an Act of 1919.

From 1915 to 1922 Lloyd George's attitude to labour varied unpredictably between authoritarian and corporatist (see e.g. Armitage 1969: 79, 80, where one such swing is tracked). There is little doubt that, before 1914, Lloyd George's sympathies in the class struggle were on the side of labour. (See e.g. the 1908 speeches and letters quoted by Wrigley 1976: 56–7.) During and after the war, his brilliance with the undefined 'or else' was applied to prosecuting the war and running the country. His sympathies with labour—especially with trade union leaders—weakened. During the war, he was closer to individual capitalists than to individual representatives of labour. He exploited his ability to communicate direct with the working man over the heads of Ministers of Labour, employers, trade union officials. Sometimes this worked; sometimes not, as on Christmas Day 1915, when a hall full of Clydeside shop stewards shouted down his praise of the 'great Socialist factories' he had set up to make munitions (McLean 1999d: 53). At other times, Lloyd George had no scruples about repression. He suppressed the Glasgow *Forward* for reporting   meeting; he deported the leading Glasgow engineering shop stewards to Edinburgh in 1916, where presumably he thought they could not stir up revolution (McLean 1999d: chs. 5, 7).

After the war, labour affairs were in the hands of incompetent ministers who panicked ludicrously about Bolshevism. At a Cabinet conference in

February 1920, for instance, the Unionist leader Bonar Law said that 'All weapons ought to be available for distribution to the friends of the Government'. Auckland Geddes (the brother of one of Lloyd George's favourite businessmen, briefly in the Cabinet probably only because his brother was)

pointed to the Universities as full of trained men who could co-operate with clerks and stockbrokers. (During the discussion Bonar Law so often referred to the stockbrokers as a loyal and fighting class until [sic] one felt that potential battalions of stockbrokers were to be found in every town) (T. Jones 1969: 100–1).

Lloyd George 'throughout played the role of taking the revolution very seriously', asking the chief of the RAF 'How many airmen are there available for the revolution?' On being told that the pilots had no weapons for ground fighting, 'The PM presumed they could use machine guns and drop bombs' (T. Jones 1969: 99). As Jones (who was Assistant Cabinet Secretary and a close friend of Lloyd George) makes clear, Lloyd George was playing games. But with panickers in charge of labour relations, the games could turn serious. Luckily, the British revolutionaries were as few and as incompetent as the British ministers, so no blood was shed. But Lloyd George's hopes of becoming the leader of the British working class were shattered, especially by the miners' strike of 1920 (Arnot 1953: ii. 263–70 for LG's 'clever letter' of 5.10.20) and lockout of 1921. He used all his heresthetic wiles to split the miners from the other workers who had announced that they would strike in sympathy. He told Jones, 'I'm sorry for the miners—they're a patriotic lot. I'm not heartless enough for this sort of thing' (T. Jones 1969: 151). But whatever his private feelings, he headed a government which mobilized troops and volunteers to break the strike, organized black propaganda, and ensured the isolation and defeat of the miners (T. Jones 1969: 131–53; McLean 1974: 238).

The 1910 Coalition Proposal

The constitutional crisis was marked by several attempts on the part of the party leaders to rein in their extreme supporters. The most visionary of these was Lloyd George's proposal of August 1910 for a coalition of the two big parties, excluding their own extremists, the Irish Party, the Orangemen, and Labour. After many decades of neglect (Jenkins 1968—originally published in 1954—being for many years the only historian to take it seriously), it is now quite well known, and may be read in full in Scally 1975: 375–83. Some extracts will give the flavour:

I cannot help thinking that the time has arrived for a truce, for bringing the resources of the two Parties into joint stock in order to liquidate arrears which, if much longer neglected, may end in national impoverishment, if not insolvency. . . . None of these great problems can be effectively dealt with without incurring temporary unpopularity. . . . No settlement is possible without exciting a good many ill-informed prejudices, some of them with an historical basis.

Lloyd George goes on to discuss a number of policy areas where he thinks a coalition would work better than a single-party government:

There is Education. Not merely could the denominational question be thus much more satisfactorily disposed of, inasmuch as the Parties are committed to certain controversial solutions which may not be the very best; but there are questions like the raising of the age limit, which is quite essential . . . The whole question of National Defence ought to be boldly faced. I doubt whether we are getting our money's worth in any direction. I am strongly of opinion that even the question of compulsory training should not be shirked. No Party dare touch it.

And, as a footnote to a section on imperial problems, Lloyd George writes:

In this connection the settlement of the Irish Question would come up for consideration. The advantages of a non-party treatment of this vexed problem are obvious. Parties might deal with it without being subject to the embar[r]assing dictation of extreme partisans whether from Nationalist or Orangeman. (All extracts from LG Papers, C/6/5/1)

As the secret coalition talks continued, Lloyd George always managed to persuade each person he talked to that he had come round to that person's point of view (Searle 1995: 73–7). By October, Lloyd George was writing that

A settlement of the Irish Question and of the difficulties of congestion in the House of Commons to be attempted on some such lines as were sketched by Mr Chamberlain in his speech on the first Reading of the Home Rule Bill of 1886. Ireland to be treated as a unit for the purpose of any measure of self-government. This settlement to be of a kind which might form a nucleus for the Federation of the Empire at some future date. (LG, 'Supplementary memorandum', 29.10.10, in Scally 1975: 384–6, quoted at p. 384)

The scheme collapsed because A. J. Balfour, after consulting a former Conservative chief whip, told Lloyd George, 'I cannot become another Robert Peel in my party!' Lloyd George tartly comments,

It was not rejected by the real leaders of the [Unionist] Party, but by men who, for some obscure reason best known to political organisations, have great influence inside the councils of a party without possessing any of the capabilities that excite general admiration and confidence outside. (Lloyd George 1938: i. 23)

By the time he wrote that, he too had become their victim.

Getting Rid of the Irish Question

By 1905, the Irish–Liberal alliance was a curse to both allies. Linked together, they seemed doomed to bring one another down. The cause of Irish Home Rule was desperately unpopular in England, and hardly any more popular in

Scotland and Wales, whatever Scots and Welsh politicians may have said. Even when the Unionists were doing badly, as in December 1905, their combination of imperialism and xenophobia was heady stuff. The Empire mattered. The middle classes could get jobs there; the working classes could hope to emigrate to one of the white Dominions. At home, the Irish were hated because they were at the bottom of the pile. Those just above the bottom of the pile, who saw the Irish as the main threats to their jobs and their housing, tended to hate them most of all. Even the young Keir Hardie said it (McLean 1975: 9).

But Lloyd George saw that the Union was not an unmitigated boon to the Unionist leaders either. In the nineteenth century, Irish landowners such as Wellington had been at the heart of Tory high politics. By 1910 they had gone. Since the anti-landlord agitations of the 1880s, there had been no money, and no future, in Irish landlordism. Great houses were falling into decay; estate incomes were plummeting. The Salisbury and Balfour governments bought out the Irish landlords in Irish Land Acts. By 1910 the Unionist party had no material interest in Catholic Ireland. In the Protestant north, there was a material Unionist interest. However, it lay not in the traditional ruling class and not, therefore, to any degree in the House of Lords. It lay with the representatives of Protestant capital and Protestant labour. Not till the Ulster-Scots-Canadian Bonar Law became Conservative leader in November 1911 was Ulster (as opposed to Irish) Protestantism heard at the top. His accession led Unionist opposition to Home Rule to take a harder, darker turn. In July 1912 Bonar Law told a meeting at Blenheim Palace (the home of Randolph Churchill, who in 1886 had said without weighing the consequences, 'Ulster will fight and Ulster will be right') that 'I can imagine no length of resistance to which Ulster can go in which I would not be prepared to support them' (Jenkins 1964: 278). Coming from the leader of the Conservative Party, that threat had far more force than coming from an unreliable gadfly. The Ulster Protestants needed no encouragement in their military preparations. In July 1914, civil war in Ulster looked imminent. It was prevented only by the outbreak of the First World War. All the Protestant paramilitaries and most of the Catholic ones enlisted in the British army. The Protestant Ulstermen were cut down in their thousands at the Somme in July 1916.

But even Bonar Law (see e.g. Ramsden 1978: 83), to say nothing of his colleagues, knew that hardline Unionism came at a price. Canada and Australia, not to mention the United States, had large Irish Catholic communities. Sustained by the collective memory of the Famine that had forced their grandparents to emigrate, they had no love for Britain, nor for Britain's continued rule over resentful Catholic Ireland. They were a powerful electoral force in all three countries. If the Unionists wanted to pursue Chamberlain's dream of a united Empire, even they had to settle the Irish question somehow. Lloyd George was on good terms with his fellow outsider Bonar Law. He used all his wiles to come to a cross-party solution of the Irish question from 1910 to 1921. How he did so is the subject of Chapter 7.

7

The Patriot Game: Rhetoric and Heresthetic in the Anglo-Irish Treaty Negotiations of 1921

British–Irish Relations from 1910 until the Truce, July 1921

On 26 August 1921, Lloyd George's faithful go-between Tom Jones, Assistant Secretary to the Cabinet, visited his boss.

P.M. in bed in a dressing gown. His head looked bigger than ever. A large room with huge pieces of red mahogany furniture and a hotch potch of feeble pictures higgledy piggledy on the walls. Above his bed two longish rows of books—chiefly light novels but also I noticed *Letters of Luther* and Roget's *Thesaurus*. Below the bookshelves was a framed text from the Book of Job worked in silk threads: 'There is a path which no fowl knoweth and which the eye of the vulture hath not seen.' (T. Jones 1971: 103)

Most of this chapter is devoted to showing how Lloyd George found a path which no fowl knew and which the eye of the vulture had not seen, in November–December 1921. He probably found both Luther and Roget handy. But, to understand the crisis, we need first to know some background. There are many histories of Irish–British relations between 1912 and 1922 (see e.g. Foster 1988: chs. 18–20 and the sources cited there). This section gives only as much detail as is required to frame the games described below, and Lloyd George's role in them.

The Asquith government presented the Third Home Rule Bill in 1912. As the government depended on Irish votes for its parliamentary majority, it was bound to do so, however little enthusiasm it retained for Irish Home Rule. Under the Parliament Act, the House of Lords could no longer prevent its passage, but could delay it until 1914. This duly happened. There was violent opposition to the Bill among Ulster Protestants. The Unionists supported the Ulster revolt. They included not only Bonar Law at Blenheim and elsewhere, but also the constitutional expert A. V. Dicey, and Major-General Sir Henry Wilson, director of military operations at the War Office. In March 1914 a large consignment of arms was run in for the Ulster Volunteer Force at Larne, unimpeded by the authorities. In July 1914 Erskine Childers, who recurs in this chapter, ran a much smaller contingent in to Howth near Dublin, for the use of the Irish Volunteer Force (but essentially for propaganda, at which Childers excelled). Childers was a sailor and adventurer, author of the best-selling spy thriller *The Riddle of the Sands* (Childers 1986, originally published in 1903), which aimed to alert Britain to the German threat. By 1914, although he was to serve with distinction in the British forces throughout the First World War, he had become a convinced Irish nationalist. The authorities impeded the Howth consignment, and three bystanders were shot dead in Dublin. Although an amending bill to suspend Home Rule temporarily in the six counties to the north-east of Ireland had been passed in June, civil war in Ireland seemed imminent. An all-party conference at Buckingham Palace (see next section) achieved nothing. Then, luckily, the First World War broke out. The Ulster Volunteers (the unionist paramilitaries, mostly in the north) and most of the Irish Volunteers (the nationalist paramilitaries) followed their leaders into the British army. An uneasy coalition of objectors, including the anti-militarist Sinn Fein, lead by Arthur Griffith, the militarist and secret Irish Republican Brotherhood, and the (initially small) group of Irish Volunteers who objected to the decision to join the British army, took part in the Easter Rising of April 1916. The Rising itself was militarily hopeless, as its leaders knew. The reaction of the British military exceeded their wildest expectations. They executed all the leaders of the Rising, creating martyrs whose names have become immortalized in railway stations.

This swung Irish public opinion away from Home Rule towards independence, a swing confirmed by the attempt to extend conscription to Ireland in 1918. In the 1918 General Election, the Irish Party of Parnell and John Redmond was wiped out in southern Ireland. Although its share of the vote was not derisory, the plurality electoral system gave it only one seat outside the north-east. All the others went to Sinn Fein, whose elected members refused to take their seats in London, but declared themselves the first Dáil (parliament) of *Saorstat Éireann* (literally, 'the Free State of Ireland' although much blood and ingenuity surrounds the translation). The Dáil created an administration that gradually became the effective government of most of the country. In 1920, the Lloyd George coalition government, numerically dominated by Unionists, passed a Government of Ireland Act that made the exclusion of the northern six counties permanent unless and until they joined, in the Council of Ireland provided for by the Act, with the parliament of southern Ireland to form an all-Ireland assembly.

The election in southern Ireland provided for by the 1920 Act took place in May 1921. 124 members of Sinn Fein were elected unopposed, and constituted themselves as the second Dáil. The four Unionists elected for Trinity College, Dublin attended one meeting of the Southern Parliament and dissolved it. There was now no southern Irish representation in any parliament that acknowledged UK rule. Meanwhile, resistance to British rule had turned into war, looting, reprisal, and counter-reprisal. Until the middle of 1921 Lloyd George apparently believed the claims of his civil and military advisers that the British forces, including the notorious 'Black-and-Tans' and 'Auxiliaries', were winning the war. Quite suddenly, in June and July 1921, he and his government decided that they were not, or at least that any military gains came at an unacceptable price. Much opinion in Britain and worldwide was appalled at British indiscipline, looting, and reprisals. The Lloyd George government arranged a truce with Sinn Fein and the forces of Dáil Éireann.

Of Kings and Conferences

From his accession in 1910 until 1914, George V felt the Home Rule crisis very personally. Buffeted by Asquith and Bonar Law, he complained that 'Whatever I do I shall offend half the population. One alternative would certainly result in alienating the Ulster Protestants from me, and whatever happens the result must be detrimental to me personally and to the Crown in general' (George V to Asquith, 11.08.13, in Nicolson 1952: 223). That rather one-sided comment tends to show that, despite Asquith's magisterial response (Jenkins 1964: 543–9) the King was more open to the views of His Majesty's Opposition than to those of His Majesty's Government. Whether or not he acted rightly during the crisis is still disputed. The best statement for the prosecution is Jenkins 1964: ch. 18, and for the defence Bogdanor 1995: 113–35. Luckily for the monarchy and (probably) for peace, he stopped short of actually using his veto on the Home Rule Bill or of dismissing the Asquith government. He sponsored a Buckingham Palace Conference in July 1914, modelled on the abortive constitutional conference of 1910 (see previous chapter). By this time all parties had accepted that, if there was any solution, it must involve the partition of Ireland, with some area in the north-east (but how big an area?) excluded from Home Rule. Lloyd George had proposed this in 1910 and again in 1914, although he had opposed, with the rest of the government, a backbench amendment to the Home Rule Bill in 1912 providing for the exclusion of the four most Protestant and Unionist counties.

The conference failed, as Asquith had acerbically predicted it would. Drawing the boundary proved impossible, even if the disputed counties of Tyrone and Fermanagh were to be split into smaller units. The First World War stilled the acute Irish problem but not the chronic one, which flared up again after the Easter Rising. Asquith appointed Lloyd George as a mediator between the Nationalists and Unionists to look for common ground in the summer of 1916. This mediation again threw up the idea of exclusion of the four majority-Protestant counties (Antrim, Down, Derry, and Armagh) together with the two in which Catholics formed a narrow majority, Fermanagh and Tyrone. These negotiations foundered on two new rocks— the southern Unionists and the northern Catholics (Fair 1980: 125)—but not before Lloyd George had given the Unionist leader Carson the impression that exclusion of Ulster from Home Rule would be permanent and the Nationalist leader Redmond the impression that it would be only for the duration of the war.

In 1917 Lloyd George, by now Prime Minister, tried again, this time with a constitutional convention for Ireland. This body of ninety-five sat for seven months and achieved nothing except to show that an attempt at mediation that did not include Lloyd George in person had even less chance of success than one that did.

Thus when the two sides in the guerrilla war agreed a truce in July 1921 it was abundantly clear that any settlement must involve Lloyd George in person; and it must, somehow, deal with Ulster, deciding how large an Ulster should be excluded from the new Free State.

July to 6 December 1921

The South African Prime Minister (and member of Lloyd George's War Cabinet) J. C. Smuts was the first successful intermediary. As a leader of the Boer guerrilla forces in the South African War, Smuts had moral authority with the Irish provisional government. He persuaded the Irish Cabinet not to reject the idea of talks out of hand, dangling in front of them the idea that Ireland might become a Dominion like South Africa (T. Jones 1971: 82–4). Dominion status was already in the air. For instance, the Oxford academic A. D. Lindsay was pressing it on Erskine Childers, whom Lindsay wrongly thought to be sympathetic to it. Lindsay presented it to Smuts in June (Ring 1996: 238; Scott 1970: 93–6; Childers MSS, TCD, 7487–7851, nos. 626–7).

In fact, the Irish Cabinet was already divided between those who would be willing to accept Dominion status and those who would not. The President, Eamon De Valera, seemed to be in the latter camp. The first face-to-face negotiation took place on 14 July 1921. The following is by Tom Jones, the Welsh-speaking confidant of Lloyd George who became the secretary to the British delegation. Jones sent it to Winston Churchill, who used it almost verbatim in his book (Churchill 1929), the most colourful of the participants' accounts.

Mr Lloyd George, never a greater artist than in the first moments of a fateful interview, received the Irish Chieftain cordially as a brother Celt. Mr De Valera was guarded and formal. He handed Mr Lloyd George a document in Irish, and then a translation in English. The Irish document was headed 'Saorstat Eireann' and Mr Lloyd George began by asking modestly for a literal translation, saying that 'Saorstat' did not strike his ear as Irish. Mr De Valera replied 'Free State'. 'Yes', retorted Mr Lloyd George, 'but what is the Irish word for Republic.' While Mr De Valera and his colleague [Art O Briain, the representative of the Irish Government in London] were pondering in English on what reply they should make Mr Lloyd George conversed aloud in Welsh with one of his Secretaries [viz. Jones himself] to the discomfiture of the two Irishmen and as Mr De Valera could get no further than Saorstat and Free State Mr Lloyd George remarked 'Must we not admit that the Celts were never Republicans and have no native word for such an idea.' (T. Jones 1971: 89; cf. Churchill 1929: 297–8)

A deconstruction of this story is in the section at p. 181 below. The negotiations with De Valera got nowhere. Lloyd George described them as 'like picking up mercury with a fork', to which De Valera retorted 'Why doesn't he try a spoon?' (Birkenhead 1960: 372). A long exchange of letters followed in which the British insisted that nothing more than Dominion status was on offer and De Valera retorted that the Irish government would never accept association with the British Crown. Finally, the British offered the Irish a conference 'to ascertain how the association of Ireland with the community of nations known as the British Empire can best be reconciled with Irish national aspirations'. De Valera chose the Irish plenipotentiaries, and stayed at home himself—a decision that still evokes controversy. The conference met on 10 October and stayed in session until the small hours of 6 December.

There were seven British delegates, but only four who counted: Lloyd George, Winston Churchill, Austen Chamberlain, and the Earl of Birkenhead (formerly F. E. Smith). Chamberlain and Birkenhead were Unionists, and Churchill should be regarded as virtually one at this period. This balance reflects the position in Parliament. A majority of MPs in the governing coalition were Unionists. They comprised more than half of the House of Commons, and so at any time they could reject their own leaders and the coalition with the 130-odd Coalition Liberals led by Lloyd George. They were to do just that in October 1922.

De Valera deliberately chose a balanced delegation—or so he told an American supporter after the Treaty was signed:

Having decided that I should remain at home, it was necessary that [Michael] Collins [the leader of the Irish forces in the guerrilla war] and Griffith should go. That Griffith would accept the Crown under pressure I had no doubt . . . I felt certain that [Collins] too was contemplating accepting the Crown, but I had hoped that all this would simply make them both a better bait for Lloyd George—leading him on and on, further in our direction. I felt convinced on the other hand that as matters came to a close we would be able to hold them from this side from crossing the line.

The letter goes on to explain that De Valera thought that the two uncompromising members of his Cabinet, Cathal Brugha and Austin Stack, were unsuitable.

The only thing left was to send [Robert] Barton. I felt that he would be strong and stubborn enough as a retarding force to any precipitate giving way by the delegation. Childers, who is an intellectual Republican, as Secretary would give Barton, his relative and close friend, added strength. . . . [Eamon] Duggan and [George Gavan] Duffy were mere legal padding. Duggan was certain to be influenced by Michael Collins, but Duffy was more likely to be on the Childers–Barton side. (To J. McGarrity, 21.12.1921, in Cronin 1972: 109–11)

Albeit with hindsight, this indicates that De Valera expected that the delegation would split as it did. Barton and Childers were first cousins, Anglo-Irish Protestants, who had been brought up together at Glendalough, Co. Wicklow. Childers did not have a vote, so the delegation could be expected to split 3:2 in favour of accepting Dominion status. In the end, Griffith, Collins, and Duggan accepted the final terms. The other three refused to. *But all five delegates signed the Treaty.* When they returned to Dublin, the Cabinet discussed it. Griffith, Collins, and Barton were members of the Cabinet; the others were not. The Cabinet accepted the Treaty by 4 votes to 3, *with Barton, who opposed the Treaty he had just signed, voting in the majority.* The Dáil accepted it by 64 votes to 57 *with Barton and Duffy among the 64*; De Valera, Brugha and Stack repudiated the Treaty and left the Cabinet. In the ensuing Civil War, Griffith died of heart failure, Collins was killed in an ambush by anti-Treaty forces, and Childers was captured at Glendalough, and later executed by pro-Treaty forces for possession of a revolver he had been given by Michael Collins.

Two deeply counter-intuitive facts therefore need explanation. Why did all five delegates sign? And why did Barton swing the Cabinet decision by voting against his convictions?

There are two day-by-day accounts of the proceedings, with equal authority, one from the British and one from the Irish side. They agree in almost all particulars. Jones (1971) is the diary of the British secretary. Pakenham (1967) may not appear to be a first-hand account, but it is. It is compiled from contemporary documents, including the frequent letters exchanged between Griffith and De Valera, sometimes changing nothing except to turn sentences from the first to the third person. (For instance, compare Pakenham 1967: 216–17, with the letter this is based on: Griffith to De Valera 4.12.21, in Childers MSS, Trinity College, Dublin, 7790/83/10). From these and other sources we draw only the events which were crucial to the ultimate game of the night of 5/6 December.

In early November, the negotiations seemed to be getting nowhere. The Unionists were due to hold their annual conference in Liverpool, a centre of Orange—that is, militant Ulster Protestant—opinion, on 17 November. Lloyd George thought that the conference might repudiate Chamberlain and Birkenhead, withdraw from the Coalition, and pave the way for a hard-line Unionist government under Bonar Law. He mused to Jones on whether a reorganization of the anti-Conservative parties was likely.

I argued that his personal power was great enough to dominate the situation but made no impression. He then said—'There is just one other possible way out. I want to find out from Griffith and Collins if they will support me on it; namely that the 26 counties should take their own Dominion Parliament and have a Boundary Commission, that Ulster should have her present powers plus representation in the Imperial

Parliament . . . I might be able to put that through if Sinn Fein will take it. Find out.' (T. Jones 1971: 155: 7.11.21)

Jones found out—he was the one person whom the leaders of both delegations trusted. Griffith told him, 'It is not our proposal, but if the P.M. cares to make it we would not make his position impossible. . . . we are not going to queer his pitch' (T. Jones 1971: 157, 9.11.21; cf. Pakenham 1967: 170). Lloyd George then met Griffith alone. Griffith's account of the meeting states that Lloyd George was now

offering to create an all-Ireland Parliament, Ulster to have the right to vote itself out within twelve months; but if it did, a Boundary Commission to be set up to delimit the area, and *the part that remained after the Commission had acted* to be subject to equal financial burdens with England.

Griffith went on to repeat that he recognized that this was a tactical proposal for the anticipated fight between the Government and its hard-line Unionists in Liverpool:

I could not guarantee its acceptance, as, of course, my colleagues knew nothing of it yet. But I would guarantee that while he was fighting the 'Ulster' crowd we would not help them by repudiating him. (Griffith to De Valera, 12.11.21, quoted by Pakenham 1967: 174–5; our italics)

Jones's minute of the meeting contains a significant difference. If Ulster opted out,

it would be necessary to revise the boundary of Northern Ireland. This might be done by a Boundary Commission which would be directed to adjust the line *both by inclusion and exclusion* so as to make the boundary conform as closely as possible to the wishes of the population (Jones minute, 13.11.21, quoted by Pakenham 1967: 178; our italics)

Griffith saw this minute and did not comment on it. On 17 November the Unionist Conference endorsed the policy of Chamberlain and Birkenhead by a very large majority.

By the end of November, the sides seemed as far apart as ever. De Valera was drafting a new form of association with the Crown, which came to be known as 'External Association'. A formula was devised by Childers' assistant John Chartres, whereby the Irish government would recognize that the Crown was the head of the British Empire, with which Ireland would be associated, but not the Crown of Ireland (Pakenham 1967: 195–7). In 1949, the Chartres formula would pacify everyone except Enoch Powell when India declared itself a republic (Chapter 5). But in 1921 every Unionist was a Powell. Membership of the Empire, together with British control of the seas around Ireland and the naval bases on Irish soil, was a non-negotiable principle for the Unionists. In the next few days, the British nevertheless made a substantial concession on the Crown, promising that the Crown in Ireland would comprise a governor-general nominated on the advice of the Irish government: neither the monarch nor the British government would have any power to intervene in Irish domestic politics.

However, this was still not external association. The delegates returned to Dublin at the weekend for briefing. On the way, their steamer hit another boat off Holyhead, drowning some of its crew, and had to put back. It was a very tired delegation, very short of time, that consulted the Irish Cabinet. In an inconclusive meeting, Griffith apparently promised to sign nothing which involved accepting the Crown in Ireland without reference back. However, this pledge was not minuted. In any case, the delegates seem to have brought no minutes of the Dublin meeting back to London with them. Collins said on his way back to the boat, 'I've been there all day and I can't get them to say Yes or No, whether we should sign or not' (Rex Taylor 1958: 183). The three compromisers—Griffith, Collins, and Duggan—returned to Holyhead on the Kingstown (Dun Laoghaire) boat, the three uncompromising republicans—Barton, Duffy, and Childers—on the rival Dublin boat.

Many of the participants wrote down their recollections of the high drama of 4–6 December. The most colourful is Churchill (1929: 305–7). The most reliable are Jones (1971: 179–84); the original documents in Pakenham (1967: 213–37), and Childers' diary and papers (see Appendix 7.2)—all of them written at the time. There is no disagreement between British and Irish sources as to what happened. On 4 December Griffith presented Irish counter-proposals. Lloyd George rejected them flat. Griffith tried to 'work . . . on Ulster again but could not get it into its proper place'. Gavan Duffy said, ' "our difficulty is coming within the Empire". They jumped up at this and the conversation came to a close' (Both extracts from Griffith to De Valera, 4.12.21, Childers MSS 7790/83/10). Austen Chamberlain said 'That ends it'. The British went off to prepare documents stating that the conference had broken down.

Collins had not attended this meeting, out of disgust at the unclarity of the Irish delegation's instructions. In October, Lloyd George had told C. P. Scott that 'Collins was an uneducated rather stupid man, but he [LG] liked him . . . and if he had him and Griffith alone to deal with could settle in five minutes' (Scott diary for 28–29.10.21, in Scott 1970: 405). Now Lloyd George tried twice to talk to him alone, and succeeded the second time, on the morning of Monday 5 December. On returning to the rest of the Irish delegation, Collins immediately wrote a note of what had happened:

[Lloyd George] remarked that I myself pointed out on a previous occasion that the North would be forced economically to come in. I assented but I said that the position was so serious . . . that for my part I was anxious to secure a definite reply from [Sir James] Craig [Prime Minister of Northern Ireland] and his colleagues, and that I was agreeable to a reply rejecting [entry to the proposed Free State] as [to a reply] accepting. In view of the former we would save Tyrone and Fermanagh, parts of Derry, Armagh and Down by the Boundary Commission. . . . Mr Lloyd George expressed the view that this might be put to Craig. (Memo by Michael Collins, 5.12.21, in Dáil Éireann [1972]. pp. 304–6).

At 3 p.m. the four leading British delegates faced Griffith, Collins, and Barton. The meeting lasted five hours. Childers 'sat outside reading Lincoln'. A new oath was agreed, drafted by Collins and amended by Birkenhead. The British made some concessions on defence. Lloyd George made a sudden and total concession on trade, withdrawing all objections to Irish autonomy in trade and tariff policy. Griffith kept trying to 'work on Ulster'. But Lloyd George dramatically reappeared with Jones's minute of 13 November (he had been away searching all his pockets because nobody could find it). Griffith said, 'I said I would not let you down on that, and I won't', to the astonishment of his fellow delegates. He said that he would sign the agreement whether any other delegate did or not. For this, Churchill (1929: 306) described Griffith as 'this little quiet man of great heart and great purpose', continuing, 'Michael Collins rose looking as if he was going to shoot someone, preferably himself. In all my life I have never seen so much passion and suffering in restraint.' Chamberlain (1935: 149) added, 'A braver man than Arthur Griffith I have not met.' Lloyd George then issued his ultimatum, producing two letters:

I have to communicate with Sir James Craig to-night. Here are the alternative letters which I have prepared, one enclosing Articles of Agreement reached by His Majesty's Government and yourselves, and the other saying that the Sinn Fein representatives refuse to come within the empire. If I send this letter it is war, and war within three days. Which letter am I to send?[1] Whichever letter you choose travels by special train to Holyhead, and by destroyer to Belfast. The train is waiting with steam up at Euston. Mr Shakespeare [the messenger, a member of Lloyd George's political staff] is ready. If he is to reach Sir James Craig in time we must know your answer by 10 p.m. tonight. You can have until then, but no longer, to decide whether you will give peace or war to your country. (Pakenham 1967: 239–40)

He 'particularly addressed himself to' Barton,

and said very solemnly that those who were not for peace must take the full responsibility for the war that would immediately follow refusal by any Delegate to sign the Articles of Agreement. (R. Barton, Note of Sub-Conference of 5.12.21, in Taylor 1958: 300. Cf. also Barton's speech to the Dáil, (Dáil Éireann [1922]: 49); and ' The truth about the Treaty and Document No. 2. A reply to Michael Collins by Robert Barton', TS in Childers MSS, TCD, 7834/4.)

The delegates returned for their last meeting. In the taxi back to their office, Collins announced that he, too, would sign. Duggan, as predicted, followed. What happened then is recorded in Childers' diary (Appendix 7.2)—the only record not written for others' consumption. The fourth to agree was Barton, splitting with his cousin and giving the reasons shown in Appendix 7.2. The last to agree was Duffy.

Childers' diary is above all revealing for what it does not say. Every commentator on that night has asked: why did the delegation not only not tell

---

[1] Lloyd George's speech down to this point is quoted from Chamberlain's notes (see also Chamberlain 1935, p. 149); Pakenham takes the rest from Irish sources, probably including Barton's minute and conversations with Barton.

Lloyd George that they must report back before replying to the ultimatum, but also fail to telephone Dublin to explain what was going on? Two *a priori* plausible explanations are: that they guessed their phone would be tapped; and that De Valera had (surely deliberately) removed himself from contact by going to Limerick. But if either of these points had been made, Childers would surely have recorded them. The silence of the diary confirms that even he did not remind the delegation of their mandate to refer back (cf. Gallagher and O'Neill 1965: 165—written before Childers' diary became available). Part of the truth may be, banally, that they did not trust the telephone and were not used to it. Shortly before his death, Barton wrote as follows to a biographer of Childers, who had obviously asked him 'why did you not phone Dublin?':

I suggest that the telephone may have been eschewed because we suspected that it was under supervision. Being in gaol or on the run induces secrecy. Messengers were passing back and forth every night to Dublin & communication by this means was easy and secure. By the time the crisis came with the final decision to sign or refuse, Griffith & Collins had already made up their minds. Their relations with DeValera had deteriorated and with Brugha & Stack they were far from cordial. It is unlikely that they were prepared to accept authoritative advice. I find it difficult to state at this date any reason for my failing to communicate or for Erskine's not suggesting it. I was not familiar with the telephone, there was none in my house [which had also been Childers' childhood house]. (R. Barton to A. Boyle, 1975. R. C. Barton MSS, Trinity College, Dublin MS 7834/10)

The treaty was signed at 2.30 a.m. on 6 December. The British and Irish delegates shook hands for the first time. Collins wrote to a friend:

I tell you this—early this morning I signed my death warrant. . . . I believe Birkenhead may have said an end to his political life. With him it has been an honour to work. These signatures are the first real step for Ireland. If people will only remember that—the first real step. M. (To J. O'Kane, 6.12.21, in Taylor 1958: 189)

Aftermath

Erskine Childers would not have dared to put the next episode into *The Riddle of the Sands*. The envoy went out into the street with the 'peace' letter to Craig. It was already $4^1/_2$ hours beyond Lloyd George's ultimatum time of 10 p.m. He hailed a taxi for Euston. The first taxi-driver refused to take him. Presumably expensively dressed gentlemen at 2.30 a.m. were too risky. The envoy reached Euston in another taxi. He got on to his special train, put the letter under the pillow, and fell asleep. He transferred to the destroyer at Holyhead without incident. On arrival at Belfast, he went to telephone Craig but found that he had no change. However, on hearing that he was the expected English envoy, the operator put him through without charge. He found Craig intransigent as expected, and sent Lloyd George a coded message:

My strong impression is that my customer will agree to purchase, subject to satisfactory cash arrangement, but joint business not acceptable.

After returning by destroyer to Stranraer and thence to London, the envoy found that the whole journey had been described in the *Daily Mail* (Shakespeare 1949: 87–92).

The Irish delegates returned to Dublin. As described above (and see Appendix 7.2), the Cabinet decided by four votes to three to accept the Treaty. The minority ministers—De Valera, Brugha, and Stack—resigned, but by that time a wave of pro-Treaty euphoria had broken out in both countries. The Dáil debated the Treaty for a fortnight, and accepted it by 64 votes to 57. De Valera resigned as President, and was replaced by Griffith on a vote of 60 to 58. Despite an election in June, Ireland slid into civil war, during which Griffith died and Collins and Childers were killed. The anti-Treaty forces surrendered in 1923. The pro- and anti-Treaty parties have remained the two main political parties in Ireland (now, respectively, Fine Gael and Fianna Fail).

The Irish Civil War, coupled with instability in Britain where there were three elections in quick succession, delayed the start of the Boundary Commission. It finally started work in 1924 under the MacDonald Labour government. Its chairman, a South African judge, ruled that its terms of reference forbade it from making wholesale transfers out of Northern Ireland. Furthermore, he interpreted the terms of reference from the Treaty, Article 12: 'in accordance with the wishes of the inhabitants, so far as may be compatible with economic and geographic conditions' to mean that the first could sometimes be overridden by the second and third. The Commission awarded an area of Co. Donegal west of Londonderry to Northern Ireland on the 'economic and geographic' grounds that its inhabitants shopped in Derry and got their water supplies from there. Its largest award to the Free State was the area around Crossmaglen in South Armagh. Its Ulster Unionist member had been prophetically willing to concede the area:

With North Monaghan *in* Ulster and South Armagh *out*, we should have a solid ethnographic and strategic frontier to the South, and a hostile 'Afghanistan' on our northwest frontier [i.e. Co. Donegal] would be placed in safe keeping (J. R. Fisher, 1922, in Gwynn 1950: 215–16; stress in original).

However, its award was leaked to the right-wing Unionist *Morning Post* in November 1925. The Free State member resigned. All three governments agreed that publishing the award was likely to cause more bloodshed than suppressing it. The boundary was left as it was. South Armagh remained in the North, and has harboured the most militant Republican paramilitaries in Ireland ever since. The Unionists got their defensible North-West Frontier at the expense of a bloody and uncontrollable South Central Frontier. The report was suppressed until 1968 and published for the first time in 1969 (Hand, 1969). It would have moved (on 1911 Census figures) 31,319 people from Northern Ireland to the Irish Free State, and 7,594 the other way. It would have moved 32,673 people the 'right' way (Catholics into the Free State plus non-Catholics out of it), and 6,240 people the 'wrong' way (Catholics into Northern Ireland plus non-Catholics out of it). (Hand 1969, computed from tables. The numbers in the end-paper map differ slightly.) In proportion to the populations of the two territories (about 3 million in the Free State; about 1.5 million in Northern Ireland), these numbers are small.

Analysis

We now turn to analysis of the narrative. Recall that Lloyd George had to persuade, or hoodwink, three cabinets and three parliaments. He controlled a majority in none of the three, as Table 7.1 shows. Although Lloyd George's Coalition Liberals held a bare 10:9 majority in the UK Cabinet over the Conservatives (Table 7.1), one of the ten was Winston Churchill, whose views on Ireland placed him much closer to the Conservatives than to Lloyd George. Alternative Commons majorities were always possible. An ideologically close one would have comprised the 335 Coalition Unionists (minus perhaps

Table 7.1. Composition of the three legislatures and Cabinets, 1921

	UK	Northern Ireland	Southern Ireland

Legislature	Unionist 335
	Coalition (LG) Liberal
	   133
	Coalition Labour 10
	   (total Coalition 478)
	Other Conservative 37
	Irish Unionist 28
	Oppn. Liberal 28
	Labour 63
	Irish Nationalist 7
	Other 10
	(total Opposition 173)
		Unionist 40	Sinn Fein 124
			   (later to split:
			   Pro-Treaty 64
			   Anti-Treaty 57
			   unknown 3)

Cabinet	Coalition Lib 10
	Conservative 9
		Unionist	Sinn Fein 7
			   (later: Pro-Treaty 3;
			   Anti-Treaty 3;
			   Anti-Treaty but
			   voted for it 1)

Sources:
Legislatures: UK: Butler and Butler 1994: 218. 1918 figures; Northern Ireland: Buckland 1979; Wallace 1971: 72. 1921 figures; Southern Ireland: Jones 1971: 72. 1921 figures.
Figures exclude abstentionist MPs who refused to attend the Parliament to which they were elected (UK Sinn Fein 73; NI Nationalist 6; NI Sinn Fein 6).
Cabinets: UK, Butler and Butler 1994: 6–9; Southern Ireland, see text.

Chamberlain, Birkenhead, and a few others) plus the thirty-seven other Conservatives and the twenty-eight Irish Unionists, led by Bonar Law (for whose pre-war views on Ulster see above). At several points, Lloyd George threatened the Irish delegation with the consequences of his resignation or defeat.

The British knew about the divisions on the Irish side throughout the negotiations. Although Irish military intelligence (headed by Michael Collins) was better than British, the reverse was true of civil intelligence, whose British head in Ireland was 'Andy', later Sir Alfred, Cope, Assistant Under-Secretary for Ireland and a former detective. However, one thing that British intelligence failed to pick up was the depth of Irish hostility to inclusion in the British Empire.

What did 'Unionism' imply, in 1921? Every Unionist had, in varying degrees, a commitment to the Empire and a commitment to Ulster. Ulster Unionists, naturally, tended to care more about Ulster; British Unionists cared more about the Crown and the Empire. As there was a potential alternative Unionist government in Britain, Lloyd George had to try to finesse the role of the Crown, as he first did in his July meeting with De Valera.

Picking up Mercury with a Fork—LG's First Heresthetic

Consider again the two Welshmen, the two Irishmen, and the meaning of 'Saorstat Éireann'. It has been variously interpreted. Jones, its originator, and Churchill (1929) see it as a trap and embarrassment of De Valera; Pakenham (1967) as an attempt to form a bond between brother Celts against the English. The language Jones uses suggests the former. The story is not quite plausible as it stands. De Valera and O Briain were fluent enough to have spoken in Irish if they had chosen to. There is an Irish word for 'Republic'—*poblacht*. It had been used in the heading of the Declaration issued at the start of the Easter Rising. It would have been surprising if Lloyd George had not known this. He was in government at the time of the Easter Rising. He must have seen copies of the 1916 declaration of the Irish Republic—*Poblacht na h'Éireann*. The Welsh *pobol*, 'people', is from the same root as Irish *poblacht*. Both derive from Latin *populus*. (On the other hand, the modern Welsh *gweriniaeth*—literally 'folk association'—for *republic* is an artificial coinage.) Lloyd George was pointing out that the Irish had freely chosen to call their state *Saorstat Éireann*. This literally meant 'Free state of Ireland', as Lloyd George surely well knew. At the end Griffith would say, 'You may prefer to translate *Saorstat Éireann* by *Free State* [instead of *Republic*]. We shall not quarrel with your translation', to which Birkenhead said 'The title, Free State, can go into the Treaty' (24.11.21; in Pakenham 1967: 197). It did (Appendix 7.1, Article 1). In the Dáil debate on the Treaty, an Irish-speaking pro-Treaty deputy announced that since he had taken his oath of allegiance to

SaorStat na hÉireann (literally, Irish Free State), he was being consistent in voting for the settlement. If the debate had been held in Irish rather than English there would have been no disagreement over the meaning of words (Liam de Roiste, 22.12.21; Dáil Éireann 1922: 158). That also provided a way out for some Unionists. But not for De Valera, in July or later. Lloyd George's first attempt at heresthetic, wishing away the republic by translation, failed.

Seeking a Break

The tactical language of Lloyd George and Arthur Griffith is strikingly similar. Both of them repeatedly say 'If there is to be a break, it must be on . . . and not on . . .'. The difference lies in the words in the gaps. For Lloyd George, it was essential to avoid a break on Ulster, therefore if there was to be a break it should be on the title of the new state, or on military or trade provisions. For Griffith, it was essential that the break, if break there be, *should* be on Ulster. Lloyd George explains why, in his summary to the Cabinet in September:

[I]f the Conference started without securing in advance Irish allegiance to the Crown and membership of the empire, the discussion would become entangled in the Ulster problem; . . . De Valera would raise the question of Fermanagh and Tyrone, where we had a very weak case, the Conference might break on that point, a very bad one. (7.09.21; T. Jones 1971: 111)

As already noted, Griffith continually wanted to 'work on' or 'work around to' Ulster. 'Ulster' had been excluded under the 1914 and 1920 Acts on the basis of county boundaries. Everybody knew that was unsatisfactory. There were predominantly Protestant areas outside, and predominantly Catholic areas inside. All attempts to draw a line more acceptable to both sides had failed. In the words of Churchill's well-known speech:

I remember on the eve of the Great War we were gathered together in a Cabinet Meeting in Downing Street, and for a long time . . . after the failure of the Buckingham Palace Conference, we discussed the boundaries of Fermanagh and Tyrone. Both of the great political parties were at each other's throats. The air was full of talk of civil war. Every effort was made to settle the matter and bring them together. The differences had been narrowed down, not merely to the counties of Fermanagh and Tyrone, but to parishes and groups inside the areas of Fermanagh and Tyrone, and yet, even when the differences had been so narrowed down, the problem appeared to be as insuperable as ever, and neither side would agree to reach any conclusion. Then came the Great War. . . . Every institution, almost, in the world was strained. Great Empires have been overturned. The whole map of Europe has changed. The position of countries has been violently altered. The mode and thought of men, the whole outlook on affairs, the grouping of parties, all have encountered violent and tremendous changes in the deluge of the world, but as the deluge subsides and the waters fall we see the dreary steeples of Fermanagh and Tyrone emerging once again. The integrity of their quarrel is one of the few institutions that have been unaltered in the cataclysm that has swept the world. (Speech introducing the Irish Free State Bill, 16.02.22; quoted in Churchill 1929: 319–20)

Seventeenth-century governments had put Protestants into the towns to watch over the Catholics in the countryside. And there they remained, as they do to this day. (For the situation in 1921 see the end-paper maps in the Boundary Commission report—Hand 1969.) But Fermanagh and Tyrone had Catholic majorities. They were reluctant members of 'Northern Ireland'. In the rest of the world, and indeed in Britain outside the ranks of determined Unionists, their position was in flagrant breach of the principles of self-determination that the Allies had so loudly put forward in the Versailles Peace Conference, while overturning the great empires of the defeated powers. If the Conference were to break on Ulster, the Irish would have world opinion on their side.

If it were to break on the Empire, they would not. All of the existing Dominions, even including South Africa after the defeat of the Boer republics, had accepted membership of the Empire, and none of them had a significant republican movement. Although Irish-American pressure had been important and would be again, in 1921 American foreign policy was moving towards isolationism after the Senate rejection of the League of Nations treaty and defeat of Woodrow Wilson in 1919–20. Potential allies of the Irish neither understood nor cared about the distinction between membership of the Empire and external association with it, that mattered so much to De Valera and the republican faction within the Dáil.

The Entrapment of Griffith and Collins

The idea that Griffith might write a letter to help Lloyd George deal with the intransigent Unionists surfaced at the end of October. Lloyd George was threatening to resign, as he often did—apparently not as a bluff for Irish ears, as he mentioned it to confidants unconnected with the Irish (see Scott 1970: 402–9, diary for 28–29.10.21).[2] However, the republican faction in the delegation prevented Griffith from sending any personal letter. Griffith thought the letter that then went from the whole Irish delegation kept Ireland out of the Empire; the British thought it brought Ireland in.

It is hard to judge how credible was Lloyd George's threat of resignation. At one level it was utterly credible. He could have resigned and walked away, to be succeeded without a General Election either by Chamberlain and a moderate coalition or by Bonar Law and a hard-line Unionist government. Lloyd

---

[2] But Scott immediately went off to see Michael Collins, whom Scott's diary reveals that he utterly failed to understand. So perhaps Lloyd George's resignation threat *was* indirectly intended for Irish ears.

George told his Press friends (C. P. Scott and Sir George Riddell) in October and November that 'Bonar Law has come out as the advocate of Ulster' (Scott 1970: 403; Riddell 1986: 355). Law came out in public on 12 November, when he said:

If L.G. goes on with his present proposals I will oppose them. I shall try to get the Conservative Party to follow me. . . . I am certainly not going to do what Disraeli did after the passing of the Corn Laws—attempt to build up a new Conservative Party (quoted from Blake 1955: 432).

Certainly, Lloyd George was in pensive mood—see his discussion with Jones on 7 November quoted above. This elicited Griffith's letter on the Boundary Commission and Jones's minute, also quoted above. As Pakenham says, (1967: 174) 'If there had been no 12th of November there might have been no Treaty.' On 5 December Griffith felt himself trapped by the undertaking he had given Lloyd George on 12 November, viz., to accept the Boundary Commission if Ulster refused to come under the Irish parliament. And that Boundary Commission was to be a Jones minute Commission, not a Griffith aspiration Commission. That is, it would have powers to move the boundary either way. It would not move the whole of Tyrone and Fermanagh, and parts of other counties, out of Northern Ireland.

However, the entrapment of Griffith was not enough. As all the sources show (see e.g. Appendix 7.2), his revelation of the 12 November deal on the night of 5 December astonished and horrified all his colleagues, including Collins. Therefore Lloyd George's interview with Collins on 5 December is equally crucial. This interview is one of Lloyd George's heresthetic masterpieces. Read Collins's memorandum very carefully. Note that Lloyd George is never recorded as promising that the Boundary Commission would actually do what Collins hoped it would. He merely bounced Collins's fervent hope back to him, nevertheless clearly leaving the astute Collins with the impression that Lloyd George had in fact promised that the Boundary Commission would strictly delimit Northern Ireland.

LG's Incredible Threat

We are now ready to start to characterize the games of November–December, 1921. The information given so far enables us to derive the preference ordering of the players among the possible outcomes.

The full game had sixteen players—seven British delegates, five Irish delegates, and a secretary and an under-secretary on each side. All four secretaries (Jones, Childers, Lionel Curtis, and Chartres) were important in shaping the proposals. Childers, as Appendix 7.2 and De Valera's letter to McGarrity show, was intended to be decisive over his cousin Barton, but at the last moment failed to be. The secretaries had no votes, so the players in the final game may be reduced to twelve.

They may then be reduced in stages to six. Three of the seven British delegates, the three who were absent on the night, were dummies. There is no evidence that Lloyd George sought their opinions at any time, including in the end game. There was no meeting of British delegates after those present on 5–6 December agreed the final terms. The three missing British signatures were simply added later.

All four of the non-dummy British negotiators were members of the British Cabinet. Three of the five Irish delegates—Griffith, Collins, and Barton—were members of the Irish Cabinet. Duggan and Duffy—dismissed by their own principal De Valera as 'mere legal padding'—were not. Furthermore, Duggan never acted independently of Collins. Duffy never acted independently of Barton and Childers, except for a few minutes near midnight on 5 December. With that exception, Duggan and Duffy are treated as clones of Collins and Barton respectively.

Chamberlain and Birkenhead may be treated as a single player with two votes. At the beginning of the negotiations they met and agreed that, as the outcome was so crucial to the Unionist party, they should speak and act as one (Chamberlain 1935: 144). All the evidence confirms that they did. We end up with a weighted voting game of the following six blocs:

Irish players

- Griffith
- Collins + Duggan
- Barton + Gavan Duffy

British players

- Lloyd George
- Chamberlain + Birkenhead
- Churchill

The First Game, from the Start of Negotiations until November 12

We suggest that the preferences of the actors were as shown in Table 7.2. *Griffith's* background was anti-militarist. He disliked the militarism of some of his colleagues (see Appendix 7.2, entry for 21.11.21). He took no active part in the Easter Rising. He founded Sinn Fein to be a movement of passive resistance, refusing to attend Westminster and setting up institutions of self-government in Ireland. He was not against Crowns in principle. His original model had been the Dual Monarchy of Austria and Hungary. If his own preferences only were at stake, therefore, he would have ranked the options *SUE* in descending order. However, he was a delegate of the Dáil with instructions to detach Ireland from the Empire. *Collins* did not share Griffith's principled objection to war, but he believed that the Irish forces were close to defeat when the Truce was agreed. He had little time for politicians or for (what he

Table 7.2. Suggested preference orderings from the outset to 12 November

	AG	MC, EJD	RB, GD	LG	AC, B	WSC
Best	*U*	*U*	*E*	*S*	*S*	*E*
Mid	*S*	*S*	*U*	*E*	*U*	*S*
Worst	*E*	*E*	*S*	*U*	*E*	*U*

Notation for Tables 7.2 to 7.6: *U* = break up on Ulster. *S* = settle on current British terms. *E* = break up on Irish membership of Empire

saw as) the small print of fine constitutional differences. For *Barton*, as for De Valera, Childers, and Collins, the difference between Dominion status and a Republic was paramount; settlement on the proposed terms was quite unacceptable. *Lloyd George* sought a settlement, but if there were to be a break preferred it to be on Empire status rather than on Ulster. *Chamberlain and Birkenhead* also wanted a settlement. But their position as leaders of the Unionist Party required them to support Ulster if it came to a break—otherwise their MPs would depose them in favour of Bonar Law. *Churchill*'s thinking was dominated by military considerations throughout. The once and future First Lord of the Admiralty regarded the continuation of British access to Irish harbours as paramount. His speech about dreary steeples shows that he did not care about Ulster substantively.

The vote matrices (Tables 7.3 and 7.5) are to be read as follows. The preferences of the two delegations are added up separately. (An overall addition would be meaningless. The structure of any treaty was not going to be decided by majority rule of those present.) The votes for option *i* against option *j* are shown in row *i*, column *j*. The horizontal sum of votes is then the *Borda score* for each option. The number of victories (disregarding margin of victory) for each option can be calculated by comparing each cell in the first block with the cell diagonally opposite. This lets us calculate the *Copeland score* for each option, which is a way of measuring whether a Condorcet winner exists. The Borda and Condorcet winners sometimes differ, but in our two cases they do not.

Table 7.3 therefore shows that in this first game the Irish delegation collectively sought a break on Ulster. If they could not get that, they would, by a majority, prefer to settle than to break on the Empire. The British delegation wanted to settle. But if there had to be a break, it was collectively indifferent on which subject the break should come.

The Second Game, from November 17 until December 4

On 12 November Griffith gave Lloyd George his pledge not to obstruct a Boundary Commission. At the Unionist conference on 17 November the Ulster hard-liners were routed. We suggest that two actors' preference orders change. *Griffith* would now back a settlement over a break on Ulster if forced

Table 7.3. Vote matrix for Table 7.2

	Irish position					British position				
	U	S	E	Borda	Copeland	U	S	E	Borda	Copeland
U	—	5	3	8	2	—	0	2	2	0.5
S	0	—	4	4	1	4	—	3	7	2
E	2	1	—	3	0	2	1	—	3	0.5

Table 7.4. Suggested preferences from November 17 to December 4

	AG	MC, EJD	RB, GD	LG	AC, B	WSC
Best	S	U	E	S	S	E
Mid	U	S	U	E	E	S
Worst	E	E	S	U	U	U

Table 7.5. Vote matrix for Table 7.4

	Irish position					British position				
	U	S	E	Borda	Copeland	U	S	E	Borda	Copeland
U	—	4	3	7	2	—	1	0	1	0
S	1	—	3	4	1	3	—	3	6	2
E	2	2	—	4	0	4	1	—	5	1

to. And *Chamberlain and Birkenhead* no longer had any reason to support Ulster intransigence (Tables 7.4 and 7.5).

Table 7.5 suggests that this did not change the Irish collective preference ordering, although it weakened the delegation's preference for a break on Ulster over a settlement. However, it did change things for the British delegation. If there were to be no settlement, the British would now prefer the break to come on Empire, not on Ulster. Just that seemed to happen on the night of 4 December, when Gavan Duffy said 'Our difficulty is coming into the Empire', and Chamberlain jumped up and said 'That ends it!' (Pakenham 1967: 217).

The Third Game, on 5 December

The first event of 5 December was Lloyd George's turning of Michael Collins by giving Collins the impression that the Boundary Commission would

Table 7.6. Revealed preferences, 5 December, 8 p.m.

	AG	MC, EJD	RB, GD	LG	AC, B	WSC
Better	S	?	E	S	S	S
Worse	E	?	S	E	E	E

decimate Northern Ireland. In the afternoon conference, the British made three concessions. First, they accepted an Oath revised by Collins and Birkenhead. Then, they made substantial concessions on defence, to produce the wording of clauses 6 to 8 of the final Treaty. On this point, either Churchill was overruled or he voluntarily gave in. Finally, Lloyd George abruptly withdrew all British objections to Irish autonomy on trade policy: 'he was prepared to agree provisionally that there should be freedom on both sides to impose any tariff either liked' (Barton's minute of 5.12.21, in Taylor 1958: 300).

This concession was directly aimed at Barton, the Irish trade specialist. It is full of irony. To concede to Ireland the right to impose protection was to concede it the right to damage its own economic interests—and the interests of substantial dairy farmers, such as Robert Barton, perhaps more than any other group in the Irish economy. That is, at any rate, what happened when the British and Irish governments did become locked in economic war after De Valera's return to power in 1932. Mutual retaliation harmed the Irish economy far more than the British.

Nevertheless, Barton was no Beardian promoter of his, or his class's, economic interests (cf. Beard 1913). He and Childers were delighted by the concession (see Appendix 7.2 and Barton's minute). But it brought the British not an iota closer to them on the constitutional question.

The game changed dramatically with Griffith's revelation of his promise to Lloyd George. It immediately became clear to all that there could not be a break on Ulster. The game reduced to that shown in Table 7.6, with Collins's position unknown to Lloyd George. Lloyd George then issued his ultimatum, with its demand for unanimous signature.

The Credibility of Lloyd George's Threat

Prima facie, Lloyd George's threat was utterly incredible.

- Why did the Irish not insist that they could not sign an amended document without reference back to their Cabinet?
- Why did they not telephone Dublin?
- How did they come to believe Lloyd George's absurd rigmarole of the special train and the destroyer? Any message to Craig could be telephoned to him. In the end the envoy phoned it in from Belfast docks, even though he had

forgotten to bring twopence for the call box (see above). He could have called from 10 Downing Street, where he would not have needed the twopence.

Some possible answers are suggested above. There is no denying that the element of pure theatre, added to the desperately high stakes and the exhaustion and internal division in the Irish camp, may have blinded them to the immediate incredibility of the threats.

But the threat behind the threat was credible. At least, it was believed. That was the threat of resumption of the war. In the short term, the Irish would lose more than the British from a resumption of war. Their relative populations, plus the absence of any real Irish armed forces, would see to that. In the medium term, Britain would be unable to hold on to Ireland by force. But the Irish delegates, even Barton, could not wait for the medium term on 5 December. Nobody with a vote was willing to restart the war on a point as abstract as Ireland's constitutional status. By ensuring that the break would come on that and not on Ulster, Lloyd George had sharply cut the amount of external support the Irish could expect. On Ulster, Britain was isolated; on Dominion status, the other Dominions would support Britain, for a few months at least.

The acid test of Lloyd George's threat is: was it time-consistent? If the Irish had failed to sign unanimously, would he still have been rational to carry it out? Recall that before he issued the ultimatum he already had Griffith's unconditional promise to sign. Therefore, the very incredibility of the Jeffrey Archer plot about special trains and destroyers might have worked to Lloyd George's advantage. He could have forgotten about any supposed promise to tell Craig the news by a particular time on a particular day. He could then have restarted preparing for war in a relatively leisurely manner, perhaps starting with a blockade of Irish ports and of the Ulster border, while waiting to see whether the division between Griffith and the other delegates led to Sinn Fein splitting into a peace party and a war party. At worst, Lloyd George could resign and allow Bonar Law to lead a Unionist war government. This would have been an immediate failure for Lloyd George, but could have left him in a position to spring back to power once the war started to go badly for the British, as it most certainly would have done within a few weeks or months.

Lloyd George's bluff, if it was a bluff, was not called, so the counterfactuals are untestable. But his underlying threat was time-consistent and therefore rationally credible.

The Sequential Signature Game

In Appendix 7.3, we set out a summary of the decision sequence for the Irish team, and suggestions about the utility function of each actor in turn.

Once Griffith had unconditionally agreed to sign, the other Irish delegates were in the appalling dilemma that all the contemporary accounts, from both sides, certify. More correctly, each of them faced a different appalling dilemma. *Collins* first. He was appalled by the way the option of breaking on Ulster had been closed off. But he had an independent assurance—so he thought—from Lloyd George on the Boundary Commission. He knew that he was a marked man whatever happened (see his well-known letter to O'Kane—'early this morning I signed my death warrant'). Having avoided being photographed throughout the guerrilla war, he was now identified. If there were an Anglo-Irish war, he would almost certainly be shot by the British. If there were an Irish civil war, he would probably be shot by the other side. He knew that if he signed, Duggan would almost certainly sign and that if he refused Duggan would almost certainly refuse. He cannot have expected that Barton or Gavan Duffy would sign, although if he signed he would try to persuade them.

So his best guess was that his signature made the difference between a treaty signed by one Irishman and a treaty signed by three (with high probability) or five (with low probability). It is widely believed that he thought the Irish guerrilla forces were unready to restart the Anglo-Irish war. (See e.g. Costello 1997: 69. But this is not a direct quotation.) One signature or three implied certain Anglo-Irish war, with widespread Irish loss of life and property and Collins's probable death, unless Lloyd George suspended his threat and accepted a three-signature agreement. But that, and also a five-signature agreement, implied a likely civil war.

A note found in Collins's papers of a discussion between him and Griffith, unfortunately undated, is nevertheless highly revealing.

MC: I will not agree to anything which threatens to plunge the people of Ireland into a war—not without their [the Irish Cabinet's] authority. Still less do I agree to being dictated to by those not embroiled in these negotiations . . . The advantages of Dominion status to us, as a stepping stone to complete independence, are immeasurable.
AG: Once signed, we are committed. But are they?
MC: No, we are not committed—not until both the Dáil and Westminster ratify whatever agreement is made. (Taylor 1958: 177–9)

Lloyd George's ultimatum forced Collins to decide without the Irish Cabinet's authority. But their indecisiveness on 3 December persuaded him that the delegates must decide without reference back. If normal politicians are utility maximizers in a conventional sense, Michael Collins was not a normal politician. The standard utility framework has difficulty with somebody who believed he was going to be killed whatever happened. His strictly altruistic preference was to minimise the damage to Ireland. He signed.

Given Collins's signature, *Duggan*'s task was easier. The payoff from signing strictly dominated that from not signing, whatever probabilities Duggan may have attached to the possible outcomes were he to sign. Not to sign would make him personally responsible for the ensuing Anglo-Irish war. Duggan was a solicitor, not a soldier. His own life would not be at risk, but not to sign would be to commit Ireland for sure to costly military action. He signed.

Barton now had to take the decision of his life.

Bob refused to sign & GD. Then long and hot argument—all about war and committing our young men to die for nothing. What could GD get better? Etc etc. GD answered quietly [?quickly] Bob shaken. Asked me out. I said it was principle and I felt Molly was with us. Suddenly he said 'Well I suppose I must sign'. (Appendix 7.2)

Griffith and Duggan already had put their coats on three times to announce to the British that they would sign and the others would refuse. Each time, according to Childers, it was Collins who called them back to continue the discussion.

A simple psychological explanation is readily available: that Barton cracked under intolerable pressure. But, if that is the explanation, why did he vote in both Cabinet and Dáil to ratify the Treaty? He was no longer under Lloyd George's sway by then. And his Cabinet vote is the most important single vote in twentieth-century Ireland. It swung the Cabinet in favour of the Treaty, and made the euphoric bandwagon unstoppable.

If Barton refused to sign, Anglo-Irish war was certain, and he would have sole responsibility, or at most responsibility shared only with Gavan Duffy, for launching it. If he signed, he could predict that Duffy would find it impossible not to. Then the Dáil would have the opportunity to decide. As Childers noted the next day:

But chief reasons seem to have been his belief that war was really imminent & inevitable—real war—this was the personal effect upon him of the British at the last— & of him feeling that he had no right to prevent the Dáil from deciding.

Thus, Barton had both a personal and an altruistic rationale for signing in the face of his convictions.

Duffy's situation now resembled that of Duggan on the other side some hours earlier. Not to sign would make him, a non-soldier, solely liable for the outbreak of war. Although if he signed a civil war was still likely, it was less likely by a two-vote margin in the Dail than if Barton signed (and voted for the treaty) and he did not. Signing clearly dominated not signing. He signed.

Conclusion

Analytic narratives aim to do all that conventional narratives can, but to add some further value. The narrative of what happened between July and December 1921 has been well established for many years, and even Childers' diary adds relatively little to the *what, when, and how*. But an analytic narrative in the rational choice tradition adds some points to the *why*. For instance, if the preference orderings in Tables 7.2 to 7.6 are correct, they show why the moderate Unionists Chamberlain and Birkenhead were ready to break on 4

December in the face of Duffy's apparently innocent remark 'Our difficulty is coming into the Empire'. And the analytic narrative both focuses attention on the surprisingly overlooked importance of Barton's swing vote for the Treaty in the Irish Cabinet on 8 December and gives a fuller explanation than that he cracked. Above all, the case enables us to see just what was so wizard-like about the Welsh Wizard in his prime (in J. M. Keynes's well-known description, 'this goat-footed bard, this half-human visitor to our age from the hag-ridden magic and enchanted woods of Celtic antiquity'—Keynes 1933: 36). Lloyd George achieved the Irish settlement that had eluded every front-rank British politician since 1800. To succeed where Peel, Gladstone, and Salisbury had failed is an achievement still worth close analysis.

Some of Lloyd George's stratagems are already well known. He played on Irish hopes from a Boundary Commission, letting them understand that it would coerce the North while British minutes, which the Irish saw, gave no such promise. Lloyd George told no lies. His heresthetic was subtler than that. He also saw, from early on, which Irishmen to deal with and which to freeze out. In the bitter words of the irreconcilable Cathal Brugha, 'the British Government selected its men' (Minute of Irish Cabinet meeting, 3.12.21, in Pakenham 1967: 208. Griffith forced Brugha to withdraw the remark). He even seems, extraordinarily, to have confided his view of the Irish delegation to Collins:

[He is] not sure how far he can go with me. Confided that Arthur G. was altogether too dour for dealings. That Barton was suspicious of him—as I am. But that Duffy and Duggan were pigeons for the plucking. . . . Hopes this affair will gain him political prestige—which apparently he desperately needs. (Collins memo, n.d. (? 11.21), quoted by Taylor 1958: 154)

In the last month, Lloyd George dealt only with Griffith and Collins. He brought in Barton just when a switch by Barton was necessary (and sufficient) for a treaty—on the afternoon of 5 December.

The nonsense about the special train and the destroyer permitted him to enforce a decision sequence on the Irish, in the common knowledge that Griffith had agreed to sign. The sequential signature game ensured that each delegate in turn had responsibility for war on his own shoulders. None of them ranked the subjective utility of starting the war above the subjective utility of signing. Therefore each of the four in turn had a rational motive for signing, given that those ahead of him had signed. The Irish Treaty was signed by induction.

Unfortunately for Lloyd George, his great Irish triumph was embedded in a great British failure. He was still the prisoner of the Unionists, who could topple him at any time. His effort to form a hegemonic centre party petered out, blocked by (among other things) the resilience of the alliance between Labour and the trade unions, and his failure, despite the proceeds from selling peerages, to finance and staff a centre party. In October 1922, a backbench Conservative revolt, led by Stanley Baldwin, ended the power of Lloyd

George—for ever, as it turned out, although nobody expected that at the time. The Conservative backbenchers threw out their own Coalitionist leaders Chamberlain and Birkenhead, and substituted the already mortally ill Bonar Law, who was willing to take revenge on his wartime ally for various offences, including Ireland. Lloyd George had succeeded in reducing the dimensionality of British politics, getting rid of the poisonous Irish dimension. He had led the transition from centre–periphery politics to class politics. However, not he, but Baldwin and his Conservative successors picked most of the fruits from the promised land.

APPENDIX 7.1

Articles of Agreement for a Treaty between Great Britain and Ireland, December 6, 1921

1. Ireland shall have the same Constitutional status in the community of Nations known as the British Empire as the Dominion of Canada, the Commonwealth of Australia, the Dominion of New Zealand, and the Union of South Africa, with a Parliament having powers to make laws for the peace, order, and good government of Ireland, and an Executive responsible to that Parliament, and shall be styled and known as the Irish Free State.
2. Subject to the provisions hereinafter set out, the position of the Irish Free State in relation to the Imperial Parliament and Government and otherwise shall be that of the Dominion of Canada, and the law, practice, and Constitutional usage governing the relationship of the Crown or the representative of the Crown and of the Imperial Parliament to the Dominion of Canada shall govern their relationship to the Irish Free State.
3. The representative of the Crown in Ireland shall be appointed in like manner as the Governor-General of Canada, and in accordance with the practice observed in the making of such appointments.
4. The Oath to be taken by members of the Parliament of the Irish Free State shall be in the following form:—
   I . . . do solemnly swear true faith and allegiance to the Constitution of the Irish Free State as by law established, and that I will be faithful to H. M. King George V, his heirs and successors by law, in virtue of the common citizenship of Ireland with Great Britain and her adherence to and membership of the group of nations forming the British Commonwealth of Nations.
5. The Irish Free State shall assume liability for the service of the Public Debt of the United Kingdom as existing at the date hereof and towards the payment of War Pensions as existing at that date in such proportion as may be fair and equitable, having regard to any just claim on the part of Ireland by way of set-off or counter-claim, the amount of such sums being determined in default of agreement by the arbitration of one or more independent persons being citizens of the British Empire.
6. Until an arrangement has been made between the British and Irish Governments whereby the Irish Free State undertakes her own coastal defence, the defence by sea of Great Britain and Ireland shall be undertaken by His Majesty's Imperial Forces, but this shall not prevent the construction or maintenance by the Government of the Irish Free State of such vessels as are necessary for the protection of the Revenue or the Fisheries. The foregoing provisions of this Article shall be

reviewed at a conference of Representatives of the British and Irish Governments, to be held at the expiration of five years from the date hereof with a view to the undertaking by Ireland of a share in her own coastal defence.

7. The Government of the Irish Free State shall afford to His Majesty's Imperial Forces

   (a) In time of peace such harbour and other facilities as are indicated in the Annex hereto, or such other facilities as may from time to time be agreed between the British Government and the Government of the Irish Free State; and

   (b) In time of war or of strained relations with a Foreign Power such harbour and other facilities as the British Government may require for the purposes of such defence as aforesaid.

8. With a view to securing the observance of the principle of international limitation of armaments, if the Government of the Irish Free State establishes and maintains a military defence force, the establishments thereof shall not exceed in size such proportion of the military establishments maintained in Great Britain as that which the population of Ireland bears to the population of Great Britain.

9. The ports of Great Britain and the Irish Free State shall be freely open to the ships of the other country on payment of the customary port and other duties.

10. The Government of the Irish Free State agrees to pay fair compensation on terms not less favourable than those accorded by the Act of 1920 to judges, officials, members of Police Forces, and other Public Servants who are discharged by it or who retire in consequence of the change of government effected in pursuance hereof. Provided that this agreement shall not apply to members of the Auxiliary Police Force or to persons recruited in Great Britain for the Royal Irish Constabulary during the two years next preceding the date hereof. The British Government will assume responsibility for such compensation or pensions as may be payable to any of these excepted persons.

11. Until the expiration of one month from the passing of the Act of Parliament for the ratification of this instrument, the powers of the Government and of the Irish Free State shall not be exercisable as respects Northern Ireland, and the provisions of the Government of Ireland Act, 1920, shall, so far as they relate to Northern Ireland, remain in full force and effect, and no election shall be held for the return of members to serve in the Parliament of the Irish Free State for constituencies in Northern Ireland, unless a resolution is passed by both Houses of Parliament of Northern Ireland in favour of holding of such elections before the end of the said month.

12. If, before the expiration of the said month, an address is presented to His Majesty by both Houses of Parliament of Northern Ireland to that effect, the powers of the Parliament and the Government of the Irish Free State shall no longer extend to Northern Ireland, and the provisions of the Government of Ireland Act, 1920 (including those relating to the Council of Ireland) shall so far as they relate to Northern Ireland continue to be of full force and effect, and this instrument shall have effect subject to the necessary modifications.

    Provided that if such an address is so presented a Commission consisting of three persons, one to be appointed by the Government of the Irish Free State, one to be appointed by the Government of Northern Ireland, and one who shall be Chairman to be appointed by the British Government shall determine in accord-ance with the wishes of the inhabitants, so far as may be compatible with economic and geographic conditions, the boundaries between Northern Ireland and the rest of Ireland, and for the purposes of the Government of Ireland Act, 1920 and of this instrument, the boundary of Northern Ireland shall be such as may be determined by such Commission.

13. For the purpose of the last foregoing article, the powers of the Parliament of South-ern Ireland under the Government of Ireland Act, 1920, to elect members of the Council of Ireland shall after the Parliament of the Irish Free State is constituted be exercised by that Parliament.

14. After the expiration of the said month, if no such address as is mentioned in Article 12 hereof is presented, the Parliament and Government of Northern Ireland shall continue to exercise as respects Northern Ireland the powers conferred on them by the Government of Ireland Act, 1920, but the Parliament and Government of the Irish Free State shall in Northern Ireland have in relation to matters in respect of which the Parliament of Northern Ireland has not power to make laws under that Act (including matters which under the said Act are within the jurisdiction of the Council of Ireland) the same powers as in the rest of Ireland, subject to such other provisions as may be agreed in manner hereinafter appearing.

15. At any time after the date hereof the Government of Northern Ireland and the provisional Government of Southern Ireland hereinafter constituted may meet for the purpose of discussing the provisions subject to which the last foregoing article is to operate in the event of no such address as is therein mentioned being presented and those provisions may include:—

    (a) Safeguards with regard to patronage in Northern Ireland;
    (b) Safeguards with regard to the collection of revenue in Northern Ireland;
    (c) Safeguards with regard to import and export duties affecting the trade or industry of Northern Ireland;
    (d) Safeguards for minorities in Northern Ireland;
    (e) The settlement of the financial relations between Northern Ireland and the Irish Free State;
    (f) The establishment and powers of a local militia in Northern Ireland and the relation of the Defence Forces of the Irish Free State and of Northern Ireland respectively,

    and if at any such meeting provisions are agreed to, the same shall have effect as if they were included amongst the provisions subject to which the powers of the Parliament and the Government of the Irish Free State are to be exercisable in Northern Ireland under Article 14 hereof.

16. Neither the Parliament of the Irish Free State nor the Parliament of Northern Ireland shall make any law so as either directly or indirectly to endow any religion or prohibit or restrict the free exercise thereof or give any preference or impose any disability on account of the religious belief or religious status or affect prejudicially the right of any child to attend a school receiving public money without attend-ing the religious instruction at the school or make any discrimination as respects State aid between schools under the management of different religious denomina-tions or divert from any religious denomination or any educational institution any of its property except for public utility purposes and on payment of compensation.

17. By way of provisional arrangement for the administration of Southern Ireland during the interval which must elapse between the date hereof and the constitu-

tion of a Parliament and Government of the Irish Free State in accordance there-with, steps shall be taken forthwith for summoning a meeting of members of Parliament elected for constituencies in Southern Ireland since the passing of the Government of Ireland Act, 1920, and for constituting a provisional Government, and the British Government shall take the steps necessary to transfer to such Provisional Government the powers and machinery requisite for the discharge of its duties provided that every member of such provisional Government shall have signified in writing his or her acceptance of this instrument. But this arrangement shall not continue in force beyond the expiration of twelve months from the date hereof.

18. This instrument shall be submitted forthwith by his Majesty's Government for the approval of Parliament and by the Irish signatories to a meeting summoned for the purpose of the members elected to sit in the House of Commons of Southern Ireland and if approved shall be ratified by the necessary legislation.

Signed
On behalf of the British Delegation:—
D. LLOYD GEORGE
AUSTEN CHAMBERLAIN
BIRKENHEAD
WINSTON S. CHURCHILL
L. WORTHINGTON EVANS
HAMAR GREENWOOD
GORDON HEWART

On behalf of the Irish Delegation:—
ART. O. GRIOBHTHA
MICHEAL O. COILEAIN
RIOBARD BARTUN
E. S. O. DUGAIN
SEORSA GABHAIN U1 DHUBHTHAIGH

6th December, 1921

APPENDIX 7.2

Extracts from the Diary of Erskine Childers (1870–1922), Secretary to the Irish Delegation

Key

The Irish delegation
  AG = Arthur Griffith
  MC = Michael Collins
  Bob, RCB = Robert Barton
  EJD = Eamonn J. Duggan
  GD = George Gavan Duffy

Members of the Irish Cabinet who repudiated the Treaty
  Dev = Eamonn De Valera, President of Dáil Éireann
  Cahal = Cathal Brugha
  Austin = Austin Stack

Other Irish actors
  Cosgrave = William Cosgrave, pro-Treaty politician, later President of Irish Free State
  Molly = Mrs M. A. Childers, the author's wife and Barton's cousin-in-law

Members of the British delegation
  LG = David Lloyd George
  Birkenhead = F. E. Smith, 1st Earl of Birkenhead
  Churchill = Winston Churchill

Diary 1921

Nov 16 GD suggests writing tonight to LG saying treaty unacceptable & we will draft another. AG refuses for his part . . . AG refuses to discuss treaty tonight. We press for cause of sending treaty today—day before Liverpool meeting. Says he doesn't know, reminds Bob of his expression about 'dirty politics' the other night and seems resentful.

Nov 18 Sub-conference AG, MC, LG, Birkenhead. They seem as usual to have put up no fight.

Nov 21. AG attacks me about *Riddle of Sands*. Says I caused one European war & now want to cause another.

Nov 22 . . . AG broke out about Allegiance saying he was willing to give it to save country from war.

Dec 5 Amendments made—those on Defence little use—principles unchanged. But they [the British] surrender on *trade*—full rights . . . Meeting lasted 4 hours. I sat outside reading Lincoln. Meeting of delegates 9 pm. Final discussion. AG spoke almost passionately for signing. It seems other side insist *all delegates* shall sign and *recommend treaty to Dáil*. Monstrous demand. AG said we were on top of wave. Never such terms again. MC said nothing. Bob refused to sign & GD. Then long and hot argument—all about war and committing our young men to die for nothing. What could GD get better? Etc etc. GD answered quietly [?quickly] Bob shaken. Asked me out. I said it was principle and I felt Molly was with us. Suddenly he said 'Well I suppose I must sign'. I stopped him and said at least ⟨They said it was bedrock on defence⟩[1] you only do it under duress [some lines missing,] [RCB] went in and said he would sign under duress and solely because, if he didn't, country would get no opportunity to decide. AG then said he would say they signed under duress and if they refused tell them to go to the devil. EJD strongly contested this (weakest of all, all team). [missing—presumably 'MC'] supported EJD and it was dropped. [missing—presumably 'GD'] couldn't hold out if 4 signed. [missing, presumably 'MC,'] AG and RCB to go. We left at 11 pm (an hour late). . . . My chief recollection of these inexpressibly miserable hours was that of Churchill in evening dress moving up and down the lobby with his loping stoop & long strides & a huge cigar like a bowsprit. His coarse heavy jowls making him a very type of brutal militarism. Duggan left by 5.30 am mail for Dublin with signed Treaty.

Dec 6 Woke desperately dreary and lonely. . . . Privately today RCB said that my allusion to Molly's support for refusal to sign last night made him sign—deciding element—because her home reminded him of thousands of homes to be [illegible, ???ransacked, ruined]! Strange reason! But chief reasons seem to have been his belief that war was really imminent & inevitable—real war—this was the personal effect upon him of the British at the last—& of him feeling that he had no right to prevent the Dáil from deciding.

We agreed that Duggan's behaviour and speeches were miserably ignominious and hypocritical. AG jarred too with his perpetual harping on men who had died. MC said too little, but it was he who prevented a break, several times suggesting delay when it had been practically decided to break—coats on etc.

Dec 7 . . . Notes of both the last sub-conferences (AG also but brief and jejune).[2] Most important document. Allusion in it to strange episode of the production by LG of a memo on Ulster said to have been agreed to by AG (date?) Also report of direct threat of war.

Dec 8 . . . Cabinet Meeting at 12. Went in & found Dev head on hands reproaching MC with having signed . . . Dev said Del[egation] had broken instructions not to make a serious decision without consulting Cabinet . . . He also said that AG promised not to sign (giving allegiance) but to submit to Dáil. AG said Dev had refused to come to London himself. Dev said that this was because he trusted no undertaking. MC said they had only recommended it to Dáil. Dev said really much more. 'He would have to oppose Treaty'. AG said alternative was war. GD, RCB, & MC all said question of referring Treaty to Cabinet didn't arise. They had not thought of it. . . . Dev said it

---

[1] This phrase is obviously out of place. It is surrounded by the account of the meeting between Childers and Barton, which was written around it in the space available on the page. 'They' clearly refers to the British delegation. The phrase probably belongs with the précis of Griffith's views, just above.

[2] These notes were made by Barton. They can be found in full in Rex Taylor (1958: 297–303).

was not team-work. GD said no choice. The Treaty was then gone through clause by clause. . . . GD said he had signed because he was told *all* must sign and recommend . . .

Cabinet asked their opinions in turn. Cahal and Austin against Treaty. Bob, AG, and MC for it—all hung on Cosgrave's vote. He gave it for Treaty.

Source: Trinity College, Dublin, MSS 7814. Six small notebooks, 6′ × 4′ in. (15 × 10 cm.) approx, 32 pp. approx. per notebook.

APPENDIX 7.3

Preference Orderings

U = break up on Ulster; S = settle on current British terms; E = break up on Irish membership of Empire

3.1 Suggested preference orderings from the outset to 12 November

	AG	MC, EJD	RB, GD	LG	AC, B	WSC
Best	U	U	E	S	S	E
Mid	S	S	U	E	U	S
Worst	E	E	S	U	E	U

Vote matrix for 3.1

	Irish position					British position				
	U	S	E	**Borda**	Copeland	U	S	E	**Borda**	Copeland
U	—	5	3	**8**	2	—	0	2	**2**	0.5
S	0	—	4	**4**	1	4	—	3	**7**	2
E	2	1	—	**3**	0	2	1	—	**3**	0.5

3.2 Suggested preferences from 17 November to 4 December

	AG	MC, EJD	RB, GD	LG	AC, B	WSC
Best	S	U	E	S	S	E
Mid	U	S	U	E	E	S
Worst	E	E	S	U	U	U

Vote matrix for 3.2

	U	S	E	Borda	Copeland	U	S	E	Borda	Copeland
		Irish position					British position			
U	—	4	3	7	2	—	1	0	1	0
S	1	—	3	4	1	3	—	3	6	2
E	2	2	—	4	0	4	1	—	5	1

3.3 *Revealed preferences, 5 December, 8 p.m.*

	AG	MC, EJD	RB, GD	LG	AC, B	WSC
Better	S	?	E	S	S	S
Worse	E	?	S	E	E	E

APPENDIX 7.4

The Irish Decision Sequence, 5 December, 1921

1. 8 p.m. AG announces decision to sign unconditionally. Pro signing: chance of peace, high probability of civil war, not breaking his word. Anti signing: certainty of Anglo-Irish war, breaking his word.
2. In taxi returning to Hans Place. MC decision.
   Sign ⇒ with high prob. majority will sign ⇒ civil war, own death warrant. With low prob. all will sign, ⇒ (less certainly) civil war, own death warrant.
   Don't sign ⇒ certainty of Anglo-Irish war—no treaty, many dead including self.
   MC signs
3. Back at Hans Place. EJD decision.
   Sign ⇒ majority will sign ⇒ civil war, many dead (but not self)
   Don't sign ⇒ certainty of Anglo-Irish war—no treaty, many dead.
   EJD signs
4. After AG and EJD have put on coats three times to return to announce that three have signed and two refused, RCB decision:
   Sign ⇒ civil war not certain, responsibility transferred to Dáil. If civil war, then many dead
   Don't sign ⇒ certainty of Anglo-Irish war, self responsible for break.
   RCB signs
5. Shortly afterwards (*c.*11 p.m.). GD decision
   Sign ⇒ civil war less likely, responsibility remains with Dáil. If civil war, then many dead
   Don't sign ⇒ certainty of Anglo-Irish war, self responsible for break.
   GD signs

8

'There is no alternative': Margaret Thatcher and Tony Blair

The Long (but Vulnerable) Conservative Hegemony

The long Conservative hegemony that followed Lloyd George's failure was surprising. With the demise of the Liberals in the 1924 General Election, British politics settled into a two-class, two-party mould. Politics was about issues of wealth and welfare, the classic single dimension that dominates politics in those democracies where it is not cross-cut by religion or ethnicity. Class politics is the default option, and in Britain from 1924 to 1974 there was no other issue dimension. Of course, there were huge and dramatic changes of political fortune. Labour split and collapsed in 1931. The Second World War, like the First, led to an all-party coalition government. Labour ministers, in charge of most of the domestic departments, gained experience and credibility that helped to pave the way for the Labour victory in 1945. All of these were movements along the main issue dimension, as one or other party positioned itself closer to the electoral median (for instance, Labour in 1945), or had a more competent reputation than the other (the Conservative-dominated National Government in 1931; Labour in 1964).

But in a two-class, two-party world, the party representing the larger class should have been the hegemon. Throughout this period (except possibly at the very end) the working class outnumbered the middle class in the British electorate, however these contentious terms are defined. Why were the Conservatives—the party of the smaller class—so much more successful in this period than Labour—the party of the larger class? Historians normally put this down to competence and luck. But that is unsatisfactory. In a world of rational office-seeking politicians, it beggars belief that competence and luck should have been overwhelmingly concentrated on one side for so long.

The electoral system helped the winning party. But that does not dispose of the mystery. The British electoral system helps *whichever* of the two big parties wins the plurality of votes. The responsiveness component of the system exaggerates the winner's vote lead into a larger seat lead. Responsiveness benefits whichever party is ahead in votes. The bias component has favoured Labour most of the time since 1945, although not in 1950 or 1951 (I have found no reliable calculations of it for the period 1924–35). So neither component of the system can explain Conservative hegemony.

What, in particular, are we to make of Margaret Thatcher's period in power from 1979 to 1990? The lazy explanation is that there is nothing much to explain. Labour had lost its reputation for competence in the circumstances of the 1979 General Election (through loss of its flagship devolution policy and extensive industrial unrest). Like the Conservatives in 1906 (and 1997), it then turned in on itself, moved sharply to a set of extreme positions which satisfied activists but not the electorate, and paraded its divisions in public. The ensuing defection of the Gang of Four (Roy Jenkins, Bill Rodgers, Shirley Williams, and David Owen) led to the formation of the Social Democratic Party (SDP). (See Butler and Kavanagh 1980: 18–46, 119–28; Crewe and King 1995: Part I). In 1983, the SDP, in alliance with the Liberals, came within two percentage points of the Labour vote. But their even distribution across the country restricted them to twenty-three seats (Table 8.1). The Alliance slid from this peak, and split after 1987. Most of the members of the SDP were absorbed into the Liberal Democrats in 1988, but a minority under Owen refused to join. The continued split of the opposition forces paved the way for the Conservative victories of 1987 and 1992.

But this account of the Thatcher years jumps too quickly to the conclusion that with a united opposition the Conservatives would not have won their four general elections in a row from 1979 to 1992. On the best evidence, from the British Election Survey, the Conservatives would have won in 1983 and 1987 because they were then the *Condorcet winners*. That is, when each party is put into a pairwise comparison with each other, the electorate preferred the Conservatives in each pair (Fisher 1999: Table 3.4). In 1992, the Liberal Democrats were the Condorcet winners, but the Conservatives ran them close.

Moreover, to discuss the Thatcher years without Thatcher would be to put on *Hamlet* without the Prince. Mrs Thatcher was very different from her predecessors. She differed in style and in policies. She was a brilliant rhetorician.

Table 8.1. Seats and votes, General Election of 1983

Party	Seats (% of total)	Votes (% of total)
Conservative	61.08	42.43
Labour	32.15	27.57
Lib/SDP Alliance	3.54	25.37
All others	3.23	4.63

Source: Calculated from Butler and Kavanagh (1984: Tables A1-1 and A1-2).

She was a more hesitant heresthetician, but this chapter argues that she was one. Like Salisbury, she saw the need to expand the social base of the Conservative Party. She did so in part by changing the issue space of British politics. At the turn of the millennium, the change of issue space looks like her enduring achievement. The rebasing of the Conservatives looks like a total failure.

But why, as the Conservatives were the more successful class party and as demographic, social, and economic change continued to shrink Labour's core class, should there be any need to widen the Conservatives' class base? Because, we shall argue, the legacy of Salisbury was slowly but surely fading, and it needed to be replaced. The first sociologists to tackle the question, 'Why are the Conservatives a consistently more successful class party than Labour?' had come up with the explanation 'deference'. The socially deferential working class, it was held, dearly loved a lord, and voted for their social betters, the Conservatives. The evidence for this is vivid (see especially McKenzie and Silver 1968: chs. 1 and 2) but anecdotal. Butler and Stokes (1969: 104–22) showed ingeniously that a cohort effect gives a much better explanation than a deference effect for the excess of working-class Conservatives over middle-class socialists. In the 1960s, the oldest generations in the electorate had come of age before Labour was a contender for power. In many parts of the UK, they were socialised into W. S. Gilbert's world where every boy and every gal that was born into this world alive was either a little Liberal or else a little Conservative (fa la la). The Conservative working-class advantage was concentrated in those generations. Teenage socialization was very powerful. But the Conservatives' advantage was dying out fast. The 1945 cohort, who came of age during the Second World War or the Attlee government, contained more middle-class Labour supporters than working-class Conservatives. One of the reviews of Butler and Stokes (1969) was headed 'Make a baby for Labour'.

Not only were deferential workers on the decline, but the Conservatives' class heartland was under threat. The loyalty of the middle class, however defined, to the Conservatives, has been declining since records were first kept in the 1950s. This is a fiercely contested question, the answer to which depends on the precise question one puts. Different authors use different definitions of 'middle class', and these differences can have considerable consequences. But Conservative support within the middle class has certainly declined (Table 8.2).

Two things were going on. The Conservatives were holding on to their support in the petty bourgeoisie (that is, small self-employed traders and their families), while they lost support in the salariat and the routine non-manual groups. And the salariat was rapidly increasing in size. In 1951, the groups listed by Bonham who would now be classed as the salariat comprised 19 per cent of the electorate; by 1979 this had increased to nearly 26 per cent. But, because the Conservative hold over them was weakening, their total contribution to the Conservative vote was not increasing. Their contribution

Table 8.2. Conservative support within the middle class, General Election years 1950–79

Year	Salariat		Routine non-manual		Petty bourgeoisie	
	Proportion of voters	% voting Con.	Proportion of voters	% voting Con.	Proportion of voters	% voting Con.
1950		81		66		74
1951	19.21	83	15.34	68	2.77	81
1964	19.49	62	14.33	58	7.42	75
1970	22.17	62	14.40	51	8.47	70
1979	25.70	61	14.21	52	8.84	77

Source (1950–1) Calculated from Bonham 1954: Tables 9 and 11; 1951 Census and Gallup data.

Source (1964–79) Heath *et al.* 1991: Table 5.2, British Election Study data.

to the anti-Conservative vote was increasing fast. Among routine non-manual workers, a group of static size, Conservative support was haemorrhaging. Only among the petty bourgeoisie was it holding up. (The apparent jump in that class size between 1951 and 1964 is merely due to different ways of grouping data).

The salariat was not only getting larger; it was becoming better educated. This was helping to foster a second issue dimension in the British electorate. Heath and his colleagues on the British Election Survey (see e.g. Heath *et al.* 1991: 174) identify this dimension by factor analysis of responses in the British Election Survey to a battery of opinion questions. Questions on the death penalty, stiffer sentences, third world aid, and other topics (listed in Heath 1991: Table 11.1) generate a 'liberal–authoritarian' dimension. It is orthogonal to the left–right dimension. Knowing that a voter is (say) to the left on the left–right dimension is of no help at all in predicting that voter's position on the liberal–authoritarian dimension. A voter's position on the left–right scale is explained by such predictors as the voter's class, the voter's father's class, housing tenure, age, and sex (women and the young being more left-wing than men and the old). None of these background variables predicts a voter's position on the liberal–authoritarian scale. Education, and membership of a church other than the established churches, are the predictors of liberalism; lack of education, and established church membership, are therefore the predictors of authoritarianism.

Politicians who can analyse and (still better) act against threats to their electoral base are rare. Disraeli was one, Salisbury another; Lloyd George a third. Disraeli detached the Conservatives from their over-reliance on Church and land, knowing that the landed interest would come to control fewer and fewer seats. Salisbury built up the alternative base on the villa vote and imperialism. Lloyd George saw that the social base of the Liberals was eroding and tried (but in the end failed) to build a centre party on a new social base.

During the long years of Conservative hegemony, few of the party's leaders addressed the weakness in its social base. As long as it represented the smaller class in a two-class two-party system, it was vulnerable. The best Conservative leader before Thatcher at projecting a cross-class appeal was Stanley Baldwin (1923–37). Baldwin, in real life a steel magnate, played the bucolic squire. He published, while he was Prime Minister, a book of essays called *On England* (Baldwin 1926). Baldwin evokes

The sounds of England, the tinkle of the hammer on the anvil in the country smithy, the corncrake on a dewy morning, the sound of the scythe against the whetstone, and the sight of a plough team coming over the brow of a hill. (Baldwin 1926: 7)

No matter that not a single one of these was common in 1926. Most metal-work was done in massive steelworks like Richard Thomas & Baldwins Ltd, not in country smithies (and 'tinkle' is a very odd word when you think about it). Corncrakes, and horse-drawn plough teams, were already in steep decline. But Baldwin's rhetoric was effective. By the time John Major tried it in 1993, evoking 'long shadows on county grounds, warm beer, ... and as George Orwell said, "old maids bicycling to Communion through the morning mist"' (Seldon 1997: 370) it no longer tinkled true.

Margaret Thatcher

Margaret Roberts was born in 1925, the daughter of a stern Methodist shop-keeper in Grantham, Lincolnshire. Her father was a Conservative-leaning independent local councillor. She studied chemistry in the local grammar school (because her chemistry teacher was the most inspiring—Thatcher 1995: 18–19) and then at Oxford, where she became president of the Conservative Association. On graduating, she worked for three years as an industrial chemist, having 'seriously considered', she says, going into the Indian civil service (Thatcher 1995: 24). She fought the safe Labour seat of Dartford in the 1950 and 1951 General Elections. Marriage to the business-man Denis Thatcher in 1951 enabled her to switch to the more conventional career (for a politician) of the law, qualifying as a barrister in 1953. She specialized in tax law. She failed to win a nomination in 1955, because Conservative Associations were reluctant to choose a woman with young children as their parliamentary candidate. However, she was selected for Finchley in 1958, and won it in 1959. She became a junior minister in 1961. In 1965, she joined Edward Heath's Opposition front bench. She joined the Shadow Cabinet in 1967, shadowing the Ministry of Power. She was the most effect-ive speaker in a debate on the Aberfan disaster that took place within days of her appointment. Equally characteristically, she appeared in the office of the relevant Assistant Secretary at the Ministry of Power to demand what the

Ministry had done and was doing to prevent a recurrence of the disaster. It was the only time that Lord Dearing can recall an Opposition spokesman doing so in his entire civil service career (*Hansard* 751: 1988–99, 26 October 1967; McLean 1997; Thatcher 1995: 142–3; interview with Lord Dearing, February 1998).

In 1970, Heath came to power in the circumstances described in Chapter 5. The Heath team had set out a somewhat free-market agenda at a Shadow Cabinet meeting at the Selsdon Park Hotel in Croydon. Harold Wilson seized on this, making more of it than it truly was:

Selsdon Man is designing a system of society for the ruthless and the pushing, the uncaring (quoted in Butler and Butler 1994: 273).

It later suited Thatcher's supporters (though not Thatcher 1995; see p. 160) to paint the same picture, in order to demonize Heath as the man who had run away from it. But the Selsdon programme fell a long way short of the strident free-marketry that was then called Powellism and would later be called Thatcherism. Why? Because, in 1970, it was associated with Enoch Powell. No more need be said. The 1970 Conservative manifesto, whose economic policy Thatcher (1995: 160) called 'a judicious muddle', promises to 'check any abuse of dominant market power or monopoly . . . identify and remove obstacles that prevent effective competition and restrict initiative' (Craig 1975: 332). It contained no explicit promises of privatization, nor of control of the money supply.

Almost as soon as he entered government, Heath faced a severe challenge to Selsdonism. Rolls-Royce went bankrupt, having been overstretched by developing a new aero engine. Heath decided that such an icon of British industry, a national champion in the aerospace and defence industries, could not be allowed to go to the wall—'there would be serious implications for our own defence capabilities' (Heath 1998: 340). The Heath government nationalized the company in February 1971. As it turned out, this was commercially shrewd—it was successfully privatized again in 1987 (Vickers and Yarrow 1988: 164–5). But hot on Rolls-Royce's heels came Upper Clyde Shipbuilders (UCS), a hopelessly unviable group of shipyards in an unemployment blackspot. Tony Benn, who had been responsible for creating the consortium in the preceding government, leaked what Heath (1998: 347) calls a 'tactless' 1969 document by Nicholas Ridley, later a Thatcherite minister, saying that government should pull out of UCS. Heath took the view that the leak made it impossible to pull out.

But the great U-turn, as Heath's enemies have always viewed it, occurred in 1972. The Industry Act of that year offered among the most generous support ever to failing industry in areas of high unemployment. At the same time, the Industrial Relations Act, which had attempted to remove the immunity from tort actions granted to trade unions by the Trade Disputes Act 1906, was proving unworkable. The National Industrial Relations Court lacked legitimacy and those who defied its rulings were seen as heroes and martyrs.

Finally that year, the Heath government took powers to control incomes, prices, and dividends—a more thoroughgoing incomes policy, at least on paper, than its predecessor had attempted. Enoch Powell said that Heath had 'taken leave of his senses' (*Hansard* 845: 631; 6.11.72).

Throughout the Heath government, Thatcher served as Secretary of State for Education and Science, where she 'showed not the smallest inclination to curb' the growth of the public sector (Young 1990: 66). Her white paper 'Education: a Framework for Expansion' (Dept of Education and Science: Cmnd 5174/1972) foreshadowed a 50 per cent increase in real terms on education spending. She did not protest against the U-turns on industrial policy. If the administration of 1970–4 was a great betrayal, then Margaret Thatcher was one of the betrayers.

After the two General Election defeats of 1974, Heath could survive no longer as Conservative leader. However, his refusal to resign immediately, which tied most of his leading colleagues to silent support until February 1975, made Thatcher's succession possible. To begin with, Sir Keith Joseph was the standard-bearer of the free-market right, but he disqualified himself with a speech apparently advocating compulsory birth control among feckless poor mothers (and showing an inability to understand how percentages are presented in statistical tables). In the first ballot of the leadership contest, Thatcher ran against Heath and beat him. In the second ballot, Heath's right-hand man and obvious successor, William Whitelaw, stood. But by now Thatcher was unstoppable. She swept him aside by 146 votes to 79, with 49 votes going to a trio of minor candidates.

Nevertheless, her first years as Conservative leader were curiously tentative. In her memoirs, she projects herself as a leader of the opposition within the Opposition. For instance, she states that she wanted to join the rebels in her parliamentary party against her own Shadow Cabinet's Rhodesia policy, and that she 'had broken ranks' against her own employment spokesmen by pressing for a less conciliatory line on trade union reform (Thatcher 1995: 418, 425). For this reason among others, the 1979 Conservative manifesto held few hints of what was to come. Of three key economic policies that were to define her governments—trade union reform, monetarism, and privatization—only the first features at any length in Mrs Thatcher's 1979 manifesto. The only privatization commitment was 'We aim to sell shares in the National Freight Corporation' (Conservative Manifesto 1979, in Times Books 1979: 282–94, quoted at p. 287). Partly because she had not yet established control over her own party, partly because there was no need, partly because her public relations adviser tried to stop her from making policy speeches, Mrs Thatcher offered relatively few commitments. The 1978–9 'winter of discontent' was marked by extensive strikes against the Callaghan government's incomes policy. Refuse collectors, lorry drivers, and gravediggers were among those who struck. Union committees decided what was essential transport, and issued permits. A deputation of cancer patients was pictured on TV news pleading with the strikers to let supplies through to their hospital. The Conservatives' most memorable poster, in the first election campaign run for them by Saatchi and Saatchi, proclaimed, 'Labour isn't working'.

Winning the election enabled Mrs Thatcher to get her own way more often. She gradually purged the Cabinet of those who did not share her economic outlook (see Young 1990: chs. 9–15; Thatcher 1993 *passim*). From the millions of words of commentary that have been written on Thatcher and Thatcherism, a few (very few) useful organizing ideas stand out. One of these is that her two ruling motifs were 'A Free Economy and a Strong State' (Gamble 1994). As with Powell, a political philosopher might be surprised at the conjunction. Surely a free economy logically belongs with a *weak* state? But politicians have more freedom of manoeuvre than political philosophers. Taking the two motifs in reverse order, we look next at their contributions to Margaret Thatcher's heresthetic.

Margaret Thatcher and the Strong State: Nation and Race

Margaret Thatcher was an unrequited admirer of Enoch Powell. She praises him for being right about the economy at least seven years before Keith Joseph and she herself were:

I can understand how difficult it was for him [Powell] to acknowledge after 1974/75 that Keith Joseph and I were genuinely committed to implementing economic policies whose contents owed so much to Enoch's own thankless advocacy in earlier years. . . . Powellism lived on in the Conservative Party and, with a number of subtractions and additions, helped generate Thatcherism. (Thatcher 1998; a review of Heffer 1998)

After the 'rivers of blood' speech, Thatcher 'strongly sympathized with the gravamen of his [Powell's] argument about the scale of New Commonwealth immigration into Britain' and objected to Heath's decision to sack Powell (Thatcher 1995: 141, 146; cf. also Gamble 1994: 81; Thatcher 1998). Her first Powellite move as leader came in January 1978, where she states that she 'offend[ed] against Party political wisdom still more fundamentally'. (Note, again, the Leader of the Opposition speaking as leader of the opposition to the Opposition.) To a TV interviewer, she said

People are really rather afraid that this country might be rather swamped with people of a different culture. . . . We do have to hold out the prospect of an end to immigration, except, of course, for compassionate cases. (Thatcher 1995: 405, 408)

This speech led to an immediate sharp rise in the Conservatives' poll rating, although not by as much as the 11 points claimed by Thatcher 1995 (p. 408; cf. Butler and Kavanagh 1980: Diagram I: 29). Why then did she not capitalize on this? The answer seems to be that she did not yet feel sufficiently in control of the Shadow Cabinet to do so. Had she persisted in a Powellite line, she might have lost some grandees from her Shadow Cabinet before she was in a position to replace them.

She was next able to embody the strong state when the Argentine military junta mounted an invasion of the Falkland Islands, to which they had a long-standing territorial claim, in April 1982. As was Churchill to the Dardanelles in 1915 and again to the Norway campaign in 1940, so was Thatcher to the Falklands in 1982. Both politicians were implicated in the failures that led to the invasion. Both emerged as triumphant war leaders. The Argentines had been misled by signals from the British government, including the withdrawal of an Antarctic survey vessel, into believing that the British would walk away from the Falklands. Margaret Thatcher was implicated in the misleading signals (see Franks [1983] 1992: paras. 281, 288; Hastings and Jenkins 1983: 79, 336.) The House of Commons met on 3 April 1982, a Saturday. Most MPs on both sides were belligerent, and demanded that heads should roll. Three ministers resigned. Mrs Thatcher immediately launched a naval-led recapture task force. It diverted to, and retook, the uninhabited island of South Georgia, at which Mrs Thatcher appeared in Downing Street to order the assembled news representatives to 'Rejoice, rejoice'. The invasion of the Falklands them-selves was touch-and-go, but once the British force succeeded in landing, its victory, in June, was only a matter of time. The worst loss of life occurred when British forces torpedoed the Argentine cruiser *General Belgrano* with the loss of over 300 lives. The *Belgrano* was sailing west, away from the Falklands, at the time, something which Mrs Thatcher and her ministers continued to deny for several years afterwards. There would have been massive British losses if the Argentine forces had managed to find and sink the British troopships.

Before the Argentine invasion, and even for the first few days of it, it seemed that Mrs Thatcher was doomed. Her government was divided and unpopu-lar. It had presided over a huge increase in unemployment, which it had addressed with economic policies opposite to those recommended by almost all commentators. Mrs Thatcher herself was receiving the lowest poll ratings of any Prime Minister to that date, bottoming at 24 per cent approval in October 1981. The only saving grace was that the Labour Party was tearing itself apart. Suddenly, during the Falklands campaign, people became more cheerful. Their subjective economies blossomed—they tended to think that things were going better for the economy and for themselves personally. This was not matched by any improvement in the objective economy. Although there is a fascinating academic wrangle on this point (Norpoth 1987; Sanders *et al.* 1987, 1990; Clarke *et al.* 1990), the inescapable conclusion is that Mrs Thatcher made people feel better because she won the Falklands war, not because of anything she or her government did for the economy. The Conservatives' recovery to win the 1983 General Election was a triumph of the strong state, not of the free economy. Mrs Thatcher was lucky. But, like Winston Churchill in 1940, she had made her own luck.

Mrs Thatcher also promoted a strong British stand against what her friend Ronald Reagan called the 'evil empire' of the Soviet Union. She took on with delight the sobriquet 'Iron Lady' hurled at her by the Red Army newspaper *Red Star*. She and her ministers faced down the revival of the Campaign for Nuclear Disarmament (CND) in the early 1980s, when American cruise missiles were brought to Britain. In a rhetorical masterstroke, her Secretary of State for Defence, Michael Heseltine, refused to call the CND policy *unilateral disarmament*, as CND itself had always labelled it. Instead, he called it *one-sided* disarmament. *One-sided*, of course, is the Anglo-Saxon for *unilateral*. But it sounded cowardly, where the other sounded statesmanlike. Thatcher's and Heseltine's strong stands were apparently vindicated, first by the arrival of the more flexible Mikhail Gorbachev (of whom Mrs Thatcher said 'we can do business together') at the helm of the Soviet Union, and then by the collapse of the Soviet Empire and the Soviet Union from 1989 onwards. Though these events came at the end of Thatcher's time in power, they posed a problem for her successors. Once the evil empire had been dissolved, there was less for them to define themselves as strong against.

If not the Soviet Union, how about the European Union? Powell, as we have seen, denounced British accession to the European Economic Community (now the European Union) as a fundamental breach of parliamentary sovereignty. Edward Heath regards it as the supreme act of his Prime Ministership (see e.g. Heath 1998: 732). As a member of Heath's Cabinet, Thatcher began her European odyssey closer to Heath's position than to Powell's. It has been a long odyssey, culminating in her declaration at a fringe meeting of the 1999 Conservative Party Conference that 'in my lifetime all our problems have come from mainland Europe and all the solutions have come from the English-speaking nations across the world' (BBC News Online, 5.10.99). One of the differences between Powellism and Thatcherism is that Powell hated the United States and Thatcher loved them.

Margaret Thatcher never acquired the *acquis communautaire*. This is the name that EU jargon gives to the convention that a new member accepts the compromises and working procedures of the Union as it has evolved up to that point. In 1973, when Britain formally became a member, the EEC was more a political than an economic community. Its founders aimed, above all, to knit France and Germany together so closely that another Western European war would become inconceivable. As a consequence, its economic policies were political. That a huge proportion of the EU budget goes on farm subsidies, and that there is on top of that extensive off-budget protection of farmers in the Common Agricultural Policy, is a result of the politics, not the economics, of the 1950s. The founders of the EEC thought that farmers, along with coal and steel workers, had to be placated to protect political stability. Otherwise, they might vote for extreme parties like the German Nazis or (in the 1950s) the French Poujadistes. Therefore, when Britain joined, the structure of subsidy and protection did not benefit British producer groups. It did not benefit consumers anywhere in the Union (or outside it, for that matter,

except perhaps for the buyers of food dumped from the EU's various sur-
pluses). Margaret Thatcher's first battle with the EU was for a budget rebate.
As she characteristically puts it, 'It was quite shameless: they were determined
to keep as much of our money as they could' (Thatcher 1993: 62–4, 78–86,
quoted at p. 81). She and her ministers negotiated a budget settlement in May
1980.

In the mid-1980s, the EU turned from politics to economics as it developed
the Single Market programme. One of its strongest promoters was Lord Cock-
field, Mrs Thatcher's nominee as a European Commissioner. Her portrait of
him—in the solitary mention of him in her memoirs—is brief and to the
point:

I was no longer able to find a place for him in the Cabinet and I thought that he would
be effective in Brussels. He was. I always paid tribute to the contribution he made to
the Single Market programme. . . . Unfortunately, he tended to disregard the larger questions of politics—constitutional sovereignty, national sentiment and the promptings of
liberty. . . . Alas, it was not long before my old friend and I were at odds. (Thatcher
1993: 547)

The programme has been highly successful at turning the EU into a single
market with free movement of capital and labour. It has gone a considerable way to offset the damage done to European welfare by the Common
Agricultural Programme. Unfortunately, as Mrs Thatcher recognizes, it could
not be divorced from questions of sovereignty. If the single market was to
succeed, the EU had to have powers to override national governments when
they obstructed it. These powers were granted in the Single European
Act (SEA), ratified by Mrs Thatcher in December 1985, and by the UK Parliament in 1986. The European Communities (Amendment) Act (1986 ch. 58)
amends the European Communities Act 1972 in order to incorporate certain
provisions of the Single European Act. Margaret Thatcher voted but did not
speak for it. It was carried through Parliament, whipped and guillotined, by
substantial majorities.

All governments have protectionist instincts. Those who would gain from
protection know who they are, and know how much free trade hurts them.
Therefore they lobby effectively. In any one case, and in all cases put together,
the beneficiaries from free trade outnumber the beneficiaries of protection.
But the beneficiaries of free trade often do not know who they are, nor how
much they would gain from it, therefore they do not lobby effectively. The
British government probably has, or at least tries to implement, fewer protectionist instincts than do those of most EU member states. But it was an
inevitable and necessary consequence of the SEA that when a British action
was found to be in breach of European single-market law, the courts would
rule that Community law overrode British. It was likewise an inevitable corol-
lary of the SEA that it should reduce the scope of national vetoes in the European Council of Ministers, and substitute qualified majority voting. Under
the SEA, 'Mrs Thatcher agreed to an extension of qualified majority voting.

... She was quite right to do so. ... Mrs Thatcher ... told Parliament, "We wished to have many of the directives under majority voting because things which we wanted were being stopped by others using a single vote"' (Heath 1998: 706, quoting Mrs Thatcher's oral answer to Dennis Skinner (Lab. Bolsover), *Hansard* 6s 153:166).

British protectionism led to the Merchant Shipping Act 1988. Under its Common Fisheries Policy, the EU had adopted fishing quotas for each member state in an attempt to prevent overfishing. Spanish fishing companies bought up some of the British quotas. This practice became known as 'quota-hopping'. It caused fury in British fishing communities (although some British fishermen saw it as a way to sell out of a declining industry by selling their boats and the attached quotas to Spanish companies). The 1988 Act sought to end quota-hopping by providing that only British-owned boats could count as part of the British fishing fleet. The Spanish companies, one of which was called Factortame, applied to the courts for relief, saying that the 1988 Act was contrary to European law, and therefore contrary to the 1972 Act as amended in 1986. Both the European Court of Justice and the British Law Lords found in their favour. Nationalist defenders of parliamentary sovereignty were appalled. Had not Enoch Powell been proved exactly right? Had not Britain abandoned parliamentary sovereignty (and also the rule that no Parliament may bind its successor)? No, said the Law Lords:

Thus, whatever limitation of its sovereignty Parliament accepted when it enacted the European Communities Act 1972 was entirely voluntary. Under the terms of the Act of 1972 it has always been clear that it was the duty of a United Kingdom court, when delivering final judgment, to override any rule of national law found to be in conflict with any directly enforceable rule of Community law. (Reg.v. Transport Sec., Ex p. Factortame Ltd. (No. 2) (H.L.(E.)) Lord Bridge of Harwich, 1 A.C. 603–83 at 659)

Long before *Factortame* finished its long and winding way through the courts, Mrs Thatcher was giving sharp expression to her Euroscepticism. In Bruges, Belgium, in 1988, she said, 'We have not successfully rolled back the frontiers of the state in Britain only to see them reimposed at a European level' (Thatcher 1993: 744–5). In the 1989 European Parliament election, the Conservatives campaigned (unsuccessfully) against 'a diet of Brussels' (Adonis 1989). The poster carried a picture of a pile of overcooked Brussels sprouts.

Meanwhile, Nigel Lawson, the Chancellor of the Exchequer, was shadowing the exchange rate mechanism of the infant European Monetary System. Mrs Thatcher made known her displeasure with this, and Lawson resigned in October 1989. A year later, her longest-serving and most loyal supporter, Sir Geoffrey Howe, whom she had already demoted for refusing to endorse her Euroscepticism, followed him. In his resignation speech he complained that her attitude to her ministers was

rather like sending your opening batsmen to the crease only to find, the moment the first balls are bowled, that their bats have been broken before the game by the team captain. . . . The time has come for others to consider their own response to the tragic conflict of loyalties with which I myself have wrestled for perhaps too long. (Howe 1994: 702–3)

Mrs Thatcher was now doomed, although she was one of the last to realize it. Labour had a huge lead in the polls. The Conservatives were patently torn down the middle on Europe, and also over the poll tax (on which see 'Margaret Thatcher's statecraft' below). Conservative MPs, the electorate for the Conservative leader, stood to lose their seats in droves. Mrs Thatcher put herself up for re-election as leader and Prime Minister. She just failed to win the required majority over Michael Heseltine in the first ballot. She announced, from Paris, that she would fight on. One by one, her Cabinet told her 'that they themselves would back me, of course, but that regretfully they did not believe I could win' (Thatcher 1993: 851). The following day— Thanksgiving Day 1990 in the USA—she resigned.

Margaret Thatcher and the Free Economy

What we now think of as Thatcherite economics had already been spelt out, first by Enoch Powell, and then by Keith Joseph, when Mrs Thatcher became Prime Minister. Some of it had been embodied in the Seldson programme of 1970. But Heath had failed to press ahead with it, because he (like everybody else at the time except Powell) thought that selling free-market capitalism to the electorate was impossible if unemployment soared to one million. Also like most commentators at the time, Heath had moral difficulties with what he called 'the unpleasant and unacceptable face of capitalism' (*Hansard* 5s. 856: 1243, 15 May 1973; Heath 1998: 419). Powell and Joseph failed because they never captured power. Thatcher succeeded. Nevertheless, that Thatcherism was not a unified ideology—or, if it was, only in retrospect— emerges most clearly from the hesitant start to her economic liberalism in office.

It is convenient (but perhaps over-schematic—see Gamble 1994: ch. 4 for an alternative scheme) to divide economic Thatcherism into three eras, defined by her three General Election victories. Thatcherism I lasted from 1979 to 1983, Thatcherism II from 1983 to 1987, and Thatcherism III from 1987 to her fall in 1990.

Thatcherism I, 1979–83

The Conservatives had ample room to manoeuvre in 1979, since they came to power as a result of Labour losing the election rather than of themselves winning it on their own policies. As already noted, their election manifesto was tentative, and their most successful poster ('Labour isn't working') was an attack on Labour rather than a promise to do better. This was just as well, as during Thatcherism I, unemployment rose to levels last seen in the 1930s. By the second quarter of 1983 it had reached 2.9 million on seasonally adjusted figures (12.1 per cent). Up to and including Callaghan, all modern Prime Ministers had assumed that unemployment at that level was incompatible with a stable and civilized society. By experiment, Mrs Thatcher showed that it was compatible with stability (civilization is a moral matter not susceptible to experiment). There were riots in inner-city Liverpool and London in 1981, but no general threat to public order. The unemployed were politically excluded and never became an electoral force either. Although the 1981 levels of unemployment and economic decline would certainly have led the Conservatives to defeat had the Falklands war not come along, it did. Under Thatcherism I, the government which had presided over three million unemployed was re-elected. Unemployment continued to rise until the third quarter of 1986.

Many commentators see the huge surge in unemployment as an inevitable consequence of the macro-economic policy of Thatcherism I. Mrs Thatcher and her Chancellor, Geoffrey Howe, resolutely turned their backs on Keynesian economics. They met the rise in unemployment not with an increase in public spending but with a tightening of the money supply. Some commentators accuse them of deliberately letting unemployment rip in order to kill the power of the trade unions. This is to go too quickly for conspiracy where (as usual) cock-up is the likelier explanation. It is better to assume that Thatcher and Howe did not anticipate that their monetarism would take such a huge toll on employment. If they had anticipated it, they would have known that they would have to modify it to have any hope of winning the next election.

Unlike monetary policy, union policy was prominent in the 1979 election manifesto. It was not nearly as radical as Mrs Thatcher wished, because the policy area was still controlled by James Prior, her Heathite first Secretary of State for Employment. But in monetarism, and the associated policy of controlling public spending by setting cash limits (Pliatzky 1989: 53), the Conservatives found by experiment the means to destroy trade union power that had eluded the head-on assault of the Heath government. Yet again, this success was anticipated by the then unlistened-to Enoch Powell. Controlling inflation by a consensual agreement on incomes policy had patently failed in 1979. The Conservatives could quite truthfully say to trade unions and their members that they would abandon it, and restore free collective bargaining. They did not reveal to unions and their members—because nobody asked them to—what they would do instead. In the event, allowing unemployment to let rip cowed unions in all sectors. Cash limits cowed those in the public sector, as they imposed a very direct tradeoff between pay rates and employment levels throughout the public service. And the 'winter of discontent' of 1978–9 gave the overt restrictions on union activity introduced by Thatcher the legitimacy that the 1971 Industrial Relations Act had lacked. Even so, she proceeded very cautiously, restrained by Prior until she felt strong enough to move him in 1981. Radical change to the legal position of unions came later. And in a crucial strategic retreat, the Government backed away from a confrontation with the National Union of Mineworkers (NUM) in 1981, increasing subsidies to the coal industry rather than insisting on closures or reductions of the industry's losses.

Privatization was hardly a feature of Thatcherism I at all. As noted, it was barely mentioned in the 1979 manifesto. The first few privatizations were mostly of profitable state holdings. They were done in order to raise money, not for any of the wider and more diverse motives that appeared under Thatcherism II and III. They realized under £500 million a year (Vickers and Yarrow 1988: ch. 6 and Table 6.1). One of the most significant privatizations, which *was* political rather than economic, occurred almost by accident. This was the sale of council houses—that is, local authority-owned houses—to their tenants at deep discounts. This was labelled the Right to Buy. It was in the 1979 manifesto, but apparently it was a last-minute addition as the Conservatives discovered from their focus group research how popular the idea was (Butler and Kavanagh 1980: 190; Garrett 1994: 109). From a political point of view, it had two advantages. It gave some voters a powerful vested interest in Conservative victory, and it broke up a concentrated electoral force with an equally powerful vested interest in Labour victory. The effect should not be exaggerated. Careful analysis (Heath and Garrett 1991; Garrett 1994) shows that council tenants who bought their homes under the Right to Buy were already more pro-Conservative than the remainder. But the effect was real. Council house buyers remained more loyal to the Conservatives as other groups slipped back in 1987 and 1992.

Thatcherism II, 1983–7

Privatization took centre stage after the 1983 General Election. In this phase its objectives were political rather than economic. There were two main ones. One was the extension of popular capitalism; the other was the break-up of a united public sector interest group.

The extension of popular capitalism was typified by the 'Tell Sid' advertising campaign used to sell shares in British Gas. Sid was presented as a working man, slow on the uptake, who had failed to realize what a bonanza he would join if he bought shares in British Gas. For the shares to be a bonanza they had to be underpriced. They were. Table 8.3 shows the immediate gains made by share purchasers in the main privatizations of Thatcherism II.

The immediate gains were even greater than Table 8.3 shows, because in most cases only part of the price of the shares had to be paid in advance. A ruthless investor who sold the partly paid shares immediately could therefore make gains about three times those shown in Table 8.3. Having sold these shares at a huge discount, the Conservatives then put a double argument to their purchasers. 'You have made a huge gain with us—reward us. And you

Table 8.3. Principal privatizations 1983–7: immediate profits

Company	Gross proceeds of sale (£m)	Date of share offer	First day premium (%)
British Telecom	3,916	03.12.84	33
British Aerospace	550	14.05.85	12
Cable & Wireless	602	13.12.85	0.5
TSB	1,360	10.10.86	35.5
British Gas	5,603	08.12.86	9
British Airways	900	11.02.87	35
Rolls-Royce	1,360	20.05.87	36

Source: Vickers and Yarrow 1988: Table 7.1; cases which occurred between the 1983 and 1987 General Elections and where the gross sale proceeds were £500 million or more.

might make a huge loss if Labour wins the next election—protect yourself. For both reasons, vote Conservative.' The finest example of this was the letter sent in November 1986 by Norman Tebbit, then Chairman of the Conservative Party, to those who had brought British Telecom shares. He was legally able to do this despite the company's objections because the share register of a public company is a public document. The letter stated:

We . . . believe in putting these companies into real 'public ownership', by which we mean ownership, through shares, by members of the public like yourself. . . . The most effective way to stop Labour's attack on your savings, and your pension, is to make sure they don't get back into power. Think how much a Labour government could cost you. Then send me a donation for our Fighting Fund. (Facsimile reproduced in McLean 1989: Fig. 3.4)

For all that, the extension of popular capitalism was of limited electoral impact—unlike council house purchasers, holders of privatization share issues did not take a permanent step to the right (Heath and Garrett 1991). The second effect of these privatizations was more important. All pre-1979 attempts to control wage inflation had foundered on the rock of public sector pay bargaining. Once one group of workers had settled for a given percentage wage increase, no other organized group would settle for less. This effect was not confined to the public sector. But in the public sector, the government was the paymaster. It would be blamed for any of the resulting strikes and disruption that followed from any attempt to impose wage restraint. That was what had happened most recently in the Winter of Discontent that made Prime Minister Thatcher possible. After privatization, it was no longer up to the government to set the wages of telephone, gas, or airline staff. And cash limits (see above) enabled the government to put a stark choice to workers in the core public sector, including the civil service: 'you can have more pay and fewer jobs, or the same number of jobs and no more pay. The choice is yours.'

Facing down the mineworkers complemented privatization. A piece of folk wisdom attributed to Harold Macmillan ran 'Never alienate the Pope, the nurses, or the NUM.' Mrs Thatcher was the first politician since Lloyd George to break the last rule, and then only at the second attempt. In 1981, as we saw, the Government bought its way out of confrontation with the miners with taxpayers' money. This emboldened the union's leaders to think that they could repeat 1972 and 1974, when they had struck successfully against the maximum wage awards possible under the Heath government's incomes policy. But the circumstances were very different by the time the NUM leader, Arthur Scargill, called an all-out strike in the spring of 1984. The economy was less dependent on coal. The Government had built up coal stocks and ensured that the nuclear power industry could meet the baseload demand for electricity. It could now stop secondary picketing of sites other than coal mines, which had been very effective against Heath. And the union itself was divided by Scargill's tactics, and had split into two. As it is now easy to see in retrospect, the strike was doomed from the start. It lasted twelve months and caused great deprivations in the coalfields. The effect was to hasten the end of the deep-mined coal industry in Great Britain. It would probably have been destroyed in any event. If earlier governments had not been so terrified of the NUM, the destruction would have begun earlier, as deep mining has never been profitable since nationalization. But if the year-long confrontation between Thatcher and Scargill had not occurred, the destruction would have been slower. Politically, Arthur Scargill was as useful to Mrs Thatcher as the Argentine junta had been. The disappearance of both from the political scene was equally a blow to her successors.

Thatcherism III, 1987–90

The influential critique by Vickers and Yarrow (1988) showed that whatever privatization was for—and it was for many things—it was not done in a way designed to promote economic efficiency. This had been the primary intention of the early prophets, Powell and Joseph. But under Thatcherism I and II, other, political, imperatives had taken priority. Above all, economic efficiency implied tough regulation. Otherwise, a public monopoly might simply give way to a private monopoly. If a government aims to increase economic efficiency, privatization as such is irrelevant; what matters is the opening of industry to competition.

But the popular capitalism of Thatcherism II depended on giving Sid both a quick buck and an assurance of long-term profits. The quick buck was easy—underprice the sale. But the long-term profits depended on the company being allowed to continue to make monopoly profits. Accordingly, the Thatcher II privatizations were not accompanied by compulsory breaking-up of the companies, nor by any very determined effort to ensure that new entrants could get fair access to customers of the former state monopolist. The privatization of British Airports Authority (BAA), initiated in 1985